HEALING
RELATIONSHIPS
THROUGH FORGIVENESS

*ACCEPTING GOD'S GRACE AND
GIVING IT TO OTHERS*

AN INSTRUCTOR'S MANUAL
FOR THE GROUP STUDY BOOKS
PARTS 1, 2, 3

WITH ADDITIONAL NOTES
AND THE WORKBOOK QUESTIONS
WITH SUGGESTED ANSWERS

DONALD E. JONES, PHD

J & A BOOK PUBLISHERS
www.jabookpublishers.com

(C) 2017 Donald E. Jones, PhD

Printed in the United States of America

All rights reserved. No part of this book may be reproduced in any form without permission in writing from the author, except in the case of brief quotations embodied in critical articles or reviews.

All Scripture quotations are from the World English Bible. This version was selected, because it is in the public domain and can be quoted without limit. A personal translation of a verse or passage will be designated with (DEJ).

ISBN-13: 978-1946368102
ISBN-10: 1946368105

DEDICATION

I dedicate this book to my Savior and Lord Jesus Christ. He has been with me every step of my journey upon the earth, and I so look forward to being in His presence forever and ever.

CONTENTS

(WORKBOOK QUESTIONS FOLLOW EACH CHAPTER)

Introduction to this Manual	1
Part 1 - Group Study Part 1 Experiencing God's Grace for Ourselves	15
Part 2 - Group Study Part 2 Requesting God's Grace from Others	165
Part 3 - Group Study Part 3 Displaying God's Grace to Others	285
Conclusion to This Manual	439

ACKNOWLEDGMENTS

I want to thank my wonderful and gracious wife Carol who has supported me in this ministry with sacrifice, enthusiasm, encouragement, and accountability. Most of all, she has been a constant blessing because of her willingness to listen. I was always sharing with her the truths God had been teaching me as I studied His word and wrote this book. It consumed many hours. Thank you, Carol and I deeply love you.

I want to thank my son Gregory R. Jones for volunteering to be the primary editor of this important book. Without his time and effort in painstakingly and meticulously going over every word and every sentence checking and rechecking the sentence structure and grammar, I would not have been able to complete it. Thank you for your ministry to me.

I want to thank my other children, Krista, Matt, and Kara for their love for Christ and His Word and their willingness to live for Him. I love you all.

AN INSTRUCTOR'S MANUAL

Introduction to this Manual

The purpose of this instructor's manual is to help the group leader facilitate the study and discussion of the group books with the same title. Since you have been given such an important responsibility as leading a group of Christians in the study of the Bible, I would like to share with you some principles utilized by the apostle Paul in his teaching and preaching ministry. These will assist you in your time with the believers God has given to you to minister to. These are in no particular order, but all are important. The Lord does not expect us to be perfect in them, but to simply do the very best that we can. If we are willing to do our part, then He will do His part through His Spirit.

In 1 Corinthians 12:5-7, Paul explains, "There are various kinds of service, and the same Lord." Here Paul, the apostle, acknowledges that the saints can minister to one another in a variety of ways. Then he adds, "There are various kinds of workings, but the same God, who works all things in all." As each person ministers, they will have a different impact than others, but it is all the work of the Holy Spirit. Finally, he continues, "But to each one is given the manifestation of the Spirit for the profit of all." Your service in this ministry is coming from the giftedness which is a work of God's Spirit to benefit all. Do the best you can with these principles and let the Spirit do the rest.

Additional Notes: Here is the Bible reference I cite:

1 Corinthians 12:5-7
There are various kinds of service, and the same Lord. There are various kinds of workings, but the same God, who works all things in all. But to each one is given the manifestation of the Spirit for the profit of all.

Your Unceasing Prayer

Paul prayed for the Christians that he served in God's Word. In Romans 1:9-10, he writes, For God is my witness, whom I serve in my spirit in the Good News of his Son, how unceasingly I make mention of you always in my prayers, requesting, if by any means now at last I may be prospered by the will of God to come to you." Paul depended on prayer and so should you. Pray for every person in your study by name and ask God to work powerfully through His Word as you share it in these materials.

Additional Notes: Here is the Bible reference I cite:

Romans 1:9-10
For God is my witness, whom I serve in my spirit in the Good News of his Son, how unceasingly I make mention of you always in my prayers, requesting, if by any means now at last I may be prospered by the will of God to come to you.

Your Persistent Practice

As Paul taught the Scriptures, he always practiced what he preached. As you study the biblical principles in these books you should practice them yourself. The believers will look to you to see if you are attempting to apply the truths as they are. In Philippians 3:17, Paul asserted, "Brothers, be imitators together of me, and note those who walk this way, even as you have us for an example." He explained to the Philippians that not only were they to listen to what he said but watch how he practiced them. In the discussions, you should describe how you are applying the principles also.

Additional Notes: Here is the Bible reference I cite:

Philippians 3:17
Brothers, be imitators together of me, and note those who walk this way, even as you have us for an example.

Your Sound Doctrine

These materials stand on their own in regard to the proper handling of God's Word. You merely have to be consistently staying within the bounds of this study. Often times, believers will desire to share opinions about what these Scriptures may mean based on personal feelings and preferences. Yet, the Bible is written by God and should be studied in light of what He meant the various Bible passages to say and how they might apply them. It is important that the discussion portion of the study remain within the limits of application rather than interpretation. I have spent many carefully interpreting the texts themselves and am confident that these are God's truths. In 1 Timothy 4:6-7, Paul writes to Timothy, his son in the faith now a pastor, "If you instruct the brothers of these things, you will be a good servant of Christ Jesus, nourished in the words of the faith, and of the good doctrine which you have followed. But refuse profane and old wives' fables.

Additional Notes: Here is the Bible reference I cite:

1 Timothy 4:6-7
If you instruct the brothers of these things, you will be a good servant of Christ Jesus, nourished in the words of the faith, and of the good doctrine which you have followed. But refuse profane and old wives' fables. Exercise yourself toward godliness.

Exercise yourself toward godliness." The word translated "good" means "sound" and speaks of the solid truths and principles of the Scriptures rather than human opinions of what people may feel they mean to them.

Your Confidential Interaction

You should set up from the very beginning of the study that what is shared is confidential. There are times for public discussion for all to hear, but in small groups it is best to keep things private. In Acts 23:18-20, Paul had been arrested and his nephew had found out there was a plot to ambush and kill him. So, Paul has him taken to the commander. Luke records what happened next, "So he took him, and brought him to the commanding officer, and said, 'Paul, the prisoner, summoned me and asked me to bring this young man to you, who has something to tell you.'" Now, notice what the commander does, "The commanding officer took him by the hand, and going aside, asked him privately, 'What is it that you have to tell me?' He said, 'The Jews have agreed to ask you to bring Paul down to the council tomorrow, as though intending to inquire somewhat more accurately concerning him.'" Here, Paul's privacy is guarded for his protection. You should guard the privacy of the members of the group.

Additional Notes: Here is the Bible reference I cite:

Acts 23:18-20
So, he took him, and brought him to the commanding officer, and said, "Paul...summoned me and asked me to bring this young man to you. He has something to tell you." The commanding officer took him by the hand, and going aside, asked him privately, "What is it that you have to tell me?" He said, "The Jews have agreed to ask you to bring Paul down to the council tomorrow, as though intending to inquire somewhat more accurately concerning him.

Paul also encouraged Pastor Timothy to exhort his flock not to become involved in any gossip (1 Timothy 3:11; 5:13). The sharing of difficulties outside the group can certainly lead to this grievous behavior. Please check with the laws in your land and the policies in your local church concerning when confidentially can and cannot be breached. Usually, this involves the harming of oneself or others.

Additional Notes: Here is the Bible reference I cite:

1 Timothy 3:11
Their wives...be reverent, not slanderers, temperate, and faithful in all things.

1 Timothy 5:13
Besides, they also learn to be idle, going about from house to house. Not only idle, but...gossips and busybodies, saying things which they ought not.

Your Flexible Strategy

Sometimes you will not be able to stick directly to the materials because you will have a "teachable moment" occur. Please take advantage of these moments. These may involve a particular situation shared or even a difficulty occurring on the day or week of the study. It is perfectly fine to depart occasionally. It is best to not allow members of the group to dominate it due to frequent issues. If this occurs, team them up with others outside the group to assist them individually. In Acts 17:23, Paul entered Antioch and was struck by all of the statues of idols in the city.

Additional Notes: Here is the Bible reference I cite:

Acts 17:23
For as I passed along and observed the objects of your worship, I also found an altar with this inscription: 'TO AN UNKNOWN GOD.' What therefore you worship in ignorance, I announce to you.

He found one identified as an "unknown god" and shifted his preaching strategy to begin with his proclamation of the "unknown god" as the God of the Universe. Luke records Paul's words to the leaders of that city, "For as I passed along, and observed the objects of your worship, I found also an altar with this inscription: 'TO AN UNKNOWN GOD.' What therefore you worship in ignorance, this I announce to you.'" He was flexible. His letters indicate that he geared them toward particular issues the churches were having rather than simple methodical instruction. We do know that he taught systematically, but his letters allow a real flexibility.

Your Loving Relationships

Christians are brothers and sisters in Christ and a study such as this can establish and develop these relationships as the saints interact with the Word, you, and each other. In 1 Thessalonians 3:12, Paul speaks of the love the Thessalonian believers had for one another and for him. He describes his prayer that they would grow in this, "And the Lord make you to increase and abound in love one toward another, and toward all men, even as we also do toward you." A group of believers in a small group centered on the Word of God is a great place to grow. The believers can also practice the "one anothers" so often spoken of in Paul's letters (Romans 12:10; 14:19; 15:7; Galatians 6:2; Ephesians 4:32).

Additional Notes: Here is the Bible reference I cite:

1 Thessalonians 3:12
May the Lord make you to increase and abound in love toward one another, and toward all men, even as we also do toward you,

Romans 12:10
In love of the brothers be tenderly affectionate to one another; in honor preferring one another.

Romans 14:19
So then, let's follow after things which make for peace, and things by which we may build one another up.

Romans 15:7
Therefore accept one another, even as Christ also accepted you, to the glory of God.

Galatians 6:2
Bear one another's burdens, and so fulfill the law of Christ.

Ephesians 4:32
And be kind to one another, tender hearted, forgiving each other, just as God also in Christ forgave you.

Your Troubles Shared

You should also be willing to share your difficulties in the areas you all are studying in the Scriptures. This should be done with common sense, so you do not undermine your own testimony as you are leading the group. It is important that members of your study group know that applying these principles are a battle and not something we simply decide to do. In 1 Corinthians 9:26-27, Paul speaks of the struggle he had with his own sin, "I therefore run like that, as not uncertainly. I fight like that, as not beating the air, but I beat my body and bring it into submission, lest by any means, after I have preached to others, I myself should be rejected." Here, he compares his struggle within himself as a boxing match between his spirit and his flesh. He was constantly fighting it to be holy and righteous.

Additional Notes: Here is the Bible reference I cite:

1 Corinthians 9:26-27
I therefore run like that, not aimlessly. I fight like that, not beating the air, but I beat my body and bring it into submission, lest by any means, after I... preached to others, I myself should be rejected.

Your Intent Listening

As everyone shares make sure you listen intently to the other group members as they share the answers to the many questions in the workbook. Sometimes, teachers get so caught up in what they want to say that they do not listen to the group members. Listening provides an opportunity to share in the joys and sorrows of those involved in the group. In 1 Thessalonians 3:6, Paul explains to the church the news he had heard about them from Timothy, "But when Timothy came just now to us from you, and brought us glad news of your faith and love, and that you have good memories of us always, longing to see us, even as we also long to see you." These words convey Paul's desire to know how they were and what they were experiencing.

Additional Notes: Here is the Bible reference I cite:

1 Thessalonians 3:6
But when Timothy came just now to us from you, and brought us glad news of your faith and love, and that you have good memories of us always, longing to see us, even as we also long to see you.

Your Safe Openness

Not all believers are at the same level in their spiritual maturity. It is important that each respect the other as they share. Paul explains this principle in 1 Corinthians 8:1. He writes, "Now concerning things sacrificed to idols: We know that we all have knowledge. Knowledge puffs up, but love builds up." Here, he is not saying we should not be knowledgeable in the Scriptures of course we should. The Bible is what helps us grow as Christians. He is describing believers who look down upon and are impatient with the biblical or spiritual immaturity of other saints. Instead, they should be building them up in their love. This means loving tolerance as they lovingly correct the mistakes in their knowledge and the patterns of behavior in their Christian lives which may not be mature. You will have to guide the members of your group in this area. If you have to, you can take some aside and explain that it is through love that one helps another become more like Christ. This does not mean we are not to correct believers who are in error or in sin.

Additional Notes: Here is the Bible reference I cite:

1 Corinthians 8:1
Now concerning things sacrificed to idols: We know that we all have knowledge. Knowledge puffs up, but love builds up.

Your Gentle Correction

In any discussion there will be a wide variety of ideas and experiences that people draw upon that might be different than others. These should be embraced as the Holy Spirit leads. The only limitation on this should be when members say something that is in direct opposition to the Scriptures. These false notions and ideas should be corrected gently. If error is left without any comment, then some of the less mature members may believe them and have errors in their Scriptural understanding. This is not very popular today as people are often allowed to share anything they desire, truth or error, without correction because they are entitled to their opinion. This is not God's way. The Lord's opinion is what matters most. In 2 Timothy 2:25, Paul explains to Timothy how to deal with error, "In gentleness correcting those who oppose him." The apostle Paul spoke of those who opposed the sound teaching of Timothy from the Word. It cannot be allowed to continue because error destroys. Then Paul adds, "Perhaps God may give them repentance leading to a full knowledge of the truth."

Additional Notes: Here is the Bible reference I cite:

2 Timothy 2:25
In gentleness correcting those who oppose him: perhaps God may give them repentance leading to a full knowledge of the truth.

As you or members of the group gently correct people, the Lords will work and turn them from the error to the full knowledge of the truth. If you are not sure if someone said something that may not be correct, you will have to consult some resources to help you. Then when you are ready, you can gently bring up the topic at the beginning of a study and correct it. If it is concerning differences among churches, then you would have to take the position of the church sponsoring the group.

Your Limited Discussion

As you follow these study books, there may be those who may want to discuss controversial, philosophical, or political issues. You must gently, but firmly guide them back to the study. Why? What God says is what matters in the meeting. He speaks through his Holy Scriptures, and this must have priority. This would include questions that are off topic. In 1 Timothy 1:4, Paul asserts, "And not to pay attention to myths and endless genealogies, which cause disputes, rather than God's stewardship, which is in faith." Your stewardship is to deliver the Word of God to others, not become involved in endless discussions that go nowhere. To respond to such people you might say, "That's a good question or issue and let's talk about that after the meeting."

Additional Notes: Here is the Bible reference I cite:

1 Timothy 1:4
And not to pay attention to myths and endless genealogies, which cause disputes, rather than God's stewardship, which is in faith.

Your Constant Encouragement

When people are deal with life-changing principles from God's Word, they will need much encouragement to keep trying to follow the Word. They must battle old habits and notions which may give them trouble. Your encouragement can go a long way in helping them continue trying to apply these supernatural principles. In Acts 15, the church had dealt with a major controversy over the salvation of Gentiles. When the decision was made, Paul and Barnabas were sent to share what had been decided. This encouraged the saints greatly. In verses 30-31, Luke records, "So, when they were sent off, they came to Antioch." This refers to the church in that location. Then he adds, "Having gathered the multitude together, they delivered the letter. When they had read it, they rejoiced over the encouragement."

HEALING RELATIONSHIPS THROUGH FORGIVENESS

Additional Notes: Here is the Bible reference I cite:

Acts 15:30-31
So, when they were sent off, they came to Antioch. Having gathered the multitude together, they delivered the letter. When they had read it, they rejoiced over the encouragement.

In Ephesians 6, Paul calls the Christian life a battle against dark forces. The saints will need the encouragement to continue on in their growth in Christ in the areas they are studying.

Additional Notes: Here is the Bible reference I cite:

Ephesians 6:11-12
Put on the whole armor of God, that you may be able to stand against the wiles of the devil. For our wrestling is not against flesh and blood, but against the principalities, against the powers, against the world's rulers of the darkness of this age, and against the spiritual forces of wickedness in the heavenly places.

Your Loving Nurture

This time in God's Word is a time of nurturing the faith of others. When Paul ministered to the Thessalonians and then left, he discovered that they had been growing immensely in Christ. When he wrote to them, he described the manner in which he served them. In 1 Thessalonians 2:7, he wrote, "But we were gentle among you, like a nursing mother cherishes her own children." He ministered to them with the purpose of nurturing them in the faith. His way was that of a loving mother nurturing her own children not a harsh father that is always disciplining them. We must lead in a nurturing and cherishing manner.

AN INSTRUCTOR'S MANUAL

Additional Notes: Here is the Bible reference I cite:

1 Thessalonians 2:7
But we were gentle among you, like a nursing mother cherishes her own children.

These are just a few of the numerous principles one could apply to their teaching ministry. I encourage you to gather some resources and continue this study of this subject on your own if needed. Carefully look over the format of the books and their accompanying workbooks. I have provided the basic answers to the questions, and you can add to them as you wish. I suggest as a format that each member of the group reads that chapter and fills out the questions in the workbook the week before. Then open with a short prayer and go through the questions one by one. If there is time, you can share prayer requests or have refreshments. I would focus on the study first, so you do not get sidetracked and use up the valuable time in God's Word.

AN INSTRUCTOR'S MANUAL

PART 1

*EXPERIENCING GOD'S GRACE
FOR OURSELVES*

THE GROUP STUDY BOOK
WITH ADDITIONAL NOTES

AND THE WORKBOOK QUESTIONS
WITH SUGGESTED ANSWERS

FOR EACH CHAPTER

AN INSTRUCTOR'S MANUAL

CONTENTS

Introduction to Group Study Part 1	19
Introduction to the Workbook Part 1	21
Chapter - 1. Involve God First (Study)	25
Chapter - 1. Involve God First (Workbook)	41
Chapter - 2. Leave Nothing Out (Study)	51
Chapter - 2. Leave Nothing Out (Workbook)	65
Chapter - 3. Admit Your Sin (Study)	75
Chapter - 3. Admit Your Sin (Workbook)	95
Chapter - 4. Accept God's Forgiveness (Study)	105
Chapter - 4. Accept God's Forgiveness (Workbook)	125
Chapter - 5. Forgive Yourself All (Study)	133
Chapter - 5. Forgive Yourself All (Workbook)	153
Conclusion to Group Study and Workbook Part 1	163

AN INSTRUCTOR'S MANUAL

Introduction to Group Study Part 1

This series of three books (Part 1,2,3) grew out of a desire to put the material in my main book on healing relationship through forgiveness into a format for small group study. As a result, the introductions are the same in all three books. This is primarily due to the essential nature of the content in our understanding of the truths found in each one. It also allows the books to be read and studied one after the other or to be studied independent of the other two. This provides more flexibility to the various individuals, groups, churches, and organizations who wish to use it.

After Moses had received the Ten Commandments, the prophet and leader requested that God show him His glory. The Almighty explained to Moses that no human could see Him and live. Nevertheless, God would grant his request by allowing His servant Moses to experience the passing of His "goodness" by him and the actual viewing of the "backside of His glory." On the next morning, he stood upon a rock and called upon the name of the Lord. The Lord God descended in the form of a cloud, shielded Moses in the cleft of the rock, and covered him with His divine hand. As God displayed His divine glory visibly, He declared the many attributes of His supernatural, divine character.

In Exodus 34:6-7, Moses described this amazing moment and the words that he heard the Lord declare about Himself. The prophet recorded, "Yahweh [I AM THAT I AM] passed by before him...he proclaimed, 'Yahweh! Yahweh, a merciful and gracious God, slow to anger...abundant in His loving kindness and truth, keeping loving kindness for thousands, forgiving iniquity and disobedience and sin.'" A book that is written on healing relationships through forgiveness by its nature must begin with the proclamation that the God of the

universe is not only the merciful, gracious, patient, loving, kind, truth-filled, just, and righteous Lord but an Almighty deity who "forgives iniquity, transgressions, and sin." This Lord God announced that He is a "forgiving" God.

This by no means negates the fact that He is also a just and righteous one; therefore, this forgiveness comes with a price that had to be paid. So, He sent His Son to die to pay the penalty for our sins in order to pour out His forgiveness upon all mankind. Through faith in Jesus Christ, men and women experience the full extent of His forgiveness that was proclaimed to Moses many years ago on that mountain top. Once this has occurred in our lives, we are to live for Him. We are to act like Him, and we are to obey Him. One of the critical ways in which God desires His forgiven people to live for, act like, and obey Him is *to forgive others as we are forgiven*. This is the key point of these books. As the Lord God has forgiven us and healed our relationship with Him, He requires us to forgive and heal our relationships with others. This is found in several passages in the Scriptures. Two of them are mentioned by our Lord and one from the apostle Paul. All three clearly explain the important truth that relationships are to be "reconciled" and "restored" to "gain back" one's brother, sister, or neighbor. This is done primarily through forgiveness.

In Matthew 5, the Lord Jesus discusses the heart attitudes people in His kingdom should possess. After speaking of anger, the Lord presents a general principle of living in His kingdom on earth. In verses 23-24, He explains, "If therefore you are offering your gift at the altar, and there remember that your brother has anything against you, leave your gift there before the altar, and go your way. First be reconciled to your brother, and then come and offer your gift." The Greek word translated "reconciled" means "to make changes." It originates from a Greek root word that was a banking term

meaning "to render accounts the same." There would be a discrepancy between two bank ledgers, and all the mistakes would have to be found and corrected in order for them to agree. We express this between people as "being on the same page." The Lord Jesus indicates that the Father desires His people to come to Him fully reconciled with each other. If we, as Christians, know that someone harbors something against us, we are to take the initiative and go to them and reconcile with them. We should not wait for them to come to us. We take our responsibility and go to them. We must once again "settle accounts." They have the same responsibility.

In Matthew 18, Jesus discusses those who are sinning in the church and what all believers should do. In verse 15, the Lord commands, "If your brother sins against you, go, show him his fault between you and him alone. If he listens to you, you have gained back your brother." The Greek word translated "gain" refers "to obtaining or securing something." When a relationship is restored, we gain back everything that the other parties contributed. In this particular case, we have something against our brother, rather than the reverse. If this does happen, we are to take the initiative and confront our brother or sister to gain him or her back and restore the relationship. So, whether someone has something against us, or we have something against someone else, the procedure is essentially the same. Christians must take the initiative and reconcile with them.

The third passage involves the restoration of a sinning brother in the church. In Galatians 6, Paul opens the chapter with an explanation of how to help a sinning saint. In verse one, Paul asserts, "Brothers, even if a man is caught in some fault, you who are spiritual must restore such a one." The Greek word translated "restore" means "to render fit, sound, or complete; to mend or repair what has been broken." The word is used of a physically broken fishing net. In Mark 1:19

and Matthew 4:21, when Jesus called James and John into ministry with Him, they were in the process of "mending" their fishing nets. They were mending the holes in their net so the fish would not fall through. This restoration could easily involve a conflict between two people. The holes in their relationship need to be mended. This process involves healing relationships through forgiveness. These passages will be referred to as you read.

These books are my original works on reconciliation and forgiveness. It is not based on other books that I have read and simply collated. To produce this work, I carefully read through the entire New Testament verse by verse. Then, I meticulously perused the Old Testament paying particular attention to the Psalms and Proverbs. As I read, categories were built from the individual passages, rather than a set of preconceived notions. These numerous categories became the individual biblical principles found in every chapter. Each passage was studied in its historical, grammatical, and scriptural contexts. After this, I compared my interpretations with those of past and present scholars. After this study, I have attempted to follow these biblical principles in my own personal life and also utilize them in my pastoral counseling practice. I have seen the Holy Spirit use them to transform relationships of all kinds.

One last thought. At the end of each chapter, I discuss a counseling experience. Due to confidentiality, none of these are based on one particular counseling situation. Instead, I have mixed together common elements I have seen, details from books and films, bits from my own life and the lives of people I have known, and thoughts from my imagination to create a situation where the biblical principles discussed in the chapters can fully be applied. These are composites of real-life situations. Read, learn, and apply. I commend you to the Lord and His Word (Acts 20:32).

AN INSTRUCTOR'S MANUAL

Introduction to the Workbook Part 1

This workbook is designed to aid in the comprehension and application of the truths from the Scriptures which are found in the book of the same name. It has a question-and-answer format because asking questions was a powerful teaching method that the Lord used to reveal God's divine truth. Jesus asked over one hundred and thirty questions as He instructed the people of God and others. These are only the recorded ones. We can only speculate as to how many questions He might have actually asked. The Lord used His questioning techniques to prompt His listeners to focus, understand, analyze, evaluate, and apply the principles He was proclaiming to them. The same has been done in this workbook.

In Mark chapter 2, Jesus enters Capernaum after a long absence. His reputation for performing great miracles had increased. His arrival caused an instant reaction, and many rushed to the home where He was residing. They desired for them or a loved one to be healed. Among the crowd were a group of Pharisees (a sect of legalistic Jews) and Scribes (a group of Jewish theologians) who had also hurried to see how they could trap Him in something He said or did. To hide their presence, they mingled among the massive crowd. It was a large town with a large crowd gathered in a small home.

Jesus was probably standing in the open courtyard which was in the center of the home surrounded by various rooms. The door or gate to the courtyard was blocked by the people. Four men brought a paralyzed man to see if Jesus would heal him. They could not enter the home due to the crowd and decided to enter another less obvious way. The roofs in ancient times were made of several beams, thick mud, and straw. The stairs to the roof were on the outside of the home attached to the side. So, these four men carried the paralyzed man on a mat up to the roof. There they began digging out a portion of the roof to drop the man into the courtyard. As the Lord was teaching, this man was being lowered down right in front of Him.

The Messiah marveled at their faith and addressed the paralyzed man. In verse 5, Mark records, "Jesus, seeing their faith, said to the paralytic, "Son, your sins are forgiven you." Though not mentioned, Jesus would have peered into the man's heart and seen his repentance and the belief in Him as Savior and Lord. Here, Jesus is demonstrating that He is God because only God can forgive sins. The Pharisees and Scribes must have gasped and thought, "Who does this man think he is? Only God can forgive sins.

As these men were pondering this, the Lord Jesus looked at them and asked a piercing question. In verse 8-9, Mark describes it in these words, "Immediately Jesus, perceiving in his spirit that they so reasoned within themselves, said to them, 'Why do you reason these things in your hearts? Which is easier, to tell the paralytic, 'Your sins are forgiven;' or to say, 'Arise, and take up your bed, and walk?'" This question forced them to the heart of the matter. Anyone could claim to forgive sins, but He was able prove it by an astounding miracle only God could do. He could make the man walk. So, Jesus commanded the man to take up his pallet and walk. Then, Son of God declared that he had demonstrated that He did have the divine power to forgive sins as He had the divine power to heal. Well, the crowd was utterly astonished and began to glorify God. As Jesus used questions, so shall we. May the questions in this book help you focus, understand, analyze, evaluate, and apply these biblical principles.

Chapter 1

Involve God First

The first important step in the reconciliation process is the recognition that no matter who else we have sinned against; we have sinned against our God first. Therefore, when we have transgressed someone, we must initially ask God for forgiveness and reconcile with Him before we reconcile with others (see Introduction). It is His law that was broken.

A Typical Scenario

Have you ever had or heard a conversation with a spouse, parent, child, or friend that went something like this? You say or hear, "Oh, I will also tell you something else! (Person responds.) No, that is not the way it was! (Person responds again.) No, that is what you think it was, but it is not at all the way we had decided! (Person responds again.) No, I'm not going to do it that way! (Person responds again.) No, at the very beginning we did not decide to do it that way!"

Even as we are arguing, we know thirty minutes later the conviction of the Holy Spirit in us will come upon us. As we expected, the argument is over, and no one has won. We are sitting alone reviewing the conversation in our minds in a self-righteous state blaming the other person. Then the Holy Spirit begins His convicting work in our hearts. We think, "Okay, maybe we contributed to the argument." Then we stop ourselves and realize that we actually started the whole argument in the first place. Either way, we must return to the person we transgressed and work things out with them. This is God's will; yet this is not the first step.

A Scriptural Principle

Before we take the important step of reconciling with the person, we must first ask our God for forgiveness. The first principle in the forgiveness and reconciliation process is "we must recognize that our sin is first against God." Yes, we are arguing with our spouse, parent, friend, or neighbor, and we have violated that relationship but that's not the first issue. Our relationship with Almighty God, our relationship with our Master and Lord comes first, and we have transgressed Him as we transgressed the other person.

A Biblical Explanation

As we are arguing with our spouse, parent, or friend, we are actually disrupting our relationship with God first. Why? It is His standards and laws that we are violating. Therefore, before we can go to our spouses we must deal with Him. This is found in Psalm 51. David has just committed the sins of adultery and murder which have been exposed. David opens the psalm crying out for God's mercy. He begs God for the forgiveness of these horrible transgressions and asks Him to wash him thoroughly from these sins and make him clean again. Then in Psalm 51:4, David utters, "Against you, and you only, have I sinned, and done that which is evil in your sight; that you may be proved right when you speak, and justified when you judge."

The word translated "only" in the English does not refer to God as the only one transgressed. Instead, it has the idea of "separate from." David is stating that His transgression against God is completely separate, wholly different, and stands alone when compared to anyone else that has been transgressed. He had sinned against Bathsheba, Uriah, their families, and even the nation of Israel as their leader, but this cannot be compared to the gravity and the seriousness of his sin against God. Why? God is above all else in the universe (Psalm 115:3). He is the ruler of all nations (Psalm 22:28) and the sovereign God (Ephesians 1:11). God is the law giver, and His law has been transgressed (James 2:10; 4:12). Most of all, His Son is our Lord (Romans 10:12-13). He was present listening to the conversation as we argued. He stands before us in every transgression. He must be asked for forgiveness.

Additional Notes: If asked about the sovereignty of God given as a gift from the Father to the Son, here are the Bible references I cite:

Psalm 22:28
For the kingdom is Yahweh's. He is the ruler over the nations.

Ephesians 1:11
In whom also we were assigned an inheritance, having been foreordained according to the purpose of him who does all things after the counsel of his will.

James 4:12
Only one is the lawgiver, who is able to save and to destroy. But who are you to judge another?

Romans 10:12-13
For there is no distinction between Jew and Greek; for the same Lord is Lord of all, and is rich to all who call on him [God]. For, "Whoever will call on the name of the Lord will be saved."

The others transgressed do not set standards of behavior. God alone does. The Lord must be dealt with on a separate and utterly divine level before all others in the transgression. In Psalm 41:4, David again takes up the lament of his sins which brought reprisal from his enemies. The king cries, "I said, 'Yahweh, have mercy on me! Heal me, for I have sinned against you.'" Then this great king paints a beautiful picture of the relief he experiences in forgiveness. In Psalm 41:11-13, he shouts, "By this I know that you delight in me, because my enemy doesn't triumph over me. As for me, you uphold me in my integrity, and set me in your presence forever. Blessed be Yahweh, the God of Israel, from everlasting and to everlasting! Amen and amen."

As Solomon is dedicating the temple he had just built for God, He brings the sins of his people before the Holy One. The king begs God for their forgiveness as he anticipates the many prayers that will proceed from this new structure. In 2 Chronicles 6:21, he asserts, "Listen to the petitions of your servant, and of your people Israel, when they shall pray toward this place: yes, hear from your dwelling place, even from heaven; and when you hear, forgive." Then in verse 25, he adds, "Forgive the sin of your people Israel." In verse 27, he continues, "Then hear in heaven, and forgive the sin of your servants." In the same prayer in verse 39, he repeats, "Then hear from heaven, even from your dwelling place, their prayer and their petitions, and maintain their cause, and forgive your people who have sinned against you." Here in the great temple dedication, Solomon recognizing the constant and continual sin of his people. When they come before God in prayer, they must recognize their sin and repent before God. When transgressions occur, they are first against God, and this must be acknowledged.

In Psalm 79:9, the psalmist cries, "Help us, God of our salvation, for the glory of your name. Deliver us, and forgive our sins, for your name's sake." Here again is this requesting of forgiveness by God's children as expressed by the writer. This is critical in understanding the reconciliation process with others. We must reconcile with God first because He is the Supreme Being and His Son is Lord and Master of our lives. In Matthew 6, the disciples asked Jesus to frame a prayer for them to follow. In verse 12, Jesus uttered, "Forgive us our debts, as we also forgive our debtors." An essential part of our prayers is asking God the Father for forgiveness. What an amazing thing it is to be able to come before our loving God and ask for forgiveness! When we arrive at His throne in prayer as His children, we will find a God who is ready, willing, and able to forgive any transgression! No one understood this better than King David.

In Acts 7, Stephen, one of the mighty witnesses of Christ, stood before the Jewish governing body, the Sanhedrin, and preached a powerful message of salvation. In Acts 7:54, Luke described their reaction in these words, "Now when they heard these things, they were cut to the heart, and they gnashed at him with their teeth." Then in verses 57-58, Luke added, "But they cried out with a loud voice, and stopped their ears, and rushed at him with one accord. They threw him out of the city, and stoned him. The witnesses placed their garments at the feet of a young man named Saul." This Saul, who would become Paul, watched Stephen's life pass out of him with great anticipation and full agreement. From that day forward, Saul set out to destroy the church of Jesus Christ which had just been established.

Luke describes Saul as "ravaging" the church. He went from house to house dragging off Christian men and women and had them thrown in prison. As the saints were scattered because of the persecution, Saul followed them breathing threats and murder against them. Finally, he obtained letters from the Sanhedrin to travel some 135 miles to Damascus to find more Christians, have them bound with the help of the local synagogue, and drag them back to Damascus to have them tried and killed. Most Christians know the story. On that road to Damascus, Saul was confronted by Jesus Christ, saved, and commissioned to be a servant of God. Sometime after Saul, the persecutor, became Paul, the apostle, he was reflecting back on his early days of terror. As the apostle wrote to young Timothy, a trusted companion and fellow pastor, he remembered the horrific affliction he had brought upon those innocent Christians and the mercy he received in God's forgiveness.

In 1 Timothy 1:12-15, the apostle characterizes himself as a blasphemer, persecutor, aggressor, and the foremost of all sinners. Then in verses 14-15, the apostle describes the open arms of God in forgiveness as he came in repentance. Paul writes, "The grace of our Lord abounded exceedingly with faith and love which is in Christ Jesus. The saying is faithful and worthy of all acceptance, that Christ Jesus came into the world to save sinners; of whom I am chief." The Lord came into the world to die so He could open His arms to us in abundant grace! In verse 16, Paul adds, "However, for this cause I obtained mercy, that in me first, Jesus Christ might display all his patience, for an example of those who were going to believe in him for eternal life." The apostle became a powerful and shining example of God's patience as He calls people to Himself through His grace and mercy. Once saved, we still find Him gracious and merciful as we confess our sins to Him.

Paul continues to marvel at the grace, love, and mercy he experienced as he came before the Lord in repentance. No matter how heinous the transgression is, how disgusting is the sin, or even how atrocious is the iniquity, when we come before almighty God, His arms are outstretched, his hands are open, and His heart is ready to forgive. His grace, mercy, and love will outpour into forgiveness when we come to confess our sins. Our God is a Father who is always ready to forgive.

After the people of Israel had been disciplined for seventy years in captivity, God released them from the Persians, and they once again entered the land. Once the wall was rebuilt and they were safe, they reinstated the celebration of the Feast of Booths. All the people gathered together and read from the Scriptures for a full quarter of the day and then confessed their sins and worshipped the Lord for another quarter. Then in Nehemiah 9:17, a group of priests stood up and reviewed the evil of their fathers in this way, "And [the fathers] refused to obey, neither were they mindful of your wonders that you did among them, but hardened their neck, and in their rebellion appointed a captain to return to their bondage." Then they add God's forgiveness, "But you are a God ready to pardon, gracious and merciful, slow to anger, and abundant in loving kindness, and didn't forsake them."

When we sin against God, He never forsakes us. Instead, God waits in readiness for our return to Him in repentance and confession. David acknowledges this in his Psalm 86:5, when the king wrote, "For you, Lord, are good, and ready to forgive; abundant in loving kindness to all those who call on you." This God of ours is ready to forgive when we sin. He is full of love and kindness to all who call upon Him. Then in verse 8, he shouts, "There is no one like you among the gods, Lord, nor any deeds like your deeds." In the midst of God's willingness to forgive, He only demands that we come to Him first to reconcile our relationships. He is our Lord; we must humble ourselves before Him in repentance, before we humble ourselves before others.

An Ancient Portrait

David was a mighty man of God, but he struggled with his passions. This led sometimes to terrible wickedness. His most infamous sin against God occurred in 2 Samuel 11-12. King David was the second ruler of Israel and a great King. In the days of good weather, Israel would go out to battle. In one such battle, David remained in Jerusalem. One evening the king was up on the roof of his palace relaxing (the roof was used in that part of the world much like a backyard patio is used in the western world). He noticed a beautiful woman bathing in the privacy of her home and wanted her.

David was king and could have any woman he wanted whenever he wanted her. So, he commanded his servants to bring her to him. He was the king, and she could not refuse. After he had his way with Bathsheba, David sent her home expecting absolutely no consequences. Sometime later, one of her messengers arrived and she told the foolish king that Bathsheba was pregnant. Now, what would David be able to do? Of course, he would try the first thing many people do when they are caught which is to cover it up. So, a clever idea came to him. He would call Uriah, her husband and a soldier, back from the battlefield. When he returned, Uriah would sleep with Bathsheba and think her child was his; the king directed his commander Joab to return Uriah to him. After greeting David, Uriah was sent home. The king fully expected Uriah to enjoy the fruits of his marriage.

This loyal and faithful soldier refused to enter his home while his fellow warriors were in battle. Instead, he slept at the door of the king's house with the king's servants. When his majesty was informed that Uriah did not return home, he summoned the man and questioned him. Uriah responded by indicating that he could not take any pleasures while the Ark of Israel's God was under siege. It was inconceivable to him that he should rest while his fellow soldiers fought for their lives. It was simply not be respectable.

Now what was the king going to do? David conjured up another plan; he would invite Uriah to stay in his palace for the night and enjoy a magnificent meal with much drinking. Once her husband was fully intoxicated, the man would lose this silly notion and sleep with his wife as David had. The

Scriptures indicate that King David made him drunk. This monarch probably insisted that Uriah continue to drink, even over the husband's protests. When Uriah finally left, David felt assured that his plan would work. Once again, the king underestimated this soldier of his. Even in his drunken state, Uriah refused to return to his home. He was not going to enjoy his wife and home when his fellow soldiers were in battle. Instead, he stayed with David's servants.

At this point, David was done with his attempts to coerce this man to sleep with his own wife. The king commanded Uriah to resume his duties on the battlefield. The soldier was given a letter to personally hand to Joab, the commander of David's troops. In that letter was the King's final scheme and Uriah's death knell. Joab was to assign this obstinate soldier to the front lines of battle. At an opportune time, the troops around him would withdraw, and Uriah would be killed in battle. This will make it look like Uriah was a war hero, leave Bathsheba a widow, and allow David to take her as his wife. He would be able to raise this child without disgrace. This would be the perfect solution to his dilemma.

When the news came that Uriah had been killed, it was finally over. The problem had been solved. King David must have sighed in relief. After the time of Bathsheba's mourning was over, she became David's wife. All of this was done as if the Lord had not been around. All along the way, God must have been too busy with other things to even notice what he had done. Big problem! God Almighty had viewed the entire mess, and it was evil in His sight. When no one was looking, God was still there. When secret plans were being made and executed, God was present, and His laws were being broken.

Sometime later, Nathan, God's prophet, entered David's palace with a story to tell the great king. It was time to indict David for his foul play before the Lord. Nathan stood before

David to seek his advice concerning a situation that he had encountered between two different men. Nathan described a city where two men lived, a rich man and a poor man. This rich man had much wealth, but the poor man had only one little ewe lamb. The poor man loved this lamb and treated it like his own child. When a traveler arrived and resided at the house of the rich man, a lavish meal had to be prepared and served. Rather than taking his own lamb, the rich man took the poor man's lamb, cooked it up, and served it.

King David did not even wait for the prophet to finish his story. He immediately declared that the rich man should be killed. Before he was to die, the man should make restitution fourfold for what he had done. Nathan stared directly at the king and declared that David was the rich man in his story. With this recognition of David's heinous sin came a series of judgments pronounced upon David from God Himself. How could David have done such a thing before God? It is easy he just pretended God was not there. Yet, He was. After this incident, King David repented of these sins and asked God for forgiveness. This is when he penned the inspired words of Psalm 51. This is a powerful prayer of repentance.

He did not initially rush off to reconcile with Bathsheba, her family or Uriah's, or anyone else involved. First, he had to face His Lord God. When we sin against someone, we must recognize we have sinned against God and reconcile with Him. Once this occurs, we can concern ourselves with others. In fact, we will have the right heart and mind to be truly humble enough to reconcile with them.

Additional Notes: If asked about the sins of David, here are the commandments he broke:

Exodus 20:13-17
You shall not murder. You shall not commit adultery. You shall

not steal [in the sense that he stole Uriah's wife]. You shall not give false testimony against your neighbor [in the sense that he wanted to make the child appear as if it were Uriah's]. You shall not covet your neighbor's house. You shall not covet your neighbor's wife, nor his male servant, nor his female servant, nor his ox, nor his donkey, nor anything that is your neighbor's.

A Modern Anecdote

Sometime ago, a married couple came into my counseling office to discuss a drinking problem his wife had. It came to a boiling point when the husband found his wife lying on the front lawn of his house in the morning. She was wearing her pajamas, and the lawn sprinklers were running. She was almost completely unconscious and not aware she was even getting wet. He helped her get up, and she stumbled into the house. Eventually, they got into a huge argument accusing one another of instigating the drunken behavior in the first place. As with many issues in relationships each contributed to the wife's constant drinking in different ways.

It turns out that the husband was always annoyed at her for a variety of habits she had constantly displayed during their marriage. As a result, he would pick at her and criticize her for many of the things she did. He did not like the way she left the dishes on the sink to dry or how she folded the towels. The house was not clean enough for his tastes. The list just went on and on. Rather than discussing the situation with him, the wife drank and drank. The more he picked on her, the more she drank. The more she drank, the more he criticized and picked on her. Until finally all of it had gotten so out of control, their marriage was on the line. Now, their divorce was eminent. As they faced each other in my office, they felt justified in their behavior.

After several intense sessions, I discovered the underlying drama that had motivated these actions. I stood them face to face before the Lord. He was their Savior and Master. What did Jesus think about their behavior (according to the Bible)? Once in front of the Lord, their inappropriate actions came to light. Both partners had brought into their marriage different approaches to washing dishes, the laundry, their cars, and cleaning the house among other issues.

The Scriptures do not speak to many of the issues directly but do indicate that both partners must love, respect, and understand each other (Ephesians 5:33; 1 Peter 3:7). Neither partner was taking the necessary time to listen to the other one. Instead, the husband continually argued, and the wife constantly drank. Differences between people can never be resolved through yelling and drinking.

The Scriptures are clear that believers are not to argue or quarrel (2 Timothy 2:24; Proverbs 18:19; 20:3; 22:10).

Additional Notes: If asked about arguing and quarreling as wrong solution to problems, here are the Bible references I cite:

2 Timothy 2:24
The Lord's servant must not quarrel, but be gentle towards all, able to teach, patient.

Proverbs 18:19
A brother offended is more difficult than a fortified city; and disputes are like the bars of a fortress.

Proverbs 20:3
It is an honor for a man to keep aloof from strife; but every fool will be quarreling.

Proverbs 22:10
Drive out the mocker, and strife will go out; yes, quarrels and insults will stop.

Also, Christians are never to be drunk (Ephesians 5:18; Romans 13:13; Psalm 69:12).

Additional Notes: If asked about drunkenness, here are the Bible references I cite:

Ephesians 5:18
Don't be drunken with wine, in which is dissipation, but be filled with the Spirit.

Romans 13:13
Let us walk properly, as in the day; not in reveling and drunkenness, not in sexual promiscuity and lustful acts, and not in strife and jealousy.

Psalm 69:12
Those who sit in the gate talk about me. I am the song of the drunkards.

This approach dishonored the Lord. This is not how Jesus Christ desires couples, who are fellow heirs of the grace of life, to behave toward each other (1 Peter 3:7). Instead, the Lord expects them to treat each other as He treats His own church (Ephesians 5:23,25,31).

Additional Notes: If people ask about this comparison between the husband and wife and Christ and the church, here are the Bible references I cite:

1 Peter 3:7
You husbands, in the same way, live with your wives according to knowledge, giving honor to the woman, as to the weaker vessel, as

being also joint heirs of the grace of life; that your prayers may not be hindered.

Ephesians 5:23
For the husband is the head of the wife, and Christ also is the head of the assembly, being himself the savior of the body.

Ephesians 5:25
Husbands, love your wives, even as Christ also loved the assembly, and gave himself up for it; that he might sanctify it, having cleansed it by the washing of water with the word.

Ephesians 5:31
For this cause a man will leave his father and mother, and will be joined to his wife. The two will become one flesh.

After several sessions, each one could now see what their responsibility was in the relationship and how they had to behave. This required apologizing, accepting the repentance, and beginning again. Yet, the Lord could not be left out. He comes first. I sent them to the Father to reconcile with Him. Though they had hurt each other, they were hurting Him first. His laws had been broken, and they were not following His Word. Today, they are living with each other in a more mutually loving, understanding, and respectful way before the Lord. The husband has stopped his yelling, and the wife has stopped her responding with alcohol.

They have found real harmony and unity as they work out their differences together. The key to the resolution to this entire problem was to stand before our God and answer to Him first. When we think we are only accountable to our spouses or others, then it is easy to continue the sinful and inappropriate behaviors and not reconcile. When the Lord God, master of our lives, enters the conflict, then our minds become clear, and the right response will come through the

Holy Spirit. So often, Christians in their many relationships fail to consider Christ as the Lord of their relationship. When they focus on each other alone, anything can happen.

A Personal Response

Dear Heavenly Father,

When I was sinning against (add name), I did not realize that I was first and foremost sinning against You. I did not recognize that You were right there with me, and Your laws were being transgressed. I am deeply sorry for all the sinful thoughts, words, and actions I have committed toward (add name) which were against You too. I have transgressed Your righteous law. Help me to reconcile with (add name) so we may honor and glorify You. I pray this in the name of Jesus. Amen.

Instructor's Notes

Chapter 1

Involve God First

The first important step in the reconciliation process is the recognition that no matter who else we have sinned against; we have sinned against our God first.

In the section, "A Typical Scenario," the author describes an argument someone might have had with another that could require a reconciliation.

What is the scenario about?

A Christian is arguing over something that had previously been decided with another.

What did the conflict concern?

It is unclear but could be many different issues.

What was the relationship between the parties?

They were a spouse, parent, child, or friend.

Have you had a similar experience?

(Various answers should be shared including yours.)

HEALING RELATIONSHIPS THROUGH FORGIVENESS

In the section, "A Scriptural Principle" the author presents an important biblical principle in the forgiveness process which concerns our sins against God in relationships.

How would you express this principle in your own words?

The first principle is "we must recognize that our sin is first against God."

(*Various answers should be shared including yours.*)

How would you rewrite this principle to make it even more personal to your life (using your name and situation)?

(*Various answers should be shared including yours.*)

Why do you think this principle might be important in your life right now?

(*Various answers should be shared including yours.*)

How would you rate yourself on the percentage of times you followed this principle in the past when you did something wrong in a relationship?

(*Various answers should be shared including yours.*)

Directions: Put a horizontal mark and your name where you see yourself on the percentage line.

| 0% | 25% | 50% | 75% | 100% |

In the section, "A Biblical Explanation," the author explains the reasons why our sin is first against the Lord God when we sin against others in a relationship and what we should do about it.

In Psalm 51:4, what did King David really mean when he wrote "against you and you alone" have I sinned?

David is stating that His transgression against God is completely separate, wholly different, and stands alone when compared to anyone else that has been transgressed. He had sinned against Bathsheba, Uriah, their families, and even the nation of Israel as their leader, but this cannot be compared to the gravity and the seriousness of his sin against God.

Why must the Lord God be dealt with on an "utterly divine level" when we transgress others?

Why? God is above all else in the universe (Psalm 115:3). He is the ruler of all nations (Psalm 22:28) and the sovereign God (Ephesians 1:11). God is the law giver, and His law has been transgressed (James 2:10; 4:12). Most of all, His Son is our Lord (Romans 10:12-13). He was present listening to the conversation as we argued. He stands before us in every transgression. He must be asked for forgiveness.

The others transgressed do not set standards of behavior. God alone does. The Lord must be dealt with on a separate and utterly divine level before all others in the transgression.

According to Psalm 41:4 and 11–13, what will we experience when we confess our sins to God first?

Then this great king paints a beautiful picture of the relief he experiences in forgiveness. In Psalm 41:11-13, he shouts, "By this,

HEALING RELATIONSHIPS THROUGH FORGIVENESS

I know that you delight in me, because my enemy doesn't triumph over me.

According to Matthew 6:12 (the Lord's Prayer), what must we do before we forgive others?

An essential part of our prayers is asking God the Father for forgiveness. What an amazing thing it is to be able to come before our loving God and ask for forgiveness! When we arrive at His throne in prayer as His children, we will find a God who is ready, willing, and able to forgive any transgression! No one understood this better than King David.

According to Psalm 86:5, when we come to God and ask for forgiveness what is He ready to do?

When we sin against God, He never forsakes us. Instead, God waits in readiness for our return to Him in repentance and confession. David acknowledges this in his Psalm 86:5, when the king wrote, "For you, Lord, are good, and ready to forgive; abundant in loving kindness to all those who call on you." This God of ours is ready to forgive when we sin. He is full of love and kindness to all who call upon Him. Then in verse 8, he shouts, "There is no one like you among the gods, Lord, nor any deeds like your deeds." In the midst of God's willingness to forgive, He only demands that we come to Him first to reconcile our relationships. He is our Lord; we must humble ourselves before Him in repentance, before we humble ourselves before others.

In what ways might these truths impact your relationships?

(Various answers should be shared including yours.)

In the section, "An Ancient Portrait," the author provides the unique portrayal of King David's sin with Bathsheba and its resultant cover-up.

What was David's sin against Uriah?

He noticed a beautiful woman bathing in the privacy of her home and wanted her.

David was king [of Israel] and could have any woman he wanted whenever he wanted her. So, he commanded his servants to bring her to him. He was the king, and she could not refuse.

How did David attempt to cover up his sin?

So, a clever idea came to him. He would call Uriah, her husband and a soldier, back from the battlefield. When he returned, Uriah would sleep with Bathsheba and think her child was his; the king directed his commander Joab to return Uriah to him.

Now what was the king going to do? David conjured up another plan; he would invite Uriah to stay in his palace for the night and enjoy a magnificent meal with much drinking. Once her husband was fully intoxicated, the man would lose this silly notion and sleep with his wife as David had.

In that letter was the King's final scheme and Uriah's death knell. Joab was to assign this obstinate soldier to the front lines of battle. At an opportune time, the troops around him would withdraw, and Uriah would be killed in battle.

HEALING RELATIONSHIPS THROUGH FORGIVENESS

How did God feel about what David had done?

With this recognition of David's heinous sin came a series of judgments pronounced upon David from God Himself. How could David have done such a thing before God? It is easy he just pretended God was not there. Yet, He was.

What was David's response after Nathan confronted him?

After this incident, King David repented of these sins and asked God for forgiveness. This is when he penned the inspired words of Psalm 51.

Though not mentioned, what would David have needed to do once he had reconciled with God?

We expect that David as a man of God would have reconciled in some way with Uriah's family.

Have you ever been in any situation comparable to David's who attempted to cover up his sin or Uriah's who had somebody try and deceive him? How was it different and how was it the same?

(Various answers should be shared including yours.)

AN INSTRUCTOR'S MANUAL

In the section, "A Modern Anecdote," the author discusses a situation in which a woman's alcohol consumption reached an extreme level and the problems that occurred.

How had the wife's drinking problem escalated to the point that she needed counseling for her and her husband?

It came to a boiling point when the husband found his wife lying on the front lawn of his house in the morning. She was wearing her pajamas, and the lawn sprinklers were running. She was almost completely unconscious and not aware she was even getting wet.

What individual responsibility did the wife and her husband bear for her difficulties with alcohol?

It turns out that the husband was always annoyed at her for a variety of habits she had constantly displayed during their marriage. As a result, he would pick at her and criticize her for many of the things she did.

The house was not clean enough for his tastes. The list just went on and on. Rather than discussing the situation with him, the wife drank and drank. The more he picked on her, the more she drank.

How did the both of them improperly handle the drinking problem?

The more she drank, the more he criticized and picked on her. Until finally all of it had gotten so out of control, their marriage was on the line.

What are two biblical reasons (with verses) why this was not the best approach?

The Scriptures do not speak to many of the issues directly but do indicate that both partners must love, respect, and understand each other (Ephesians 5:33; 1 Peter 3:7).

The Scriptures are clear that believers are not to argue or quarrel (2 Timothy 2:24; Proverbs 18:19; 20:3; 22:10) and Christians are never to be drunk (Ephesians 5:18; Romans 13:13; Psalm 69:12). This approach dishonored the Lord.

How did the couple begin the reconciliation process using A Scriptural Principle discussed in this chapter?

The key to the resolution to this entire problem was to stand before our God and answer to Him first. When we think we are only accountable to our spouses or others, then it is easy to continue the sinful and inappropriate behaviors and not reconcile.

Based on the truths learned in this chapter, what would you have done differently if you were the wife or the husband?

(Various answers should be shared including yours.)

In the section, "A Personal Response," the author provides a model you may use for prayer if you find it necessary after discovering the truths in this chapter.

Are you presently in a relationship where you have sinned against another and have not asked God for forgiveness? If not, is there one from the past that still needs this prayer to be prayed?

(Various answers should be shared including yours.)

Based on the truths you have just learned, what will you continue doing in your current relationships and what will you do differently?

(Various answers should be shared including yours.)

What additional thoughts would you like to share with the others?

(Various answers should be shared including yours.)

Instructor's Notes

Chapter 2

Leave Nothing Out

In the first chapter, we learned we must recognize that we are sinning against God first. Therefore, we should reconcile with Him before attempting to reconcile with the person we may have wronged in a relationship. As we walk into God's presence to ask for forgiveness, we must realize God knows the entire story and every detail of what we have done. As we confess our transgressions, we must admit to all of them holding nothing back.

A Typical Scenario

Have you ever had or heard a phone conversation with a customer representative that went something like this? You say or hear, "No! The item that you gave me is not working. First, I talked to you, and then you put me on hold, and sent me to somebody else. She also put me on hold and sent me to another person, and he placed me on hold while I was talking. Then, I was disconnected. I had to call back! This is the third time I have called about this same exact problem. Obviously, none of you know what you are doing! (Person responds.) Okay! Fine! Goodbye!"

We all have had this kind of interaction with a customer service representative of a company. Then sometime later, we suddenly start feeling guilty for how poorly we treated the representative. Then we think, "Well, nobody saw it. Nobody is here. Nobody is around! So, what is the harm?" This couldn't be further from the truth. There is one person who sees everything that we do. He is the invisible observer of all our good and evil behavior, and nothing escapes His gaze. This person is God. We may attempt to conceal a small or minute detail of what we did to others we have hurt in a relationship, but we cannot hide it from our Father. We may think unkind thoughts about people, even say something evil to someone about them, or do something in secret that is against them, but God sees it all. When we ask Him for forgiveness, these should not be left out. Everything should be confessed as the Holy Spirit brings them to mind.

A Scriptural Principle

The second principle is "we must know that God knows all our sins, so we must own up to all of them." Sometimes, when we go to ask for forgiveness from someone, we do not want to accept all of the responsibility we had in the sin. We want to leave out some of the words or actions which may embarrass us the most or lessen our responsibility. At other times, we like to alter the story slightly to make us look a little better; this is not the way God deals with things. God desires us to confess to Him everything we said or did, not just what we might feel is expedient, convenient, or even less embarrassing to us.

A Biblical Explanation

There might be times, where it would be too hurtful and not edifying to disclose everything, we thought or may have said in private to someone we have wronged, but we should confess these to God. As a result, when we confess our sins and ask for forgiveness from the ones we wronged, none of the important details will be left out. We should take the true responsibility for what happened as we go before the throne of our God in prayer.

Confession before God involves the acknowledgement of all our sin. In Psalm 32:3-4, David describes the torment he felt when he refused to confess all his sins and kept them bottled up inside. He sobs, "When I kept silence, my bones wasted away through my groaning all day long. For day and night your hand was heavy on me. My strength was sapped in the heat of summer. Selah." Then in the next verse, he finally acknowledges all his sin. In Psalm 32:5, he continues, "I acknowledged my sin to you. I didn't hide my iniquity. I said, I will confess my transgressions to Yahweh, and you forgave the iniquity of my sin. Selah." Then the king paints a beautiful picture of the relief that he experiences. In Psalm 32:11, David adds this, "Be glad in Yahweh, and rejoice, you righteous! Shout for joy, all you who are upright in heart!"

When Solomon cried out to God for the forgiveness of his people, it was for all their transgressions. In 1 Kings 8:50, he proclaimed these powerful words, "And forgive your people who have sinned against you, and all their transgressions in which they have transgressed against you; and give them compassion before those who carried them captive, that they may have compassion on them." We must admit every detail of what happened between us and the person or persons we have transgressed. God wants all confessed before Him.

In Psalm 90:8, Moses acknowledges this when he asserts, "You have set our iniquities before you, our secret sins in the light of your presence." Both Moses and the nation of Israel had a problem with sin, and he states that their iniquities and sin were before the Lord, even the hidden ones. These secret transgressions that no one knows are exposed in the light of God's presence. The light of God's holiness brings to light all our sins, even the ones hidden from all. Moses is explaining that the Lord sees all our sins. No iniquity can be hidden from Him. Once we are cognizant of His continual presence, His light exposes our sin.

God even knows the transgressions we do not realize we have committed. In Psalm 19:12, David declares, "Who can discern his errors?" Then the king cries, "Forgive me from hidden errors." When no one knows, even ourselves, a sin that we have committed, still our God knows! Then in Psalm 69:5, David cries out, "God, you know my foolishness. My sins aren't hidden from you." In Psalm 44, the sons of Korah describe how God's people had fallen into idolatry. In verses 20-21, they exclaimed, "If we have forgotten the name of our God, or spread out our hands to a strange god; won't God search this out? For he knows the secrets of the heart." God knows all that happened, and it cannot be hidden from him.

In Proverbs 15:3, King Solomon characterizes God in this way, "Yahweh's eyes are everywhere, keeping watch on the evil and the good." While God is keeping watch, our Father is pleased or displeased with what He sees. In verse 26, the king writes, "Yahweh detests the thoughts of the wicked, but the thoughts of the pure are pleasing." So not only is God viewing all our behavior but actually judging it according to His standards. He is watching how we treat the people we interact with in our lives.

Since God can look deeply into the recesses of our hearts and minds, He can also clearly see our motives and reasons for our behavior toward others. In Proverbs 17:3, Solomon adds, "The refining pot is for silver, and the furnace for gold, but Yahweh tests the hearts." In Proverbs 16:2, the wise king declared, "All the ways of a man are clean in his own eyes; but Yahweh weighs the motives." As God is weighing our hearts, we may see some thought, word, or action as of no account or even righteous, but God may judge it differently. He may see it as evil.

Why do we often attempt to cover up the evil we do from God? He knows us completely. In Psalm 139:4, David cries aloud, "For there is not a word on my tongue, but behold, Yahweh, you know it altogether." Even before any word is spoken by us, it is already before His eyes. Nothing can be hidden; everything must be confessed (if we know about it). When we start the process of reconciliation, we all must first recognize that we have transgressed God's law and should confess everything to Him.

So, we must go before God with every thought, word, and action and lay them bare before Him. How do we do this? Through prayer, we ask the Holy Spirit to convict us of any transgression in the breakup of the relationship that we have committed. One of the responsibilities of the Holy Spirit in our lives is to convict us of sin (John 16:8). How does He do this? In Psalm 139:23-24, David beseeches, "Search me, God, and know my heart. Try me and know my thoughts." Then he adds, "See if there is any wicked way in me and lead me in the everlasting way." He entreats the Lord to show Him where he has failed.

Can we imagine the power of asking the Lord to convict us of our responsibility in an incident in our relationship with a spouse, parent, friend, fellow student, teacher, or co-worker? Are we not always reviewing in our minds what they did, when we should really be reviewing what we did! As we are engaging in this prayer, we should be searching the Scripture. Conviction will come from the Holy Spirit through the truth of the Word of God.

In Hebrews 4:12, the author of Hebrews explains, "For the word of God is living and active, and sharper than any two-edged sword, piercing even to the dividing of soul and spirit, of both joints and marrow, and is able to discern the thoughts and intentions of the heart." The Scriptures can dig deep into our very hearts and discern thoughts, motives, and intentions. Then God will convict us of them.

In 2 Timothy 2:7, Paul exhorted Timothy, his son in the faith, to be a gentle, yet strong shepherd of God; then, Paul adds this request, "Consider what I say, and may the Lord give you understanding in all things." Paul was confident that the Lord would help him understand everything he had told him, including where he had gone wrong and how he could correct the situation. In Psalm 119:169, thousands of years ago, the psalmist proclaimed, "Let my cry come before you, Yahweh. Give me understanding according to your word." He knew that God's Word would convict him as he cried out to the Lord God. In Psalm 119:175-176, this psalm ends with these beautiful words, "Let my soul live, that I may praise you. Let your ordinances help me. I have gone astray like a lost sheep. Seek your servant, for I don't forget your commandments." When we go astray, these commands in His Word guide us back.

The best way to do this is to go step by step through every thought, word, and action in the transgression. We should judge each one according to the Word and depend on the Holy Spirit to guide us. Notice, we go through our actions, not the other person's. Often, when we recount a falling out between us and others, we carefully judge their thoughts (inferred by us), words, and actions; then, we get angrier and angrier, sometimes even letting ourselves off the hook in the light of their transgression. This is not God's way. We are responsible for our actions before God, not theirs.

Additional Notes: Here are excerpts from the prayer David prayed to help Him search his heart through the Word and have the Lord reveal his sins:

Psalm 139:1-4
Yahweh, you have searched me, and you know me. You know my sitting down and my rising up. You perceive my thoughts from afar. You [God] search out my path and my lying down and are

acquainted with all my ways [of living]. For there is not a word on my tongue, but behold, Yahweh, you know it altogether.

Psalm 139:7-12
Where could I go from your Spirit? Or where could I flee from your presence? If I ascend up into heaven, you are there. If I make my bed in Sheol, behold, you are there! If I take the wings of the dawn and settle in the uttermost parts of the sea; Even there your hand will lead me, and your right hand [of power] will hold me. If I say, "Surely the darkness will overwhelm me; the light around me will be night"; even the darkness doesn't hide from you, but the night shines as the day. The darkness is like light to you.

Psalm 139:17-18
How precious to me are your thoughts, God! How vast is their sum! If I would count them, they are more in number than the sand. When I wake up, I am still with you.

Psalm 139:23-24
Search me, God, and know my heart. Try me and know my thoughts. See if there is any wicked way in me and lead me in the everlasting way.

An Ancient Portrait

In Genesis 1-3, we are given the story of Adam and Eve as they walked with the Lord God in the Garden of Eden and their subsequent fall from His grace. God created man and placed him in a garden. Adam was given the responsibility to name the animals and subdue the earth. God told Adam that He could eat of all trees of the garden, except for the Tree of the Knowledge of Good and Evil. As Adam named the animals, it became evident there was not a companion suitable for him as there was in the animal kingdom. The Lord God saw that it was not good for Adam to be alone and proceeded to create a woman for him. God put Adam into a deep sleep and then took from his body one of his ribs and formed that into a companion for him.

When Adam awoke he declared that the woman was now bone of his bones and flesh of his flesh. As a result, a man is to leave his father and mother and cleave to his wife. They will join together and become one flesh. This is when God created marriage. While Adam and Eve were in the garden and enjoying its many fruits and God's presence, suddenly a serpent appeared. We know that this was the Devil, but Eve did not know. The Serpent asked Eve about the Tree of the Knowledge of Good and Evil. When she said that it would essentially kill them if they ate of it, he disagreed. Instead, he told Eve that if she ate of it, her eyes would be opened, and she would be like God. Nice thought! Be Divine! Big Lie!

So, Eve looked at the tree. She saw that it was good for food; it delighted her eyes and would make her wise like God. She grabbed its fruit and ate. Then she handed it over to Adam and he ate it also. Suddenly, they realized that they were naked. Why? For the first time, they understood lust and evil desire, so they sought to cover themselves with leaves. They wanted to remove the shame they felt at being naked. Then they heard God coming. Now what were they going to do? Of course, they decided to hide from God.

They wanted to conceal their sin from God. So off to the bushes they went. Did they really think they could get away with this? Yes. Do we really think we can hide our sin from an all-knowing God? Yes, we really do. We fool ourselves by simply committing the sin without any thoughts of God. Put Him out of our mind while we fight, argue, yell, scream at someone and pick Him up later on. Perhaps, this is exactly what Adam and Eve also did. Where were their thoughts of God while they were being tempted?

Of course, God knows exactly where they are. God knows everything. He began making sounds as He approached, so the couple would know He was on His way. This was their first chance to admit to everything they had done. Instead, they hid themselves because the two were naked. They were more concerned about the situation of their nakedness, then the fact that they had just transgressed the Lord God. Are we not like that? We can get so wrapped up in the situation; we forget He is right there being transgressed.

Then the Lord God called to Adam and asked him where he was. Here God provided another opportunity for them to spring forth from their hiding place and admit all they had done. Instead, Adam explains that they had hid themselves because they were naked. God then inquired as to how they knew they were naked and whether they had eaten from the tree. Adam responded with man's first real excuse for his sin which will lead to a long history of excuses. Adam blamed the Lord and His wife. His wife blamed the Serpent who had tricked her.

There is a whole lot of finger-pointing at each other not at themselves. Adam blames the Lord God for giving him the woman in the first place. This action created the whole mess. The woman, Eve, blames the Serpent for his trickery. It was entirely someone else's fault; of course they would think that as we do. Though not really mentioned directly, we know they admitted all of their sins, but the damage had already been done. The human race had fallen into sin which would lead to both physical and eternal death.

Believe me, we all have our excuses why the relationship was fouled up, and it is never our fault! We are the victims! Had our wives, husbands, sons, daughters, fathers, mothers, friends, acquaintances, co-workers, fellow students, or even customer service representatives acted any differently, we would not have reacted the way we did! Does this not sound familiar? We want to always be the victim! If we can blame someone else, we do not have to carry the full guilt for the destruction of the relationship. Unfortunately, that doesn't work for God, and it did not work for Adam and Eve. God desires people to take responsibility for their sins. He will not take any excuses.

Additional Notes: And we know why. Our God is omniscient (all-knowing). He cannot be fooled, though everybody else can be. That is why we must go to God first and hold nothing back from Him. This does not mean that we have to take all the responsibility. We are to be responsible for our part. If we take all the responsibility to quiet things down, then how will God be able to work in all their lives, as He is working in ours? When we have insulted, offended, or even hurt someone, we need to acknowledge that God has seen this. He knows the thoughts, intentions, words, and actions. Then we must stand before Him and confess all our sins.

We must take all of our responsibility for what happened before we ever go to the person or people involved. Then, when we go to those people who have been mistreated, the reconciliation will be full and complete without any lingering doubts or bitterness on our part or theirs. More importantly, our relationship to the Lord God ought to be reconciled first. He will have His proper place in our lives.

A Modern Anecdote

Many of my male clients have struggled with the evil of pornography. One such husband came to my office with his wife livid over his many mental affairs. While weeping, she recounted the evening she had found him in a compromised position lounging at his computer. As her emotions flooded out of her, he sat slumped over with his head down quietly muttering how difficult this all was and how embarrassed he felt. It was an utterly sad day for their relationship, but they desired to overcome this predicament with God's help. They both wanted a strong marriage once again. They had entered into a lifetime covenant and were determined to remain in it.

Unfortunately, this problem can have multiple reasons for the issue to begin and multiple different reasons for the issue to have continued. It took some time to fully discover all of the factors involved and the extent to which the husband had actually sinned. Needless to say, pornography is a sin of the heart. It is sexual immorality of the heart (Matthew 5:28; 1 Corinthians 6:18; Galatians 5:19). There were many nights and more websites than he could even recall.

Additional Notes: If asked about the sinfulness of all pornography, here are the Bible references I cite:

Matthew 5:28
But I tell you that everyone who gazes at a woman to lust after her has committed adultery with her already in his heart.

Galatians 5:19
Now the deeds of the flesh are obvious, which are: adultery, sexual immorality, uncleanness, lustfulness.

As I met with him individually, he was even too ashamed to disclose the full extent of what he had seen, nor could he admit everything he had done to his dear wife. Neither was actually necessary. This believer was accountable to His God first, and He would confess all of it to Him and Him alone. I did not need to know every detail to help him, and his dear wife did not need to be traumatized by all that he had done, since it was confined to his computer and the images alone.

Yet, to begin their healing process, this husband had to acknowledge that God had been there all along and he had done such evil in His presence. I will always remember that day he cried to the Lord in my office mumbling silently his sorrow while confessing the minute details of His sin to His Savior and Lord as I sat next to him praying. The man knew that Jesus Christ was forgiving him even as he was uttering quietly his many transgressions.

Then the healing process was initiated with his wife as he confessed to her his sins, and she forgave him. Over a course of time, these unrighteous practices were put away and fully replaced with holy ones that honored the Lord (Galatians 5:19-25; Ephesians 4:25-32). He battled with his flesh to keep from stumbling, and she battled with hers to fully forgive him.

Additional Notes: If asked about the evil deeds of the flesh that Christians struggle with, here are the Bible references I cite:

Galatians 5:19-25
Now the deeds of the flesh are obvious, which are: adultery, sexual immorality, uncleanness, lustfulness, idolatry, sorcery, hatred, strife, jealousies, outbursts of anger, rivalries, divisions, heresies, envy, murders, drunkenness, orgies, and things like these; of which I forewarn you...as I also forewarned you, that those who practice such things will not inherit God's Kingdom. But the fruit of the [Holy] Spirit is love, joy, peace, patience, kindness, goodness, faith, gentleness, and self-control. Against such things there is no law. Those who belong to Jesus Christ have crucified the flesh with its passions and lusts. If we live by the Spirit, let's also walk by the Spirit.

Ephesians 4:25-32
Therefore, putting away falsehood, speak truth each one with his neighbor. For we are members of one another. "Be angry, and don't sin." Don't let the sun go down on your wrath, and don't give place to the devil. Let him who stole steal no more; but rather let him labor, producing with his hands something that is good, that

he may have something to give to him who has need. Let no corrupt speech proceed out of your mouth, but only what is good for building others up as the need may be, that it may give grace to those who hear. Don't grieve the Holy Spirit of God, in whom you were sealed for the day of redemption. Let all bitterness, wrath, anger, outcry, and slander, be put away from you, with all malice. And be kind to one another, tender hearted, forgiving each other, just as God also in Christ forgave you.

Eventually, victory came on both their parts, and the issue was finally settled in their relationship. I must mention one last thing. During the process, the man's wife realized that some things she did and did not do concerning their sexual interactions contributed to his problem. She realized that she perhaps had not fulfilled all of her responsibilities sexually to her husband (1 Corinthians 7:1-5). This contributed to his sexually charged state when the woman's advances began.

Additional Notes: If asked about the true responsibility of spouses to each other sexually, here is the Bible reference I cite:

1 Corinthians 7:1-5
Now concerning the things about which you wrote to me: it is good for a man not to touch a woman [single]. But, because of sexual immoralities, let each man have his own wife, and let each woman have her own husband. Let the husband render to his wife the affection owed her, and likewise also the wife to her husband. The wife doesn't have authority over her own body, but the husband. Likewise, also the husband doesn't have authority over his own body, but the wife. Don't deprive one another, unless... by consent for a season, that you may give yourselves to fasting and prayer, and may be together again, that Satan doesn't tempt you because of your lack of self-control.
Though this was difficult to bear and not an excuse for his sin, she asked the Lord and her husband for forgiveness.

A Personal Response

Dear Heavenly Father,

I recognize you are present everywhere I go and view everything I do. While I was reading this chapter, I realized that I have kept back from confessing all of the sins that I committed against (add name). I now confess them to You (list them). I am so sorry. I have transgressed your holy and righteous law. Please give me the courage to admit all my wrongs to (add name). Help me to honor and glorify You in my relationship with (add name) and follow your Word. I pray this in the name of Jesus. Amen.

Chapter 2

Leave Nothing Out

As we ask for forgiveness, we must realize God knows every detail of what we have done. So, we must confess all our wrongdoing in the relationship and hold nothing back.

In the section, "A Typical Scenario," the author describes an encounter one might have with a customer representative on the phone which may require a reconciliation.

What is the scenario about?

A Christian was speaking to a customer service representative and was put on hold, then disconnected and is yelling at the person.

What did the conflict concern?

He needed to return an item that was not working, and no one was helping him adequately.

What was the relationship between the parties?

He was a customer of company and he or she was the customer service representative.

Have you had a similar experience?

(Various answers should be shared including yours.)

HEALING RELATIONSHIPS THROUGH FORGIVENESS

In the section, "A Scriptural Principle" the author presents an important biblical principle in the forgiveness process which concerns our sin against God.

How would you express this principle in your own words?

The second principle is "we must know that God knows all our sins, so we must own up to all of them."

(Various answers should be shared including yours.)

How would you rewrite this principle to make it even more personal to your life (using your name and situation)?

(Various answers should be shared including yours.)

Why do you think this principle might be important in your life right now?

(Various answers should be shared including yours.)

How would you rate yourself on the percentage of times you followed this principle in the past when you did something wrong in a relationship?

(Various answers should be shared including yours.)

Directions: Put a horizontal mark and your name where you see yourself on the percentage line.

| 0% | 25% | 50% | 75% | 100% |

AN INSTRUCTOR'S MANUAL

In the section, "A Biblical Explanation," the author explains the reasons why we should own up to all our sins against others in a relationship and what we should do about it.

According to David's words in Psalm 32:3-4, and 11, what did he feel before and then after he confessed all his sins?

In Psalm 32:3-4, David describes the torment he felt when he refused to confess all his sins and kept them bottled up inside.

Then the king paints a beautiful picture of the relief that he experiences.

What are two examples (with the passages that support them) of individuals who acknowledged that God's people should confess all of their sins before Him?

When Solomon cried out to God for the forgiveness of his people, it was for all their transgressions. In 1 Kings 8:50, he proclaimed these powerful words, "And forgive your people who have sinned against you, and all their transgressions in which they have transgressed against you; and give them compassion before those who carried them captive, that they may have compassion on them." We must admit every detail of what happened between us and the person or persons we have transgressed. God wants all confessed before Him.

In Psalm 90:8, Moses acknowledges this when he asserts, "You have set our iniquities before you, our secret sins in the light of your presence." Both Moses and the nation of Israel had a problem with sin, and he states that their iniquities and sin were before the Lord, even the hidden ones.

In 1 Kings 8:50, what key phrase is used to indicate that Solomon was asking God to forgive every sin of His people?

Solomon uses the phrase "all their transgressions."

In Psalm 90:8, what key phrase is used to indicate that Moses was asking God to forgive all the sins of His people?

In Psalm 90:8, Moses acknowledges this when he asserts, "You have set our iniquities before you, our secret sins in the light of your presence.

According to Psalm 139:4 and Hebrews 4:12, how might we discover the sins we have committed in a relationship?

Why do we often attempt to cover up the evil we do from God? He knows us completely. In Psalm 139:4, David cries aloud, "For there is not a word on my tongue, but behold, Yahweh, you know it altogether." Even before any word is spoken by us, it is already before His eyes. Nothing can be hidden; everything must be confessed (if we know about it). When we start the process of reconciliation, we all must first recognize that we have transgressed God's law and should confess everything to Him.

In Hebrews 4:12, the author of Hebrews explains, "For the word of God is living and active, and sharper than any two-edged sword, piercing even to the dividing of soul and spirit, of both joints and marrow, and is able to discern the thoughts and intentions of the heart." The Scriptures can go deep into our hearts and discern thoughts, motives, and intentions. Then God will convict us of them.

In what ways might these truths impact your relationships?

(Various answers should be shared including yours.)

In the section, "An Ancient Portrait," the author provides an example of Adam and Eve committing a sin against God and their unwillingness to own up to all that they did.

When God placed Adam and Eve in the garden, what were they to do?

God created man and placed him in a garden. Adam was given the responsibility to name the animals and subdue the earth.

What was the transgression that Adam and Eve committed which destroyed their initial relationship to God?

God told Adam that He could eat of all trees of the garden, except for the Tree of the Knowledge of Good and Evil. As Adam named the animals, it became evident there was not a companion suitable for him as there was in the animal kingdom.

She grabbed its fruit and ate. Then she handed it over to Adam and he ate it also.

They wanted to conceal their sin from God.

Rather than admit all he had done, who did Adam blame?

Adam blamed the Lord and His wife.

Adam responded with man's first real excuse for his sin which will lead to a long history of excuses. Adam blamed the Lord and His wife.

HEALING RELATIONSHIPS THROUGH FORGIVENESS

Rather than admit all she had done, who did Eve blame?

This action created the whole mess. The woman, Eve, blames the Serpent for his trickery.

Did God give them opportunities to admit all they had done wrong to Him?

This was their first chance to admit to everything they had done. Instead, they hid themselves because the two were naked.

Then the Lord God called to Adam and asked him where he was. Here God provided another opportunity for them to spring forth from their hiding place and admit all they had done.

Have you ever been in a situation that was similar to Adam and Eve's in which you or the other person blamed someone else for wrongdoing? How was it different and how was it the same?

(Various answers should be shared including yours.)

AN INSTRUCTOR'S MANUAL

In the section, "A Modern Anecdote," the author discusses a situation in which a husband had to own up to all the sins he committed in his sinful pornography habit before God.

How did the husband's pornography obsession negatively impact his relationship to his wife?

One such husband came to my office with his wife livid over his many mental affairs.

How did the husband feel after his wife found out?

As I met with him individually, he was even too ashamed to disclose the full extent of what he had seen, nor could he admit everything he had done to his dear wife. Neither was actually necessary.

What initial steps did the husband have to take to reconcile his relationship with God and then his wife?

Yet, to begin their healing process, this husband had to acknowledge that God had been there all along and he had done such evil in His presence. I will always remember that day he cried to the Lord in my office mumbling silently his sorrow while confessing the minute details of His sin to His Savior and Lord as I sat next to him praying.

Did this process come easily for the couple?

Over a course of time, these unrighteous practices were put away and fully replaced with holy ones that honored the Lord (Galatians 5:19-25; Ephesians 4:25-32). He battled with his flesh to keep from stumbling, and she battled with hers to fully forgive him.

Did the wife desire to accept any responsibility for what her husband had done? Should she have? Why or why not?

She realized that she perhaps had not fulfilled all of her responsibilities sexually to her husband (1 Corinthians 7:1-5). This contributed to his sexually charged state when the woman's advances began.

Based on the truths learned in this chapter, what would you have done differently if you were husband or wife?

(*Various answers should be shared including yours.*)

AN INSTRUCTOR'S MANUAL

In the section, "A Personal Response," the author provides a model you may use for prayer if you find it necessary after discovering the truths in this chapter.

Are you presently in a relationship where you have sinned against another and have not asked God for forgiveness? If not, is there one from the past that still needs this prayer to be prayed?

(Various answers should be shared including yours.)

Based on the truths you have just learned, what will you continue doing in your current relationships and what will you do differently?

(Various answers should be shared including yours.)

What additional thoughts would you like to share with the others?

(Various answers should be shared including yours.)

Instructor's Notes

Chapter 3

Admit Your Sin

When we have committed a transgression toward another person, we should reconcile our relationship with God first. When we approach God, we should leave nothing out. We are to take all of the sins we are responsible for in the breakdown of a relationship with someone to Him and admit our sin. This chapter explains the confession process toward God as outlined in Scripture. When this properly occurs, we will experience His full forgiveness and be ready to approach the other person we have transgressed.

A Typical Scenario

Have you ever been angry or upset because you received a traffic ticket that you perceived was unfair? Perhaps you described it to someone like this, "I am so angry and upset. The officer said I was reckless driving and gave me a ticket. Can you believe He said that I was eating a cheeseburger while I was driving? Well, you know what? I was. What's wrong that? A lot of people eat cheeseburgers while they're driving. Then, he said that I was texting, while I was eating the cheeseburger. Yeah, so what? I was texting, but I can still drive. You see, I can put my knees up on the wheel and drive that way. Oh, yes, he also wrote on the ticket that I had my dog on my lap which was distracting me. After I stopped texting, I used my electric shaver on my face. He must have been following me for a long time. How dare he give me a ticket? Doesn't he have anyone else to follow? There are a lot worse drivers out there than me. I certainly let that officer know how I felt about this ticket!"

Though the above is rather tongue-in-cheek rendering of a traffic ticket incident, it is meant to demonstrate how we often rationalize our mistakes, rather than admit them. We often try to figure out a way to get out of what we did that was wrong, instead of owning up to it and admitting that we had erred. This we must do!

A Scriptural Principle

The third principle in the reconciliation process is "we must fully repent of our sins and confess them before God." Often times, when we think of repentance, we may assume it simply means to be sorry for our sins. It actually has a fuller and broader meaning which encompasses three different aspects. True biblical repentance involves the admission of our sins, the sorrowing over those same transgressions, and the turning from those iniquities in a direction that is more righteous.

A Biblical Explanation

As God called us into His eternal kingdom, He first made us cognizant of our wretchedness and our sinfulness before Him. To become Christians, people had to proclaim sin and judgment to us, and we responded with repentance for that sin. This resulted from a real understanding of the absolute holiness of the Father, His Son, and the Spirit. As unsaved people, once we realized who Christ was, we came to fully understand just how unworthy and sinful we were before Him.

Additional Response: This was the response of the centurion when he asked Jesus to heal his servant. In Luke 7:1-10, this Roman desired Christ to heal him from afar. Why? The centurion knew he was unworthy to have Jesus [Christ] come to him because He was a wretched sinner. We should have the same sense.

People are not saved without this sense of unworthiness leading to repentance which demonstrates true belief. In 2 Timothy 2:24-26, Paul exhorts Timothy, his son in the faith, to gently correct those who are opposing him. Why? So, God will cause them to repent and lead them into knowledge of the truth. This is a reference to salvation. In Matthew 3:2, John the Baptist declared people should repent because the kingdom of God was at hand. Sometime later, in Matthew 4:17, the apostle revealed that the ministry of the Lord was preaching repentance and proclaiming the kingdom of God. Repentance is an essential part of the saving response.

2 Timothy 2:24-26
The Lord's servant must not quarrel, but be gentle towards all, able to teach, patient, 25 in gentleness correcting those who oppose him: perhaps God may give them repentance leading to a full knowledge of the truth, 26 and they may recover themselves out of the devil's snare, having been taken captive by him to his will.

Matthew 3:2
Repent, for the Kingdom of Heaven is at hand!

Matthew 4:17
From that time, Jesus began to preach, and to say, "Repent! For the Kingdom of Heaven is at hand.

It is important to note that repentance does not end at the moment of salvation. True believers in Christ will constantly be recognizing the sins that they are committing and asking God for forgiveness. This is not just an eternal issue but a relational one. When we received Christ as Savior and Lord, all of our sins were forgiven from the past, present, and future (Colossians 2:13-14; Romans 8:1). In our relationship with the Lord upon this earth in the flesh, we still confess our transgression. This restores our relationship with God in a relational sense and barriers are eliminated.

Colossians 2:13-14
You were dead through your trespasses and the uncircumcision of your flesh. He made you alive together with him, having forgiven us all our trespasses, 14 wiping out the handwriting in ordinances which was against us; and he has taken it out of the way, nailing it to the cross.

Romans 8:1
There is therefore now no condemnation to those who are in Christ Jesus, who don't walk according to the flesh, but according to the Spirit.

John speaks to this in his first letter. Some were saying in the church that they had matured to such a level that they no longer sinned in any way. John, the apostle, counters with a scathing response. In 1 John 1:8, the apostle emphatically states, "If we say that we have no sin, we deceive ourselves, and the truth is not in us." Then in verse 10, he declares, "If we say that we haven't sinned, we make him a liar, and his word is not in us." Those who claimed that they had never sinned or no longer sinned were simply lying to themselves, others, and God. The truth of His Word was not in them because this truth convicts us of sin.

Then sandwiched between these two convicting passages is what believers do when they realize they have sinned. In verse 9, he proclaims, "If we confess our sins, He is faithful and righteous to forgive us the sins, and to cleanse us from all unrighteousness." The verbs "confess" and "forgive" are in the present tense which indicates continual action in present time. Believers are continually confessing their sins, and God is continually forgiving them. Repentance and asking God to forgive us is a lifelong practice.

As we repent of our sins and experience God's constant forgiveness, then it becomes easier and easier to ask for the forgiveness of others we have transgressed. Also, it makes it much less difficult to accept the repentance of others as they transgress us. As saints, we must recognize our sinfulness or we might be destined to become angry, judgmental people.

This is exactly the point the Lord made in Matthew 7:1-5. Here Jesus spoke against the self-righteous attitudes of the Pharisees. They thought they were keeping the law perfectly and became bitter, angry, and judgmental critics of people. Jesus makes this pronouncement in verses 1-2, "Don't judge, so that you won't be judged. For with whatever judgment you judge, you will be judged; and with whatever measure you measure, it will be measured to you." Then in verses 3-4, The Lord inquires, "Why do you see the speck that is in your brother's eye, but don't consider the beam that is in your own eye? Or how will you tell your brother, 'Let me remove the speck from your eye;' and behold, the beam is in your own eye." Then in verse 5, Jesus chastises all of them saying, "You hypocrite! First remove the beam out of your own eye, and then you can see clearly to remove the speck out of your brother's eye." The beam is their rejection of Christ.

The Lord is explaining to them that they need to be taking care of their own sins first before they begin looking at the sins of another. The implication for us is astounding. As we constantly come in repentance before God and continually experience His grace, mercy, and love in forgiveness, it will create hearts in us that do the same for others. It will become easier for us to graciously and lovingly ask for forgiveness and mercifully and lovingly grant forgiveness to others. This in turn will make us people who are not so quick to judge the actions of others and condemn them. This passage is not banning judgment of any kind toward others; instead, it is requiring us to judge our own thoughts, words, actions, and attitudes first. This brings constant repentance.

As mentioned earlier, there are actually three aspects to the full concept of "repentance" in the Scripture. These are presented in various places by different writers in the New Testament. Repentance involves admitting the sins we have committed, sorrowing and mourning over their wickedness, and turning away from them toward righteousness. All of these are crucial elements in the repentance process and are expected and anticipated as the Spirit convicts us of our sin.

The first is the admission of sin. To fully repent, we must admit that we have sinned. This means that Christians are to acknowledge that the thoughts, words, and actions that they had taken were indeed sins. Notice 1 John 1:9 again, "If we confess our sins, He is faithful and righteous to forgive us the sins, and to cleanse us from all unrighteousness." John, the apostle, uses a critical word to explain his meaning. The Greek word translated "confess" literally means "to say the same thing." Our confession is to say the same thing about a thought, word, or action that God says about them. They are sinful. They are against God's law.

Additional Notes: If asked about the details concerning this rich young ruler, here is one of the three gospel references I cite:

Mark 10:17-31
As he was going out into the way, one ran to him, knelt before him, and asked him, "Good Teacher, what shall I do that I may inherit eternal life?" Jesus said to him, "Why do you call me good? No one is good except one – God. You know the commandments: 'Do not murder...commit adultery...steal...give false testimony...defraud,' 'Honor your father and mother.'" He said to him," Teacher, I have observed all these things from my youth." Jesus looking at him

loved him, and said to him, "One thing you lack. Go, sell whatever you have, and give to the poor, and you will have treasure in heaven; and come, follow me, taking up the cross." But his face fell at that saying, and he went away sorrowful, for he was one who had great possessions. Jesus looked around, and said to his disciples, "How difficult it is for those who have riches to enter into God's Kingdom!" The disciples were amazed at his words. But Jesus answered again, "Children, how hard is it for those who trust in riches to enter into God's Kingdom! It is easier for a camel to go through a needle's eye than for a rich man to enter into God's Kingdom." They were exceedingly astonished, saying..."Then who can be saved?" Jesus...said, "With men it is impossible, but not with God, for all things are possible with God." Peter began to tell him, "Behold, we have left all, and have followed you." Jesus said, "Most certainly I tell you, there is no one who has left house, or brothers...sisters...father...mother...wife... children, or land, for my sake, and for the sake of the Good News, but he will receive one hundred times more now in this time, houses, brothers, sisters, mothers, children, and land, with persecutions; and in the age to come eternal life. But many who are first will be last; and the last first."

When Jesus encountered a rich young ruler, he claimed to have kept the whole law from his youth up (Mark 10:17-31; Matthew 19:16-30; Luke 18:18-30). Could that be true? No, the rich young ruler simply refused to admit his sin. To him every single thought, word, and action from his youth up was righteous. So, Jesus told him to sell all he had which he refused to do. This manifested the real sin in his heart which was not displayed outwardly - greed. The Lord immediately exposed the iniquity which was deep within his heart, and he would not admit this was sinful.

Instead, this wealthy young ruler left Jesus with his self-righteousness and wealth intact but not saved. Kingdom people always admit their sin and ask for forgiveness on a regular basis. We must stand before the Lord God and tell him the thoughts, words, and actions we have committed and agree with Him that they were sinful and violated His law. As we do this, we are to hold nothing back that the Lord brings to our minds. Of course, He does not expect us to remember or even know all that we may have done.

The second aspect of repentance is to mourn over those sins. In the Beatitudes, the Lord Jesus speaks of the spiritual characteristics of His children. Though these qualities appear physical, they really refer to spiritual aspects of his kingdom people. In Matthew 5:3, Jesus declares, "Blessed are the poor in spirit, for theirs is the kingdom of God." There is no virtue in being poor. He was speaking of those poor in their spirit. The Greek word translated "poor" means "bankrupt" and refers to the acknowledgement that His people know they are spiritually bankrupt in sin. This is the first aspect, we just discussed.

The Lord continues in verse 4, "Blessed are those who mourn, for they shall be comforted." This remark speaks of mourning over our bankrupt condition before God as one mourns over the dead. It refers to a deep sorrow over our sin and wickedness which is the second aspect. When someone receives the Lord, they admit their sin and mourn, grieve, and sorrow over it. As we live our Christians lives, we will be constantly convicted of our sins and are to admit them to the Lord. Then we will experience a grieving process when we fully face what we did. There is sorrow and mourning over it.

In 1 Corinthians, Paul describes the sins and difficulties this church encountered because they had been prideful and rebellious. The apostle Paul was so deeply hurt because the church had taken a stand against him. False prophets had risen up and found a leader in the church. This sinful leader with most of the church stood against Paul, the apostle, and his ministry.

As a result, the apostle was forced to send a difficult and confrontational letter which is referred to in 2 Corinthians 2:3-4. When he finally visited, they did not respond well. So, he shortened his visit and departed. Later, Paul sent Titus to discover their final response to his letter of rebuke. When Titus returned, he brought wonderful news of the church's repentance for their evil stand (2 Corinthians).

In 2 Corinthians 7:9, Paul vividly described the extent of their sorrow, grief, and mourning over their sin. He wrote, "I now rejoice, not that you were made sorry, but that you were made sorry to repentance. For you were made sorry in a godly way, that you might suffer loss by us in nothing." He spoke of their godly sorrow which produces the repentance leading to salvation. This is the sorrow Christians have when they come to Christ and every day of their lives thereafter. He contrasts this with another in verse 10, "For godly sorrow works repentance to salvation, which brings no regret. But the sorrow of the world works death." The first sorrow leads to initial salvation and the other to final eternal damnation. The other is a sorrow but not a godly one. It leads to despair and guilt-ridden anguish.

The first is the sorrow expressed by the woman who came to Jesus in Luke 7:37-39. This grieving woman washed His feet with her many tears and wiped them with her hair in sorrow over her sin! Then, she kissed His feet and anointed them with expensive perfume. What humility and mourning over wrongdoing! The second sorrow produces bitterness, despair, anger, and pride. It desires to lash out at others for hurting them, rebuking them, or interrupting their sin. This emotion vents at oneself in punishment and self-hatred. It will not admit sin and plead for forgiveness.

The third aspect in repentance is the repentance of sins. Though this word is used with a fuller meaning in defining the entire concept, it also has a unique meaning of its own. The Greek word translated "repent" means "to turn around in the opposite direction or change one's mind or behavior." We must turn around from our confessed sins and move in the opposite direction. We must commit ourselves to living differently. Luke records Peter's denial of even knowing the Lord in Luke 22:62 and how the apostle wept in sorrow and remorse afterward. Later, Luke records in Acts numerous sermons that Peter preached in great boldness for Christ. Peter clearly demonstrated that he had fully turned in the opposite direction from that sin. Of course, the Holy Spirit will provide the strength needed in order to accomplish this supernatural feat (Acts 2:4; Romans 8:13).

Additional Notes: If asked about the power of the Holy Spirit to provide us strength, here are the Bible references I cite:

Acts 2:4
They were all filled with the Holy Spirit, and began to speak with other languages, as the Spirit gave them the ability to speak.

Romans 8:13
For if you live after the flesh, you must die; but if by the Spirit you put to death the deeds of the body, you will live.

Now, consider the response of Judas. In Matthew 27:3-9, he would not repent nor humble himself before the Lord Jesus and remove the guilt and sorrow through salvation. Instead, he simply killed himself to alleviate them from his life. This is the sorrow unto death.

Additional Notes: If asked about the lack of true repentance on the part of Judas, here are the Bible references I cite:

Matthew 27:3-9
Then Judas, who betrayed him, when he saw that Jesus was condemned, felt remorse, and brought back the thirty pieces of silver to the chief priests and elders, saying, "I have sinned in that I betrayed innocent blood." But they said, "What is that to us? You see to it." He threw down the pieces of silver in the sanctuary, and departed. He went away and hanged himself. The chief priests took the pieces of silver, and said, "It's not lawful to put them into the treasury, since it is the price of blood." They took counsel, and bought the potter's field with them, to bury strangers in. Therefore that field was called "The Field of Blood" to this day. Then that which was spoken through Jeremiah the prophet was fulfilled, saying, "They took the thirty pieces of silver, the price of him upon whom a price had been set, whom some of the children of Israel priced."

As we interlace the three principles we have studied in these initial chapters, we clearly see how we are to reconcile our relationship with the Lord, before we can reconcile with others. The response of all believers when they have sinned against another will be to turn toward God first and ask Him for forgiveness. This is accomplished through the admission of their wrongs, sorrow over their sin, and a turning toward righteousness while leaving no sin in the transgression out. This is how we are to reconcile with God, our Father.

An Ancient Portrait

This repentance process is distinctly seen in the story of Achan's sin in the book of Joshua, chapters 6-8. Joshua was the commander of the nation of Israel after Moses died. He brought God's people to the land of Canaan. He was told by God to wipe out the people in this wicked land. This was due to the horrible atrocities of the Canaanites. These people were so extremely wicked that even their possessions were unclean. No one was to take any plunder in the battles. Only gold and silver and a few other items were to be collected for the Lord's house. God was very serious about protecting the purity of His people and standing against their evil.

The first city to be defeated in their quest was Jericho. As most know, the walls came down through a miraculous feat of the Lord, and the city was taken. Now it was time to move on to a place called Ai. Having sent out spies, they realized this would require a small army to conquer them. So, their leader Joshua would only need 3000 men, not the normal 30,000. The army closed in on Ai with great expectations of a mighty victory.

Instead, the people of Ai ran them off killing 36 men and causing Israel to retreat in humiliating terror. Where was the power of the Lord God? What had happened? Something had gone terribly wrong. Joshua threw himself before the ark and begged the Lord to tell him what had happened. He was fearful that once the Canaanites heard of their miserable defeat, they would be run out of the country. The Lord told Joshua that one of his people had taken items from the city that was to be devoted solely to the Lord. The commander would have to find the violator and cleanse the nation from this atrocity. The Lord Himself would point him out, so all would know the seriousness of obeying the commandments of God Almighty, the God of Israel.

God told Joshua to bring the people before the Lord the next morning, and He would identify the transgressor. First, each tribe of the nation was brought before the Lord, and the Lord God singled out the tribe. Then He divided the tribe into smaller and smaller groups until He arrived at Achan and his family. So, this man Achan was required by Joshua to stand before the Lord Almighty and give Him glory and honor by admitting the sinful action he had taken. This is so crucial to our understanding of how to reconcile with God.

The admission of our wrongdoing glorifies the Lord God by recognizing His sovereignty and power over all people. Then Achan admitted his transgression in detail. In Joshua 7:20, the author recorded, "Achan answered Joshua, and said, 'I have truly sinned against Yahweh, the God of Israel, and this is what I have done.'" Notice, Achan admits he has broken God's law and sinned against God first. Then Achan describes exactly how he had sinned in verse 21. He explains this, "When I saw among the plunder a beautiful Babylonian robe, two hundred shekels of silver, and a wedge of gold weighing fifty shekels, then I coveted them and took them. Behold, they are hidden in the ground in the middle of my tent, with the silver under it."

Notice what the man did not do. He did not demonstrate any mourning over what he had done or committed himself and his family to living righteously from then on. He did not fully reconcile with God. Also, he did not reconcile with the people of Israel or Joshua. They had lost thirty-six lives and experienced a major defeat. Instead, he admits what he did, shows them where the possessions are hidden, and accepts the punishment. It appears that there was no repentance, mourning, and turning toward righteousness.

All of us deserve physical death the very first time we sin and every time after that (Romans 3:26). Yet, God displays tremendous mercy on us all. At other times, the Lord God determines that He will not show His mercy and grace in withholding physical death to teach His people an important lesson. This was one of those times. The perpetrators of this atrocity against God's holiness were taken out and stoned to death. All their possessions, including the possessions they had taken, were burned with their bodies. Then a heap of rocks was put over it as a memorial in order to teach future generations the utter seriousness of obeying the Lord God and honoring His holiness.

When we sin against others, sometimes we rationalize our actions and will not admit what we did, mourn over it, and turn the other way. This is not how God deals with us. We must stop the rationalization and make things right with the Lord which honors and glorifies Him. Once our relationship with Him is fully reconciled, we will be ready to reconcile with those we have wronged. These steps are critical in the forgiveness process.

A Modern Anecdote

Sometime ago, a young man entered my counseling office with his parents because they thought he seemed depressed and sad. Since he was twenty-three (an adult), I had to bid the parents goodbye. This young man had been through a difficult time growing up after his parents divorced. He had to live rotating weeks with each parent which made him miserable. The mother periodically dated a series of men he did not like, and the father married what he characterized as a cold and harsh woman.

Needless to say, the young man was not happy in either of these places. Whenever he spent time with his family, he was depressed and sad. Whenever he spent time with his friends, he was happy and funny. This was an important bit of information worth noting. After some sessions, it became obvious that he had failed to launch. The mother was strong and demanding and the father had barely noticed him. His opinion about issues that affected him did not matter to either parent. So, he developed the attitude that he would just "go with the flow."

Rather than asserting himself, he merely complied. This gave him a sense of imprisonment and a lack of control over anything. As a result, he became extremely dependent upon both his parents. As he continually acquiesced, the young man was unable to develop a real concept of himself and a hope for the future. He blamed his failure to launch on the fact that his mother needed him. How did he come up with this idea? As the men flowed in and out, the son basically fulfilled the role of her husband (not sexually, of course, but emotionally).

She took him places and did things only adults would do. Though he did not desire to go to coffee after a movie and talk about it, he did love feeling and acting like an adult. Yet, when decisions had to be made concerning buying clothes, or music, his school and social life, she made them. He was acting like her mother's husband in some areas and like a younger child in other areas. The two eventually developed an unnatural dependence on each other.

First, the mother had lost her husband and replaced him with her son. This is fairly common, and usually the parent is not even cognizant of the issue. God's blueprint embedded within a person is for he or she to be married (Genesis 2:18) with the exception of being singularly devoted to the Lord which Paul calls a "gift" (1 Corinthians 7:7, 32-34). When a spouse leaves, the blueprint does not automatically shut off.

Additional Notes: If asked about the God's blueprint for marriage and singleness, here are the Bible references I cite:

Genesis 2:18
Yahweh God said, "It is not good for the man to be alone. I will make him a helper comparable to him."

1 Corinthians 7:7
Yet I wish that all men were like me. However each man has his own gift from God, one of this kind, and another of that kind.

1 Corinthians 7:32-34
But I desire to have you to be free from cares. He who is unmarried is concerned for the things of the Lord, how he may please the Lord; but he who is married is concerned about the things of the world, how he may please his wife. There is also a difference between a wife and a virgin. The unmarried woman cares about the things of the Lord, that she may be holy both in body and in spirit. But she who is married cares about the things of the world – how she may please her husband.

Instead, one must replace the spouse with the Lord, not a child or a "live-in" partner (Psalm 68:4-6).

Additional Notes: If asked about the Lord God's ability to replace a spouse, here is the biblical reference I cite:

Psalm 68:4-6
Sing to God! Sing praises to his name! Extol him who rides on the clouds: to Yah, his name! Rejoice before him! A father of the fatherless, and a defender of the widows, is God in his holy habitation. God sets the lonely in families. He brings out the prisoners with singing, but the rebellious dwell in a sun-scorched land.

Second, the young man should follow the Lord's blueprint "to leave and cleave" (Genesis 2:24) or be single and live a life devoted to Christ.

Additional Notes: If asked about God's command to "leave and cleave," here is the Bible reference I cite:

Genesis 2:24
Therefore a man will leave his father and his mother, and will join with his wife, and they will be one flesh.

The Lord never intended for children to be living with their parents beyond the childhood years of life (Proverbs 22:6; Ephesians 6:4). Third, the father was distant and unwilling to raise his son in the many things of the Lord and prepare him for manhood. On the other hand, his wife was inciting and exasperating his son until he would finally give into whatever she wanted (Ephesians 6:4).

Additional Notes: If asked about the training of children without inciting them, here are the Bible references I cite:

Proverbs 22:6
Train up a child in the way he should go, and when he is old he will not depart from it.

Ephesians 6:4
You fathers, don't provoke your children to wrath, but nurture them in the discipline and instruction of the Lord.

Once this was discovered, it became time to reconcile the relationships and launch this young man into adulthood. This begins with repentance before the Lord. His mother had to be gently confronted for her mistakes. She had "to cut the umbilical cord" with her son both as her servant-child and as her surrogate husband. His father and stepmother had to be lovingly confronted for not taking the responsibility for teaching the son how to become a man and for exasperating him to the point of subservience to their every wish. Both mom and dad had to take responsibility for their divorce and his resultant predicament.

The son had to be confronted concerning his response to everything that had happened. The son had not assumed any adult responsibilities and launched himself from the nest. Instead, he had taken great advantage of the situation by relying upon the mother to meet the needs that a wife should have met, or he should have taken care of himself as a single man (e.g. preparing food, laundry, earning a living, cleaning up after himself). All responded according to their own unique timeline (not all respond immediately).

All of them mourned over their transgressions and turned from them. Then, they committed themselves to moving in a more righteous direction. So, they began the critical process of restoration with each other. Sometimes, this takes a long time and at other times a short amount of time. It depends largely on the hard work and open hearts of all involved as the Holy Spirit works. Eventually, the young man's sadness and depression began to depart and were replaced with a new enthusiasm for his future. Finally, the son was able to launch into adulthood as a single man by finding a place to live. The launching of the young man's new adult life began with the entire family taking responsibility for their actions and admitting to the mistakes and sins each had done to the other members in the family.

AN INSTRUCTOR'S MANUAL

A Personal Response

Dear Heavenly Father,

Though I have admitted my transgressions against You and (add name), I realize I have not taken them seriously. Help me to truly mourn over what I have done. Then, give me the desire to make a real commitment to the right kinds of actions. I want to be holy like You. I am sorry for breaking Your law. May I honor and glorify You in my relationship with (add name). I pray this in the name of Jesus. Amen.

Instructor's Notes

Chapter 3

Admit Your Sin

To restore our relationship with God, He desires us to confess our sins before Him. This is a three-fold process as we admit our sins, mourn over them, and turn from them.

In the section, "A Typical Scenario," the author describes an encounter one might have with a police officer that did not go well and may require a reconciliation.

What is the scenario about?

A Christian was distracted while driving and was stopped and ticketed by a police officer.

What did the conflict concern?

He did not think that texting, eating, shaving, etc. was a big deal and disagreed with the officer.

What was the relationship between the parties?

He was a citizen and the person who stopped him was a police officer.

Have you had a similar experience?

(Various answers should be shared including yours.)

HEALING RELATIONSHIPS THROUGH FORGIVENESS

In the section, "A Scriptural Principle" the author presents an important biblical principle in the forgiveness process which concerns the confession of our sins against God.

How would you express this principle in your own words?

The third principle is "we must fully repent of our sins and confess them before God."

(Various answers should be shared including yours.)

How would you rewrite this principle to make it even more personal to your life (using your name and situation)?

(Various answers should be shared including yours.)

Why do you think this principle might be important in your life right now?

(Various answers should be shared including yours.)

How would you rate yourself on the percentage of times you followed this principle in the past when you did something wrong in a relationship?

(Various answers should be shared including yours.)

Directions: Put a horizontal mark and your name where you see yourself on the percentage line.

| 0% | 25% | 50% | 75% | 100% |

In the section, "A Biblical Explanation," the author explains the reasons why we are to fully confess all the sins against others in a relationship and how to do it.

According to 1 John 1:8, what can we never say about sin in general or in our relationships?

Those who claimed that they had never sinned or no longer sinned were simply lying to themselves, others, and God. The truth of His Word was not in them because this truth convicts us of sin.

According to 1 John 1:9, once we realize we have sinned in a relationship what should we do?

The verbs "confess" and "forgive" are in the present tense which indicates continual action in present time. Believers are continually confessing their sins, and God is continually forgiving them. Repentance and asking God to forgive us is a lifelong practice.

What it the first characteristic of a repentant heart (provide a verse)?

The first is the admission of sin. To fully repent, we must admit that we have sinned. This means that Christians are to acknowledge that the thoughts, words, and actions that they had taken were indeed sins.

What it the second characteristic of a truly repentant heart (provide a verse)?

This remark speaks of mourning over our bankrupt condition before God as one mourns over the dead. It refers to a deep sorrow over our sin and wickedness which is the second aspect. When someone receives the Lord, they admit their sin and mourn, grieve, and sorrow over it.

What it the third characteristic of a repentant heart (provide a verse)?

We must turn around from our confessed sins and move in the opposite direction. We must commit ourselves to living differently. Luke records Peter's denial of even knowing the Lord in Luke 22:62 and how the apostle wept in sorrow and remorse afterward.

In what ways might these truths impact your relationships?

(Various answers should be shared including yours.)

AN INSTRUCTOR'S MANUAL

In the section, "An Ancient Portrait," the author provides a devastating situation for Israel when Achan was unwilling to confess his sin before God.

What was Achan's sin against Israel?

Instead, the people of Ai ran them off killing 36 men and causing Israel to retreat in humiliating terror. Where was the power of the Lord God?

The Lord told Joshua that one of his people had taken items from the city that was to be devoted solely to the Lord.

How did Achan cover it up?

He explains this, "When I saw among the plunder a beautiful Babylonian robe, two hundred shekels of silver, and a wedge of gold weighing fifty shekels, then I coveted them and took them. Behold, they are hidden in the ground in the middle of my tent, with the silver under it."

What did Joshua want Achan to do before he received his just punishment?

So, this man Achan was required by Joshua to stand before God Almighty and give Him glory and honor by admitting the sinful action he had taken. This is so crucial to our understanding of how to reconcile with God.

What qualities of repentance did Achan not demonstrate?

Notice what the man did not do. He did not demonstrate any mourning over what he had done or committed himself and his family to living righteously from then on. He did not fully reconcile with God. Also, he did not reconcile with the people of Israel or Joshua.

It appears that there was no repentance, mourning, and turning toward righteousness.

What was Achan's punishment and why was God so harsh?

At other times, the Lord God determines that He will not show His mercy and grace in withholding physical death to teach His people an important lesson. This was one of those times. The perpetrators of this atrocity against God's holiness were taken out and stoned to death. All their possessions, including the possessions they had taken, were burned with their bodies.

Have you ever been in a situation comparable to Israel's in which others did not own up to their sins against you or like Achan's in which you did not take any responsibility against them? How was it different and how was it the same?

(Various answers should be shared including yours.)

AN INSTRUCTOR'S MANUAL

In the section, "A Modern Anecdote," the author describes an encounter with a young man who was not able to leave the home when he became an adult.

What difficulties did the mother and father have with each other that led to their son being unable to leave the home?

This young man had been through a difficult time growing up after his parents divorced. He had to live rotating weeks with each parent which made him miserable. The mother periodically dated a series of men he did not like, and the father married what he characterized as a cold and harsh woman.

How was his joy with his parents much different than his joy with his friends? Why?

Needless to say, the young man was not happy in either of these places. Whenever he spent time with his family, he was depressed and sad. Whenever he spent time with his friends, he was happy and funny. This was an important bit of information worth noting. After some sessions, it became obvious that he had failed to launch. The mother was strong and demanding and the father had barely noticed him.

What unhealthy behaviors did the young man engage in to cope with the struggles of his parents?

His opinion about issues that affected him did not matter to either parent. So, he developed the attitude that he would just "go with the flow."

Rather than asserting himself, he merely complied. This gave him a sense of imprisonment and a lack of control over anything.

What individual responsibility should the son have taken for his own failure to leave the home?

As a result, he became extremely dependent upon both his parents. As he continually acquiesced, the young man was unable to develop a real concept of himself and a hope for the future.

The son had to be confronted concerning his response to everything that had happened. The son had not assumed any adult responsibilities and launched himself from the nest. Instead, he had taken great advantage of the situation by relying upon the mother to meet the needs that a wife should have met, or he should have taken care of himself as a single man (e.g. preparing food, laundry, earning a living, cleaning up after himself). All responded according to their own unique timeline (not all respond immediately).

How did the parents and the son reconcile with each other in order for the young man to leave the home?

All of them mourned over their transgressions and turned from them. Then, they committed themselves to moving in a more righteous direction. So, they began the critical process of restoration with each other.

The launching of the young man's new adult life began with the entire family taking responsibility for their actions and admitting to the mistakes and sins each had done to the other members in the family.

Based on the truths learned in this chapter, what would you have done differently if you were one of the parents or the young man?

(Various answers should be shared including yours.)

AN INSTRUCTOR'S MANUAL

In the section, "A Personal Response," the author provides a model you may use for prayer if you find it necessary after discovering the truths in this chapter.

Are you presently in a relationship where you have sinned against another and have not asked God for forgiveness? If not, is there one from the past that still needs this prayer to be prayed?

(Various answers should be shared including yours.)

Based on the truths you have just learned, what will you continue doing in your current relationships and what will you do differently?

(Various answers should be shared including yours.)

What additional thoughts would you like to share with the others?

(Various answers should be shared including yours.)

Instructor's Notes

Chapter 4

Accept God's Forgiveness

When we have sinned against another, we should begin the reconciliation process by approaching God. A Christian's relationship with Him has been damaged, and God must be dealt with first. To restore the relationship with Him, we are to spread out our transgressions before Him and take full responsibility for them. We are to admit that they are wrong and ask Him for forgiveness. The next step is to accept God's forgiveness with a sense of blessing and gratefulness.

A Typical Scenario

Suppose you suddenly awoke in the middle of the night and felt the full weight and burden of all your transgressions against God. Every sin you had committed started parading through your mind, and you began to write them down. You were completely honest and left nothing out. Wouldn't you write and write and write and write until your hand was so sore you could no longer hold the pen? Of course, I would too. Here is an important truth: since we are Christians, our long list of sins, transgressions, and iniquities from small to great have been forgiven! All of them are completely gone. It is important that we accept this by faith.

A Scriptural Principle

The fourth principle is "we must believe by faith that all our sins are forgiven in Jesus Christ with a sense of blessing and thankfulness." The moment we repented and received

Jesus Christ, all our past, present, and future sins and the punishment involved were washed away. What do I mean by this? At the very moment that we placed our faith in Jesus Christ, the penalty for all our sins paid at the cross was appropriated to us directly. Eternal life became ours with full, complete, and total forgiveness. Since this is a spiritual process, there may not have been a great feeling of relief or a tremendous sense of forgiveness at this defining moment in our lives. Instead, we should claim this forgiveness by faith.

A Biblical Explanation

To fully accept this forgiveness in our lives graciously and thankfully, we should understand exactly what happened at the cross. When we speak of forgiveness, we are speaking of two kinds of forgiveness. One concerns what occurred when we received Christ as Savior and Lord. Here the penalty that was paid was appropriated to us, our sins were forgiven, and we were declared righteous before God (Romans 8:1).

Additional Notes: If asked about our full forgiveness in Christ before God, here is the Bible reference I cite:

Romans 8:1
There is therefore now no condemnation to those who are in Christ Jesus, who don't walk according to the flesh, but according to the Spirit.

The second occurs in our earthly relationship and fellowship with God and occurs as we confess our sins and ask Him for forgiveness (1 John 1:9).

Additional Notes: If asked about our relational need to confess our sins and be forgiven, here is the Bible reference I cite:

1 John 1:9
If we confess our sins, he is faithful and righteous to forgive us the sins, and to cleanse us from all unrighteousness.

When I sin against my wife with an unkind word or action, she often forgives me even as I am sinning. Then, when I do go to her and ask for forgiveness and she grants it again (in a sense), all the barriers between us are [fully] removed. The relationship is fully restored because we each did our part and took our responsibility. Then I feel a great sense of blessing and gratefulness for her continual love, mercy, and grace. When the reverse happens, she feels the same.

After David had sinned against God by taking Bathsheba and murdering her husband, the king wrote psalms 32 and 51. In these two psalms he has this relational forgiveness in mind. In Psalm 32:1-2, he rejoiced, "Blessed is he whose disobedience is forgiven, whose sin is covered. Blessed is the man to whom Yahweh doesn't impute iniquity, in whose spirit there is no deceit." He was overjoyed with a sense of blessing for God's forgiveness of Him. This blessing was accompanied by a sense of gratefulness. In Psalm 51:8, He alludes to this when he cries, "Let me hear joy and gladness, that the bones which you have broken may rejoice." Then in verse 10, he continues, "Create in me a clean heart, O God. Renew a right spirit within me." In verse 12, he entreats, "Restore to me the joy of your salvation. Uphold me with a willing spirit." Then in verse 14-15, he says, "Deliver me from the guilt of bloodshed, O God, the God of my salvation. My tongue shall sing aloud of your righteousness." He adds, "Lord, open my lips. My mouth shall declare your praise." How can one not feel the sense of blessing and gratefulness he experiences as he confesses his sins to the Lord?

Did David know God had already forgiven Him for all His sins? Of course he did. In fact, the prophet Nathan had confirmed this very fact when he was confronted by him. In 2 Samuel 12:13, when David declared that he had sinned, Nathan responded, "Yahweh also has put away your sin." Though David knew he was forgiven from a salvation point of view, he needed his relationship with God fully restored and deeply desired the sense of blessing and thankfulness that pours out of a true confession. We all know the sense of relief and joy that comes when we have fully admitted our sin, mourned over it, and turned from it.

Additional Notes: As New Testament believers, we will not have a prophet come and confirm this because the prophets already have. The author of Hebrews affirms that in the past God spoke through the fathers and prophets, and now God has spoken through His Son (Hebrews 1:1-2). This was delivered to us by the apostles (Hebrews 2:3-4). When we come to our Father in confession, we accept His forgiveness because the Scriptures say we are forgiven.

Hebrews 1:1-2
God, having in the past spoken to the fathers through the prophets at many times and in various ways, has at the end of these days spoken to us by his Son, whom he appointed heir of all things, through whom also he made the worlds.

Hebrews 2:3-4
How will we escape if we neglect so great a salvation — which at the first having been spoken through the Lord, was confirmed to us by those who heard; 4 God also testifying with them, both by signs and wonders, by various works of power, and by gifts of the Holy Spirit, according to his own will?

This is important because from this sense of blessing and thankfulness comes the willingness on our part to forgive ourselves, others, and, if necessary, to be humble enough to ask for forgiveness.

To fully comprehend this forgiveness leading us to accept it, producing blessing and thanksgiving, and stimulating us to forgive ourselves and others, we must understand the full extent of what Christ actually did. The second person of the Trinity entered humanity for the purpose of dying for man's sins. The Father punished Jesus, the God-Man, instead of us to satisfy His just and holy wrath. God has no wrath toward us for the sins we now commit toward Him or others.

Additional Notes: In John 19:30, the apostle records the Lord's final words before his death, "When Jesus therefore had received the vinegar, he said, 'It is finished.' He bowed his head and gave up his spirit." The three words translated "it is finished" is one word in the Greek meaning "to finish, complete." The word was used in secular life as a contractual term meaning "payment in full." In ancient times, someone would borrow money and sign a contract. When the debt was fully paid, it would be stamped "Payment in Full."

We will see this same phrase stamped on receipts today. The debt for our sins was fully paid on the cross. As His life was pouring out of Him, Jesus was declaring, "The penalty is now paid in full." Jesus had come to suffer and die for us, to pay all the debts of our punishment, and it was now completed. As soon as Christ uttered these words, He gave up His spirit (John 19:30). We should remember this after our confession. When we fully repent from our sins, we can claim by faith based on this truth that the penalty was paid. The debt was gone. Now we can do the same for ourselves and others.

God will still discipline us in His deep love as a Father (Hebrews 12:7), but He will no longer punish us in His holy wrath as a Judge (Romans 8:1).

Additional Notes: If asked about God's discipline as a loving Father, here is the Bible reference I cite:

Hebrews 12:7
It is for discipline that you endure. God deals with you as with children, for what son is there whom his father doesn't discipline?

Paul deepens our concept of what happened on the cross in Colossians 2. In verses 13-14, Paul explained, "You were dead in your trespasses and the uncircumcision of your flesh. He made you alive together with him, having forgiven us all our trespasses, wiping out the certificate of debt which was decrees against us; and he has taken it out of the way, nailing it to the cross" (DEJ). Christ has taken the certificate of debt consisting of decrees against us and has nailed them to the cross. What are these "decrees?" The decrees are the many judgments against us for every transgression we ever committed, are committing, or will ever commit.

Additional Notes: These sins are written in books which Christ will open on the day of final judgment. In Matthew 16:27, the Lord Jesus proclaimed, "For the Son of Man will come in the glory of his Father with his angels, and then he will render to everyone according to his deeds." The rendering He is referring to involves these specific decrees against us for every sin. The book of Revelation describes exactly what that judgment will entail. In Revelation 20:12, John portrays it this way, "I saw the dead, the great and the small, standing before the throne, and they opened books. Another book was opened, which is the book of life." Believers are judged from the book of life but unbelievers from the other books. John continues, "The dead were judged out of the things which were written in the books, according to their works." This would have been our fate before we placed our faith in Jesus Christ and what He did on the cross for us.

Standing before a righteous and wrathful God, we would have been judged and punished for all eternity. How many decrees against us would we have with a lifetime of sinning? More than we could possibly count! Our iniquities were paid for by our Lord Jesus Christ in his death and nailed to His cross. In Hebrews 9:22, the author of Hebrews declares in the final part of the verse, "Apart from shedding of blood there is no remission." Through the shed blood of the Lord, these sins and decrees were nailed to the cross and wiped away.

After our confession, we claim this great truth by faith and accept His forgiveness. In Romans 4:8, Paul explains our blessed state when he testifies, "Blessed is the man whom the Lord will by no means charge with sin." There is the sense of blessing and gratefulness. God, our Father, will not charge us with our sin. We merely accept this. In Hebrews 8:12, the author says, "For I will be merciful to their unrighteousness. I will remember their sins and lawless deeds no more." Here he quotes Jeremiah 31:34, where God is directly speaking. Then in Hebrews 10:17, the author repeats, "I will remember their sins and their iniquities no more." In verse 22, the holy writer compares our full forgiveness to washing with pure water, "Let's draw near with a true heart in fullness of faith, having our hearts sprinkled from an evil conscience, and having our body washed with pure water." As saints confess their sins, they can imagine pure water flowing over them washing their sins away. If this truth does not bring a sense of blessing and thankfulness, what will?

Additional Notes: In Revelation 1:5, John opens the last book of the Bible in these words, "And from Jesus Christ, the faithful witness, the firstborn of the dead, and the ruler of the kings of the earth. To him [Christ] who loves us and washed us from our sins by his blood." When we received Jesus Christ, we were washed in His blood eternally; when we confess our sins, forgiveness just keeps flowing relationally. This is a powerful truth. Our sins are washed away. They are gone.

The same concept can be seen in the Old Testament when the prophets speak of God washing away or removing the sins of His people Israel after they had confessed, mourned, and turned from their sin. In Isaiah 38:17, Hezekiah says, "Behold, for peace I had great anguish, but you have in love for my soul delivered it from the pit of corruption." Then, he adds, "For you have cast all my sins behind your back." As believers accept God's forgiveness, they will experience a blessing and gratefulness of God casting those sins behind His back. In Isaiah 43:25, God emphatically pronounces, "I, even I, am he who blots out your transgressions for my own sake; and I will not remember your sins." The Lord directly speaks about blotting out their sins and remembering them no more. In Isaiah 44:22, the Lord asserts, "I have blotted out like a dark cloud your transgressions, and like a thick mist your sins. Return to me, for I have redeemed you" (DEJ). In this passage, God explains His redemption of His people as having "blotted out" their sins.

Additional Notes: The Hebrew word translated "blotted out" means "to wipe away, obliterate." He wiped away the dark cloud and thick mist of sin. When we have sin in our lives it does feel like a dark cloud or thick mist. Once we confess the sin and accept forgiveness by faith. It lifts!

In Psalm 85:2, the sons of Korah cry out with praise, "You have forgiven the iniquity of your people. You have covered all their sin." In Micah 7:19, the holy prophet describes what will happen to the sins of God's people when they turn back to Him, "He will again have compassion on us. He will tread our iniquities under foot; and you will cast all their sins into the depths of the sea." As you and I come before the throne of grace and repent of the sins we have committed in a relationship, we can know that God has covered over them, treaded their iniquities under His foot, and cast them into the depths of the sea. Will this not prepare us to accept the Lord's forgiveness, and then to forgive ourselves, others, or humbly ask for forgiveness?

Lastly, we must understand the abundant grace that was bestowed on us because the Lord will require us to bestow the same to ourselves and others. In Ephesians 1:7-8, Paul portrays what Jesus accomplished in these words, "In whom we have our redemption through his blood, the forgiveness of our trespasses, according to the riches of his grace, which he made to abound toward us in all wisdom and prudence." Notice what the apostle states concerning God's grace. The words "made to abound" is only one Greek word meaning "to exceed a fixed number of measures, to be over, abundant, excelling beyond." His grace overflowed exceedingly beyond anything that could be measured in order to forgive. Notice it is "according to the riches of His grace." Paul did not say "out of" but "according to" the riches of His grace. This grace is infinite having no bounds, and this makes His forgiveness infinite and without bounds. The word "riches" is a Greek word meaning "riches, wealth." According to the great and abundant wealth of His grace came forgiveness. It came when we received Christ. Moment by moment as we confess our sins, He forgives and forgives and forgives again and again until our very redemption.

We desperately need His "wealth of grace" because we not only sin repeatedly but commit some horribly grievous sins against God, ourselves, and others. Yet, God forgives all of them. There is not one sin that a believer can commit that was not dealt with on the cross of Christ. When we repent and accept this forgiveness, a tremendous sense of blessing and thankfulness pours forth from our lives. In Psalm 103:1-2, the psalmist testifies, "Bless the Lord, O my soul, And all that is within me, bless His holy name. Bless the Lord, O my soul, And forget none of His benefits." This sense of blessing results from all of the benefits that God bestows on us as His people. In the first part of verse 3, he mentions forgiveness, "Who pardons all your iniquities."

The psalms continue with this incredible theme. In Psalm 106:1, the writer articulates his sense, "Praise Yahweh! Give thanks to Yahweh, for he is good, for his loving kindness endures forever." What could be kinder than forgiveness? In verse 47, the writer communicates, "Save us, Yahweh, our God, gather us from among the nations, to give thanks to your holy name, to triumph in your praise!" Salvation for the nation was the forgiveness of their sins and the deliverance from captivity of their enemies on earth, our salvation is the forgiveness of our sins and the deliverance from hell for all eternity. Temporally, it is the deliverance from the weight and guilt of our sins and the restoration of our relationship with God.

In Psalm 28:7, David testifies of his thanksgiving, joy, and blessing, "Yahweh is my strength and my shield. My heart has trusted in him, and I am helped. Therefore, my heart greatly rejoices. With my song I will thank him." In verse 8, he adds, "Yahweh is their strength. He is a stronghold of salvation to his anointed." What a sense of blessing and thanksgiving! Yet, the Lord God does not want His children to stop right there. He wants us to take our experience of blessing and to pour out forgiveness upon ourselves and others. Also, as our hearts are full of all His blessings, we must use it to motivate ourselves to humbly go before those we have transgressed and ask for forgiveness, if necessary.

An Ancient Portrait

A great example of this sense of blessing and gratefulness is seen in Luke chapter seven. When Jesus was in Galilee, the Lord was invited into the house of a Pharisee named Simon.

Additional Notes: This story is different than another similar story told in the three gospels (Matthew 26; Mark 14; John 12) and should not be confused with it. The other story occurred in Judea; this story happens in Bethany of Galilee. This story was near the time of the cross whereas the other was much earlier. The host here was a Pharisee named Simon. The other story featured Simon who was a leper. Here the woman pours perfume on the feet of Jesus; there she pours it on His head. These have different places, times, and people involved. Simon was a common name at the time.

At times, Pharisees would persuade the Lord to give a talk in their homes to various dignitaries. Sometimes, He was invited for the purpose of trapping Him in something He said.

Additional Notes: The Pharisees were a Jewish sect who felt that they were guardians of the law. These laws not only involved the law of God in the Old Testament, but numerous and diverse man-made interpretations and applications of God's law which became of equal weight as God's standard. They followed Jesus everywhere He traveled to trap Him in some violation of their laws.

Other times, some Pharisees were serious about His ministry and message and wanted to learn from Him.

Additional Notes: Some Pharisees did come to believe in Jesus. Here are two Bible references which verify this:

Acts 15:5
But some of the sect of the Pharisees who believed rose up, saying, "It is necessary to circumcise them, and to command them to keep the law of Moses."

Acts 23:6
But when Paul perceived that the one part were Sadducees and the other Pharisees, he cried out in the council, "Men and brothers, I am a Pharisee, a son of Pharisees [a group of Jewish legalists]. Concerning the hope and resurrection of the dead...being judged!"

While Jesus was at Simon's table, a woman who had the reputation among the Jews of being a "sinner" (most likely a prostitute), entered the house with a jar of expensive oil. I am sure to everyone's amazement she began to wet the feet of the Lord with her tears and wipe them with her hair.

After this, she kissed Christ's feet and anointed Him with her oil. One would think that Simon and the others would be filled with empathy and compassion as they saw this poor woman kneeling before Christ. Instead, these religious men of Israel were stunned that Jesus even allowed such a sinner to touch Him. "Why did He have anything to do with her?" they must have thought. The scoffers viewed the entire scene with disgust. They reasoned that if this Jesus was truly the prophet He claimed to be, He would know how wretched that woman was.

They did not realize that she was in the middle of an act of deep repentance crying out for ultimate forgiveness. Her tears were her repentance, her anointing was her recognition of His Deity, and His acceptance was His forgiveness. As she experienced His forgiveness, her tears began to flow from her sense of acceptance, blessing, and thankfulness. To open up Simon and the others' minds to the significance of the moment, Jesus told him the story of a lender who had two people who owed him money. One of the two owed him five hundred denarii (500 day's wages) and the other five denarii (5 day's wages). The lender then forgave them both. One was forgiven a large amount and the other a smaller amount. Then Jesus asked Simon to pick the person who would love this lender more. Simon responded that it would be the one with the larger amount.

The implication was obvious. This woman, who was such a sinner, was showing a greater love for Jesus because Jesus had forgiven a greater amount of her sins than others. What a testimony of His forgiveness and her love demonstrated through repentance, acceptance, and gratefulness! Then the Lord Jesus turned the tables on Simon and compared his treatment of the Lord with her conduct toward Him. He was a self-proclaimed righteous man, and she was a proclaimed sinner. Christ told Simon that he did not wash the Lord's feet when He entered his home (a custom due to the wearing of sandals), but this woman washed them with her tears and wiped them dry with her hair. Simon did not kiss the Lord when He arrived (a common greeting at that time), but the woman continually kissed His feet. Simon did not anoint the head of the Lord with oil (a common custom to remove the smell of travel, like perfume), but she anointed His feet. The implication was clear. Here is a simple contrast between her humility and care for Christ and Simon's distaste of Jesus.

Then the Lord pronounced His forgiveness of the many sins of the woman. He acknowledged her great love for Him as Savior and Lord. Then Jesus declared exactly what had happened. He had given her the very gift she had desired all along which was forgiveness. Now Simon and his guests would clearly understand what they were viewing. Christ demonstrated through this story the love and forgiveness He has for us, and the sense of blessing and thankfulness we are to have for Him. She was welcomed, and we are welcomed. She repented and found forgiveness, and we repent and find the same forgiveness. She greatly sinned and found pardon, and we greatly sin and find the same pardon.

When we come before our Lord and Savior in repentance, sorrow, and confession, we will receive complete and total forgiveness every single time. We received it all on the cross eternally, now we receive it all relationally. We merely have to accept it all with blessing and thankfulness. Then out of that experience of full forgiveness, we must go to those who have transgressed us and demonstrate that same forgiveness toward them. To those we have transgressed, we must show the same repentance. We must display that same forgiveness toward ourselves. What a God of forgiveness we have! Now we must show it through our own forgiveness of others.

A Modern Anecdote

A young lady came into my office one day after spending weeks in rehab for a drug addiction. She told me that though she had learned some good things at the center, it had still left her empty inside. She was clean but empty. She told me that she did not know where to go from this point. The young woman went to her pastor who often refers clients to me, and she was referred. She told me that she needed God and had heard that I could help her find Him. Her story was a tragic one. She described herself, her mom, and her dad as the perfect little family living in a huge country home in the Midwest.

While her mom stayed home and took care of the house, her father was one of the managers of an equipment rental company. As a girl, she was good in school and won many achievement awards. She could not remember one time that her parents had argued or exchanged unkind words. From her perspective all was well and comfortable in her world.

Then one day when she was about eleven, her dad came home and said he had lost his job. Her mom and dad went into their room and had a terrible argument which she had never seen before. She was petrified. The police came later that night and hand-cuffed her dad and took him away. When she asked mom what had happened, she explained that her father had stolen a huge amount of money from the company to pay back gambling debts. Her mom had never worked a day in her life and did not know what to do. After a year, her parents divorced, and her life felt like it was over. Since her father had mortgaged the house to pay attorney's fees, there was no equity left. As a result, they sold the house for a loss and had nothing left. They were going to have to live with her grandparents in a big city. She told me she felt like she was living in a bad movie.

Additional Notes: Divorce can be very devastating for a child, but the results may even be worse. These encompass moving to a new home and most likely school, leaving friends and family, and even having to transition to a new life that the child did not want or choose.

At twelve, her world shattered. She felt as if it had gone from a picture-perfect home to a dirty little house in a dirty suburb where the lawns were brown, and the people were tough. The school was old and loud, and no one would talk to her. Then one day a druggy-type girl befriended her. This girl taught her how to fit in. She took her shopping for cooler clothes, showed her how to do her hair and make-up, and introduced her to drugs and older more mature boys.

Additional Notes: Though a child, she was still old enough to be responsible for the choices she made in response to this difficult situation.

From that day forward, it was one party after another, while her mother worked long hours. In high school, she was almost always high on drugs. Her relationship with her mother deteriorated until one night she just stormed off and never returned. After two husbands divorced her and three of her children were removed by social services, she decided it was time to get cleaned up.

The woman was twenty-nine and empty. Now, she was sitting in my office asking for help. So, I shared the good news of Jesus Christ with her. Our Lord God was willing to accept her with open arms in spite of what she had done. He was willing to forgive all her sins and rebuild her life into the beautiful image of His Son. The Lord would give her a new identity, a new family of God, and help her go back and reconcile with all of those she had hurt and had hurt her. When she came for the next session, she explained that she could not believe that God would forgive her. She felt she was a total "screw-up" as she called it. I told her, "When you repent and receive Jesus Christ, you have to believe that God has forgiven you by faith with blessing and gratitude. You will make other mistakes as a Christian and will again have to accept this forgiveness by faith." We prayed and she received Jesus Christ as Savior and Lord. Then we began the process of rebuilding her life now in Jesus Christ.

Additional Notes: Salvation must come first so she will have the power through the Holy Spirit to change. Those who do not know Christ must rely in their own personal strength. Here are some Bible references:

2 Corinthians 13:4
For he was crucified through weakness, yet he lives through the power of God. For we also are weak in him, but we will live with him through the power of God toward you.

Ephesians 1:19
And what is the exceeding greatness of his power toward us who believe, according to that working of the strength of his might.

Ephesians 3:16
That he would grant you, according to the riches of his glory, that you may be strengthened with power through his Spirit in the inward man.

Ephesians 3:20
Now to him who is able to do exceedingly abundantly above all that we ask or think, according to the power that works in us,

1 Thessalonians 1:5
And that our Good News came to you not in word only, but also in power, and in the Holy Spirit, and with much assurance. You know what kind of men we showed ourselves to be among you for your sake.

A Personal Response

Dear Heavenly Father,

    While I was reading this chapter, I suddenly realized that I have not fully accepted your forgiveness with a sense of blessing and thankfulness for the sins I have committed in my relationship with (add name). I am truly sorry. Father, please help me to claim your full forgiveness by faith. I struggle with this and want desperately to overcome it in Your power. May I honor and glorify You in my relationship with (add name). I do pray all of this in the name of Jesus. Amen.

Instructor's Notes

Chapter 4

Accept God's Forgiveness

The next step is to accept God's forgiveness with a sense of blessing and gratefulness. Any sin or transgression that we could commit has already been forgiven.

In the section, "A Typical Scenario," the author describes an unpleasant dream in which one may suddenly realize all the sins he or she has committed, especially in relationships.

What is the scenario about?

A Christian awakes from a bad dream, where he had to face all of his sins.

What did the conflict concern?

He was dismayed over how much he had sinned against God.

What was the relationship between the parties?

He was a Christian and God was His Father.

Have you had a similar experience?

(Various answers should be shared including yours.)

HEALING RELATIONSHIPS THROUGH FORGIVENESS

In the section, "A Scriptural Principle" the author presents an important biblical principle in the forgiveness process which concerns fully accepting God's forgiveness.

How would you express this principle in your own words?

The fourth principle is "we must believe by faith that all our sins are forgiven in Jesus Christ with a sense of blessing and thankfulness."

(Various answers should be shared including yours.)

How would you rewrite this principle to make it even more personal to your life (using your name and situation)?

(Various answers should be shared including yours.)

Why do you think this principle might be important in your life right now?

(Various answers should be shared including yours.)

How would you rate yourself on the percentage of times you followed this principle in the past when you did something wrong in a relationship?

(Various answers should be shared including yours.)

Directions: Put a horizontal mark and your name where you see yourself on the percentage line.

| 0% | 25% | 50% | 75% | 100% |

AN INSTRUCTOR'S MANUAL

In the section, "A Biblical Explanation," the author explains the reasons for accepting the forgiveness of God for our sins against others with a sense of blessing and gratefulness and how to do it.

According to Colossians 2:13-14, what has happened to the past sins we have committed in our relationships?

Christ has taken the certificate of debt consisting of decrees against us, and has nailed them to the cross. What are these "decrees?" The decrees are the many judgments against us for every transgression we ever committed, are committing, or will ever commit.

According to Hebrews 9:22, what sacrifice had to be made for our forgiveness of sins that we commit in relationships?

In Hebrews 9:22, the author of Hebrews declares in the final part of the verse, "Apart from shedding of blood there is no remission." Through the shed blood of the Lord, these sins and decrees were nailed to the cross and wiped away.

According to Romans 4:8 and Psalm 28:7, how should we feel about God's forgiveness of our relationship sins?

After our confession, we claim this great truth by faith and accept His forgiveness.

According to Hebrews 10:22, how does forgiveness compare to washing with pure water?

As saints confess their sins, they can imagine pure water flowing over them washing their sins away. If this truth does not bring a sense of blessing and thankfulness, what will?

Does God have enough grace to forgive these sins no matter how great and how do you know (provide verse)?

In Ephesians 1:7-8, Paul portrays what Jesus accomplished in these words, "In whom we have our redemption through his blood, the forgiveness of our trespasses, according to the riches of his grace, which he made to abound toward us in all wisdom and prudence." Notice what the apostle states concerning God's grace. The words "made to abound" is only one Greek word meaning "to exceed a fixed number of measures, to be over, abundant, excelling beyond." His grace overflowed exceedingly beyond anything that could be measured in order to forgive. Notice it is "according to the riches of His grace." Paul did not say "out of" but "according to" the riches of His grace. This grace is infinite having no bounds, and this makes His forgiveness infinite and without bounds. The word "riches" is a Greek word meaning "riches, wealth."

In what ways might these truths impact your relationships?

(Various answers should be shared including yours.)

AN INSTRUCTOR'S MANUAL

In the section, "An Ancient Portrait," the author provides a picture of a woman who entered Simon's home to see Jesus. The woman repented and accepted His forgiveness with a sense of blessing and gratitude.

According to Simon, what kind of person was the woman?

Other times, they were serious about His ministry and message and wanted to learn from Him. While Jesus was at Simon's table, a woman who had the reputation among the Jews of being a "sinner" (most likely a prostitute), entered the house with a jar of expensive oil.

Why didn't Simon understand what the woman was doing?

The scoffers viewed the entire scene with disgust. They reasoned that if this Jesus was truly the prophet He claimed to be, He would know how wretched that woman was.

What three actions did the woman take to demonstrate her repentance?

They did not realize that she was in the middle of an act of deep repentance crying out for ultimate forgiveness. Her tears were her repentance, her anointing was her recognition of His Deity, and His acceptance was His forgiveness. As she experienced His forgiveness, her tears began to flow from her sense of acceptance, blessing, and thankfulness.

What was the Lord's gracious response?

Then the Lord pronounced His forgiveness of the many sins of the woman. He acknowledged her great love for Him as Savior and Lord. Then Jesus declared exactly what had happened. He had given her the very gift she had desired all along which was forgiveness.

How did Simon dishonor Jesus in what he did not do?

Christ told Simon that he did not wash the Lord's feet when He entered his home (a custom due to the wearing of sandals), but this woman washed them with her tears and wiped them dry with her hair. Simon did not kiss the Lord when He arrived (a common greeting at that time), but the woman continually kissed His feet. Simon did not anoint the head of the Lord with oil (a common custom to remove the smell of travel, like perfume), but she anointed His feet.

Have you ever been in a situation similar to the woman's in which you sought forgiveness or Simon's where you may have been critical? How was it different and how was it the same?

(Various answers should be shared including yours.)

AN INSTRUCTOR'S MANUAL

In the section, "A Modern Anecdote," the author shares the good news with a woman who could not believe the Lord God would forgive all her sins.

What happened in the woman's life that made her feel so empty inside?

Her relationship with her mother deteriorated until one night she just stormed off and never returned. After two husbands divorced her and three of her children were removed by social services, she decided it was time to get cleaned up.

The woman was twenty-nine and empty. Now, she was sitting in my office asking for help.

Why did the author share the gospel with her?

A young lady came into my office one day after spending weeks in rehab for a drug addiction. She told me that though she had learned some good things at the center, it had still left her empty inside.

She told me that she needed God and had heard that I could help her find Him. Her story was a tragic one.

After a year, her parents divorced, and her life felt like it was over.

They were going to have to live with her grandparents in a big city.

What does God, the Father, provide people with when they become Christians?

The Lord would give her a new identity, a new family of God, and help her go back and reconcile with all of those she had hurt and had hurt her.

What held the woman back from receiving Jesus Christ as Savior and Lord?

When she came for the next session, she explained that she could not believe that God would forgive her. She felt she was a total "screw-up" as she called it. I told her, "When you repent and receive Jesus Christ, you have to believe that God has forgiven you by faith with blessing and gratitude.

What should the woman do if she makes more mistakes?

You will make other mistakes as a Christian and will again have to accept this forgiveness by faith." We prayed and she received Jesus Christ as Savior and Lord. Then we began the process of rebuilding her life now in Jesus Christ.

Based on the truths learned in this chapter, did you react in the same kind of way when you became a Christian or have you since felt this way when you sinned against another?

(Various answers should be shared including yours.)

In the section, "A Personal Response," the author provides a model you may use for prayer if you find it necessary after discovering the truths in this chapter.

Are you presently in a relationship where you have sinned against another and have not asked God for forgiveness? If not, is there one from the past that still needs this prayer to be prayed?

(Various answers should be shared including yours.)

Based on the truths you have just learned, what will you continue doing in your current relationships and what will you do differently?

(Various answers should be shared including yours.)

What additional thoughts would you like to share with the others?

(Various answers should be shared including yours.)

Instructor's Notes

Chapter 5

Forgive Yourself All

When we sin against another, before we go to them to ask for forgiveness, we must first approach God. We admit our sins and leave nothing out. We mourn over them and make a commitment to act in a more righteous way. With a sense of blessing and gratefulness, we accept God's forgiveness. After this, we must fully forgive ourselves. The Lord God may forgive us, but we do not always forgive ourselves. At times, when the memory of a sin rears its ugly head, we may experience all of the regret, shame, and humiliation again. Then we may beat ourselves up over and over again. This does not have to happen; we can overcome this in Christ. This is why He came to free us from sin's grip.

A Typical Scenario

Perhaps, you have had or even heard a conversation with a friend, parent, sibling, child, acquaintance, co-worker, or fellow student which went something like this, when they asked you how you were doing? You say or hear, "I am fine. I am just fine. Everything is going great. (Pause.) No, really, I am doing great. Yes, that was a big mistake, humiliating and embarrassing, but I am okay with it. (A moment of silence occurs). No, what am I saying, everything is not fine. I am miserable and depressed. I will never get over what I did. I hate myself. The embarrassment was horrible. I cannot bear it! Whatever I do reminds me of how rotten I am!

A conversation like this describes how we may feel when we commit a terrible sin against someone. There lies a heavy weight of humiliation and shame upon us. Even after the sin has been confessed, the memory keeps returning whenever we see or hear something similar, in a book, movie, song, or experience we have. This may go on for days, weeks, or even years. Christians do not have to live with this weary load and strain. God desires for us to experience full forgiveness which includes the full forgiving of ourselves for the sin.

A Scriptural Principle

The fifth critical principle in healing relationships is "we must forgive ourselves for our sin as God has forgiven us." Once we have accepted God's forgiveness, we must turn our attention toward ourselves, before we turn it toward others. It is very difficult to restore a relationship with someone else, when we are still dealing with the sin within ourselves. This will make us feel defeated, broken, and unable to build the relationship anew. We do not have to carry this burden; instead, we can be free of it once and for all. We can be fully released from these self-imposed chains. Notice, I said, "self-imposed!" This kind of bondage comes from within. It needs to be identified and then dealt with.

A Biblical Explanation

To unchain ourselves from the bonds of our own lack of forgiveness, we must understand the source of the shame, guilt, and humiliation we feel. This does not originate from the Lord Jesus Christ. Once we confess the sins and accept our forgiveness by faith, it should all flow away. If it does not, then the flesh is the culprit. In Romans 7:20, Paul calls our sinful flesh the "sin which dwells in me." The sin principle resides in our physical bodies. The flesh (common word for this principle) desires to wallow in its own sin. It can be prideful, arrogant, and boastful, but it can also be insecure, worried, and unable to trust God. In our case, it is the voice inside us that says, "You are no good, pathetic, and just plain stupid! You will never overcome this moronic act. You fool! You idiot!" It chastises us like a vicious parent. It whips saints with the memories of their own mistakes over and over again.

Additional Notes: In the movies, when someone struggles with doubts, on one shoulder is a tiny demon and on the other shoulder a small angel. Each of them is vying for attention and giving advice. This is not the case in real life. Instead, in our own minds, it is the "old man" accusing us, while the "new man" forgives us through the Spirit. In Ephesians 4:22-24, the apostle discusses this old and new life (man). Paul writes concerning the old life we lived, "That you put away, as concerning your former way of life, the old man, that grows corrupt after the lusts of deceit." Then he contrasts this with the new man, "And that you be renewed in the spirit of your mind, and put on the new man, who in the likeness of God has been created in righteousness and holiness of truth."

When we became Christians, we put on this "new man" (or woman). We became brand new creations in Christ (1 Corinthians 5:17). So, when we are haunted by any of our past sins, where does it come from? Our new man knows we are forgiven and rejoices in it, but the old man (our sinful flesh) accuses us and wallows in it. Paul writes that we must do battle with this flesh of ours.

In 1 Corinthians 9, he uses a powerful boxing analogy to explain how he handled this ugly sin principle inside him. In verse 27, he describes it in these words, "But I beat my body and bring it into submission, lest by any means, after I have preached to others, I myself should be rejected." The word "beat" in the Greek means "to beat black and blue." In our case, it would refer to hard effort to fight back against the flesh's lies. When we begin to feel angry or pity toward ourselves for some past sins, we must realize this is not the "new us" but the "old us."

The flesh has two powerful accomplices in its endeavor to lie to us: the world (1 John 2:15) and the Devil (John 8:44).

Additional Notes: If asked about these two powerful accomplices, here are the Bible references I cite:

1 John 2:15
Don't love the world or the things that are in the world. If anyone loves the world, the Father's love isn't in him.

John 8:44
You are of your father, the devil, and you want to do the desires of your father. He was a murderer from the beginning, and doesn't stand in the truth, because there is no truth in him. When he speaks a lie, he speaks on his own; for he is a liar, and its father.

The world or society of unbelievers enjoys watching God's people fall from grace and then scoffing at them (Psalm 1:1).

Additional Notes: If asked about the world's scoffing, here is the Bible reference I cite:

Psalm 1:1
Blessed is the man who doesn't walk in the counsel of the wicked, nor stand on the path of sinners, nor sit in the seat of scoffers.

The Devil loves to find God's righteous people and then test their loyalty (Job 1:11), tempt them to sin (Luke 22:31), or else accuse them of evil day and night before the Lord God (Revelation 12:10).

Additional Notes: If asked about the Devil's desire to test, tempt, and accuse righteous people, here are the Bible references I cite:

Job 1:11
But stretch out your hand now, and touch all that he has, and he will renounce you to your face."

Luke 22:31
The Lord said, "Simon, Simon, behold, Satan asked to have you, that he might sift you as wheat.

Revelation 12:10
I heard a loud voice in heaven, saying, "Now the salvation, the power, and the Kingdom of our God, and the authority of his Christ has come; for the accuser of our brothers has been thrown down, who accuses them before our God day and night."

So, believers must be aware of these two enemies coercing the flesh *(sin principle)* to lie and influencing Christians to become depressed, defeated, grief-stricken, angry, bitter, or immobilized about a transgression they have committed against other saints or even unbelievers. They do not regard reconciliation between people as a virtue.

Additional Notes: The popular magazines and websites will pay little attention to any Christian who takes a stand for the Lord in sports, acting, music, or politics until the believer slips up or makes a mistake. Then they cackle with delight and throw barbs back and forth endlessly until the person is covered in guilt, shame and humiliation. After this, they discard them for someone else.

This battle to overcome the guilt, shame, and humiliation of past actions pouring forth into full self-forgiveness can be fought using several biblical strategies. The first involves our minds. In our minds, we must "take every thought captive to Christ." In 2 Corinthians, Paul, the apostle, discussed the many false beliefs the saints possessed about him and their faith. Then in chapter 10, verse 5, he described his ultimate objective in all of his preaching and letter writing. He was "throwing down imaginations and every high thing that is exalted against the knowledge of God and bringing every thought into captivity to the obedience of Christ."

This is a simple concept when examined carefully. Every single idea or thought should be examined. Those thoughts that are contrary to the Scriptures should be discarded and those consistent should be embraced. In Romans 12, Paul explains how Christians can resist conforming themselves to the world, and it involves their minds. In verse 2, Paul states this, "Don't be conformed to this world, but be transformed by the renewing of your mind." Our mind is renewed in God's Word by discarding worldly thoughts and embracing God's thoughts. This then transforms us into His image. Christians forgive themselves and do not carry around guilt, shame, and humiliation. They continually discard thoughts that condemn and embrace thoughts that forgive.

How is this practiced in our lives? We speak to ourselves identifying where the negative thoughts are coming from and replace them with new ones. I will often say to myself, "I know these thoughts are from my flesh. God has forgiven me according to 1 John 1:9. I will not believe that God will hold this against me." This is essentially what Christ did with the Devil in His temptation in the wilderness. The Devil tempted Him, and Jesus quoted Scripture (Matthew 4:1-11).

Additional Notes: If asked about the details of the testing of Jesus by the Devil, here is the Bible reference I cite:

Matthew 4:1-11
Then Jesus was led up by the Spirit into the wilderness to be tempted by the devil. When he had fasted forty days and forty nights, he was hungry afterward. The tempter came and said to him, "If you are the Son of God, command that these stones become bread." But he answered, "It is written,' 'Man shall not live by

bread alone, but by every word that proceeds out of the mouth of God.' "Then the devil took him into the holy city. He set him on the pinnacle of the temple, and said to him, "If you are the Son of God, throw yourself down, for it is written, "He will put his angels in charge of you." and, 'On their hands they will bear you up, so that you don't dash your foot against a stone.'" Jesus said to him, "Again, it is written, 'You shall not test the Lord, your God.'" Again, the devil took him to an exceedingly high mountain, and showed him all the kingdoms of the world, and their glory. 9 He said to him, "I will give you all of these things, if you will fall down and worship me." Then Jesus said to him, "Get behind me, Satan! For it is written, 'You shall worship the Lord your God, and you shall serve him only'" Then the devil left him, and behold, angels came and served him.

When we are tempted through our flesh by a memory or some thought of our sin, we must stand against it by saying, "This is not the real me nor is it the Holy Spirit, I have been forgiven, and I will let it go. Please God help me to let it go. I discard the negative and embrace the positive.

Second, we must become strong in our faith that the Lord has forgiven us. We know we have full forgiveness of our sins at the cross eternally and the full forgiveness of our sins at confession relationally, now we must believe this critical truth intellectually and emotionally. Abraham was given a promise by the Lord God that was too fantastic to believe. After Sarah was past child-bearing years and they both were old, He told them Sarah would conceive a son and Abraham would have a true heir. This was so unbelievable to the both of them that their response was exactly the same. They responded by laughter (Genesis 17:17-19; 18:12). It was not laughter of joy but the laughter of hearing something so outrageous that it could not possibly be true. God's promise was fulfilled, and Isaac was born.

Additional Notes: If asked about the laughter of the both of them, here are the Bible references I cite:

Genesis 17:17-19
Then Abraham fell on his face, and laughed, and said in his heart, "Will a child be born to him who is one hundred years old? Will Sarah, who is ninety years old, give birth?" Abraham said to God, "Oh that Ishmael might live before you!" God said, "No, but Sarah, your wife, will bear you a son. You shall call his name Isaac. I will establish my covenant with him for an everlasting covenant for his offspring after him.

Genesis 18:12
Sarah laughed within herself, saying, "After I have grown old will I have pleasure, my lord being old also?"

When we read in the Scriptures that God forgives all our sins, it appears wonderful and easy to believe. When we do something really wicked, shameful, or humiliating, then His forgiveness can seem so outrageous that it could not be true. Deep down in the recesses of our souls, we refuse to believe it. This is the same feeling Abraham and Sarah had. How did Abraham overcome this? Paul articulated what happened in Romans 4:18-21. He wrote, "Besides hope, Abraham in hope believed, to the end that he might become a father of many nations, according to that which had been spoken, 'So will your offspring be.'" When the Lord originally told Abraham that he would have offspring, he believed God based on His Word.

In verse 19, Paul delineates what Abraham thought when he considered all of the physical evidence, "Without being weakened in faith, he didn't consider his own body, already having been worn out, (he being about a hundred years old), and the deadness of Sarah's womb." Abraham looked at the evidence of their old bodies and was not weakened in faith.

He discarded all thoughts from his flesh mocking him and telling him it was impossible. Instead, he grew stronger in faith. In verse 20, the apostle asserted, "Yet, looking to the promise of God, he didn't waver through unbelief, but grew strong through faith." Then his mind embraced the thoughts which were consistent with God's Word, "Giving glory to God, and being fully assured that what he had promised, he was also able to perform." Over and over God performed the promises He made because He has the power to do it. This was being embraced in his mind, as the Spirit was assuring Him of this truth. Then he glorified God.

How does this passage apply to us in forgiveness? God promised that as we received Him, He forgave us on the cross eternally. When we confess our sins to Him now, He forgives us relationally. When we consider the humiliation, guilt, and shame of some sin we committed, we discard the thoughts that God will not forgive us this time. We embrace the truth that the Lord God said He would forgive us and has the power to do it. Then the Holy Spirit will assure us, and we will grow strong in faith.

Additional Notes: As I proceed through this process, I often pray the words of the father who brought his demon-possessed son to Jesus for healing in Mark's gospel. The Lord proclaimed to the man that all things were possible to him who believes. Then in Mark 9:24, the father cried, "I believe. Help my unbelief!" I will pray, "Father, I believe you forgave me, help me when I am tempted not to believe it." After I consider God's promise through the death of His Son and His power demonstrated in the resurrection, then I can fully accept that forgiveness and act on it. This helps me grow in my faith.

The third way to overcome our own lack of forgiveness is guard our hearts and minds in Christ Jesus. Paul exhorts the Christians in Philippians 4:6-7 to never be anxious about anything. Instead, we are to bring everything to our God in prayer with thanksgiving. That "everything" includes the sense of disappointment and guilt over a sin against a loved one. He then promises the peace of God which will guard our hearts and thoughts in Christ Jesus. The next two verses are often left out of a discussion concerning the removal of anxiety but are equally important. After we pray and turn these requests to God, we must think and act differently.

In Philippians 4:8, Paul adds, "Finally, brothers, whatever things are true, whatever things are honorable, whatever things are just, whatever things are pure, whatever things are lovely, whatever things are of good report; if there is any virtue, and if there is any praise, think about these things." Then in verse 9, he concludes with a general statement, "The things which you learned, received, heard, and saw in me: do these things, and the God of peace will be with you." Once we turn our requests over to God, we must change our thinking and doing. Our minds must dwell on honorable, just, pure, lovely, virtuous, reputable, praise-worthy things, while we behave in a way that is consistent with Paul and the apostles (righteous ways). The result will be peace in our hearts and souls. This is a godly peace which will surpass any comprehension.

Additional Notes: The result will be a peace in our hearts and souls. This is a godly peace which will surpass any comprehension. People might gawk and say, "How can he have so much peace after what he did?" Others might respond, "He repented and is forgiven and believes it." This supernatural peace from the forgiveness he has is due to Christ's work on the cross. There is definitely sorrow over what happened, a great desire for restitution, and a bearing of all the consequences. Yet, peace comes from God's forgiveness.

The fourth way to unchain ourselves from the bonds of our own lack of forgiveness is to deal with the memories of our sin. The memory system that God has imbedded in us was to learn from our mistakes. We put our hand in a fire and get burned. Through that painful experience, we make a memory. Then, we learn never to do this again. When we see the fire again, our memory of being burned returns, and we are warned. This will work exactly the same way with our sins. When we sin, we receive the consequences of our sin which might include shame, guilt, anguish, and humiliation before repentance. When we travel through our lives, many different triggers bring up those painful memories.

We will need to rehearse what was learned and recommit to our new behavior. These are reminders to be careful. They do not have to debilitate us. They will bring up some of the feelings we experienced when the problem occurred. This is what memory is supposed to do, so we do not forget how "burned" we got. I usually say to myself, "I am glad I went through that experience. I will never do that again because the guilt, shame, and humiliation were so great." I will thank the Lord Jesus Christ for His forgiveness and rejoice in my relationship with Him always.

Additional Notes: Another way to unchain ourselves from the bonds of our own lack of forgiveness is to put away the notion that we are now tainted or stained before God. Due to the wickedness, shame, and humiliation of some sin, we may feel that we are now sort of second-class Christians. We can no longer stand with other believers before God on earth or in heaven. We think we are now "one of them." These include the shipwrecked saints, the carnal Christians, and the bygone believers. These are the Christians that are looked upon as dirty, stained, and tainted by a sinful mistake. This concept could not be further from the truth. We need to realize that we are not alone in our sin. Everyone has sinned. When we sin, we think we are the only ones who have done such a wicked deed. This is not true. In Romans 3:23, Paul makes a clear statement, "For all have sinned, and fall short of the glory of God."

Stumbling Christians are in the company of some very great men who struggled with some terrible sins. Noah drank too much (Genesis 9:20-23). Judah picked up prostitutes off the streets (Genesis 38:14-16). Joseph was a braggart (Genesis 37:1-11). Samson was a womanizer (Judges 14:3). Moses had a temper (Exodus 11:8; 32:19; Numbers 16:15; 20:10). King David was a poor father, adulterer, and murderer (2 Samuel 13-18); Solomon fell into idolatry at the end of his life (1 Kings 11:1-12). The disciples James and John had thunderous tempers (Mark 3:17; Luke 9:5) and were also momma's boys. They asked their mother to ask Jesus if the two of them could sit on either side of Him in the kingdom (Matthew 20:20-24).

The apostle Peter was terribly impulsive (Matthew 14:28-33; John 18:10) and often did not think before the man would speak (Matthew 16:22; John 13:8-9). Sometimes, we like to compare ourselves to the apostle Paul. Yet, Paul struggled deeply with his own sinful flesh, though no sins are actually mentioned after he became saved (Romans 7:13-25). One of the reasons these real people and their real transgressions are described in the Bible is to demonstrate that believers are not alone. We have all failed and will fail God at times in our lives. Sometimes, we can do this in a big way. This is why our Lord Jesus came to die! Isn't this true? Yes, it is.

Here is a Bible reference describing the struggle with the flesh:

Romans 7:13-25
Did then that which is good become death to me? May it never be! But sin, that it might be shown to be sin, by working death to me through that which is good; that through the commandment sin might become exceedingly sinful. For we know that the law is spiritual, but I am fleshly, sold under sin. For I don't know what I am doing. For I don't practice what I desire to do; but what I hate that I do. But if what I don't desire, that I do, I consent to the law that it is good. So now it is no more I that do it, but sin which

dwells in me. For I know that in me, that is, in my flesh, dwells no good thing. For desire is present with me, but I don't find it doing that which is good. For the good which I desire, I don't do; but the evil which I don't desire, that I practice. But if what I don't desire, that I do, it is no more I that do it, but sin which dwells in me. I find then the law, that, to me, while I desire to do good, evil is present. For I delight in God's law after the inward man, but I see a different law in my members, warring against the law of my mind, and bringing me into captivity under the law of sin which is in my members. What a wretched man I am! Who will deliver me out of the body of this death? I thank God through Jesus Christ, our Lord! So then with the mind, I myself serve God's law, but with the flesh, the sin's law.

An Ancient Portrait

A great illustration of this supernatural ability to forgive oneself is Peter (Matthew 26; Mark 14; Luke 22; John 18). In the Garden of Gethsemane, Jesus told His disciples that He was about to be betrayed, and all of them would fall away. Peter declared that he would never fall away. Jesus looked at Peter and told him directly that this very night before the cock crowed, Peter would deny Him three times. The apostle declared that he would die before he ever denied the Lord. Aren't we exactly the same way? At first, we think that we could never do some of the sins that others have done. Later, we find we have done the very same or similar thing.

This chief of the apostles could not even conceive of the fact that he would ever deny the Lord. Then the mob came. The leaders of the Jews dragged Jesus away. Peter followed Him to the courtyard of Annas, the former high priest. After he entered, a slave girl walked up to him and asked if he were one of the disciples of Jesus. Without hesitation, he denied that he even knew Jesus. Then Peter walked over and began to warm his hands in front of the fire. He was joined by some of the servants and officials. Again, he was asked if he knew Jesus. Again, Peter denied knowing Him. Finally, a servant of one of the officials noticed his accent. The servant proclaimed that not only did Peter have a Galilean accent, but he had actually seen him with Jesus. Peter responded by cursing, swearing, and proclaiming loudly that he did not know the man. Peter had the accent and was seen with Jesus by an eyewitness, but He still lied.

After this, Peter was so distraught that he went out and wept bitterly. He was genuinely repentant and sorrowful for this wicked deed. I am sure he confessed it to God. When he was restored by Jesus in John 21:15, it is never brought up again. It is never mentioned in his letters or in the book of Acts. Peter was a joy-filled, peace-filled, and thankful saint.

Additional Notes: If asked about the restoration of Peter by Jesus, here is the Bible reference I cite:

John 21:15
So when they had eaten their breakfast, Jesus said to Simon Peter, "Simon, son of Jonah, do you love me more than these?" He said to him, "Yes, Lord; you know that I have affection for you." He said to him, "Feed my lambs." He said to him again a second time, "Simon, son of Jonah, do you love me?" He said to him, "Yes, Lord; you know that I have affection for you." He said to him, "Tend my sheep." He said to him the third time, "Simon, son of Jonah, do you have affection for me?" Peter was grieved because he asked him the third time, "Do you have affection for me?" He said to him, "Lord, you know everything. You know that I have affection for you." Jesus said to him [Peter], "Feed my sheep. Most certainly I tell you, when you were young, you dressed yourself, and walked where you wanted to. But when you are old, you will stretch out your hands, and another will dress you, and carry you where you don't want to go." Now he said this, signifying by what

kind of death he would glorify God. When he had said this, he said to him, "Follow me."

He had accepted by faith his forgiveness and did not beat himself up over and over or churn it over and over in his mind. Peter had found joy after his confessions. We can find the same. This does not mean there were no consequences to Peter's denial. It is written in all four gospels as a testimony to what Peter did. The greater testimony was the courage and boldness Peter displayed after his fall. He went on to achieve great things for God.

Additional Notes: To achieve this kind of valor and freedom from ourselves, we simply must discard the negative thoughts of our flesh and embrace the positive thoughts of the new man. We need to grow strong in faith trusting God's promise to forgive. We must realize that when we sin, we are not alone, nor are we second-class Christians. We should protect our hearts and minds with the Word and practice righteousness. Then we should use the memory of the shame to remember what we learned from the incident and never do it again. This was exactly what Peter did.

Peter never dwelt on his colossal failure, nor did he forget it because he never denied the Lord again. In fact, on many occasions he stood boldly for the Lord Jesus. In his letters, he spoke of the courage of the other men of faith to encourage his brothers and sisters to remain strong. He also remained in truth and practiced righteousness himself while trusting God that he too was fully forgiven. Once we are able to fully forgive ourselves, we can forgive those who transgressed us or ask for forgiveness of those that we transgressed.

A Modern Anecdote

In the world today, adultery has become a fairly common occurrence. This is a difficult situation for all involved. Some Christians think that adultery should always lead to divorce, but this simply is not the case. I have seen the Holy Spirit rebuild many marriages in which adultery occurred. A while ago, a married couple entered my counseling office in the pit of this debilitating situation. The wife was weeping, and the husband was completely distraught. He had been involved in a six-month long affair, yet they both wanted to save the relationship.

As I was speaking to the husband, he began to shed tears and muttered, "Dr. Jones, I became that guy!" I asked him to explain what he meant by that comment. He told me that he was now "the guy that everyone in his community, church, job, and neighborhood, will stare at, talk about, and avoid." Unfortunately, this situation could and does actually occur, but it is a sin and transgression that can be forgiven (1 John 1:7; Colossians 2:13).

Additional Notes: If asked about the fact that all transgressions can be forgiven, here are the Bible references I cite:

John 1:7
But if we walk in the light, as he is in the light, we have fellowship with one another, and the blood of Jesus Christ, his Son, cleanses us from all sin.

Colossians 2:13
You were dead through your trespasses and the uncircumcision of your flesh. He made you alive together with him, having forgiven us all our trespasses.

The husband was a very high-ranking city official. Often, his office would take in a group of interns and provide the experience they needed to complete their university training. He usually wasn't involved directly with the interns, but the one in charge was in the hospital preparing for surgery. One particular female intern did catch his eye, but he reminded himself how happy he was in his marriage. Also, he knew the Lord was watching. She traveled with him from time to time as he continued his work in the city. Every time she returned to his office; she was dressed more provocatively.

Feelings were beginning to develop on both sides, until finally she suggested they stay a little longer at his office to finish the city project that they were working on together. They suggested that could order in dinner. He knew that everyone had gone home for the evening but gave into the temptation. This "working dinner" turned into a powerful romantic encounter leading to a six-month affair. He told me that all along he had mixed feelings about what he was doing but continued with the affair anyway. The woman was unsaved, unmarried, and was not at all bothered by it.

Finally, the wife found a receipt from a hotel in his wallet and confronted him. The husband confessed everything, and the wife demanded that he leave. He said good-bye to his four shocked children and went to stay with a friend. After some time, she realized how much she loved him and asked him to return home. He already had ended the relationship with the other woman. Over the weeks, many issues came to light from his childhood including how he was raised and the difficulties his father had with the same issue, his habits surrounding his purity, their lack of intimacy, and his lack of adequate safeguards. Many people think, "Oh, I can trust my husband or wife." The issue is not trust, it is a healthy fear of the flesh, the world (society and their values), and the Devil, and the devastation one can experience when these enemies of our righteousness are left unguarded and unchecked.

After dealing with each and every one of these factors, the process of forgiveness and reconciliation had to begin. The obstacle that caused the largest problem was not the wife and his children forgiving him, it was his unwillingness to forgive himself. He was filled with anxiety because he felt like he was wearing a large sign that read "Adulterer!" which everyone could see. He began to think every conversation was about him, and every look was a look of condemnation. Even this he could handle as part of the consequences of what he had done, but his inner voice kept condemning him.

The inner voice that haunted him was not his new man but his old man: the flesh. To relieve him of this constant condemnation, I shared with him key biblical concepts in this chapter. This provided for him the truth that the Spirit utilized to remove the mental sign and to allow him to fully forgive himself. The final and most critical step for their marriage involved the placing of various safeguards into his life which would rebuild the trust of his wife and children and prevent this sin from occurring again.

The setting up of various safeguards (Philippians 3:1) will preserve his purity and the sanctity of their marriage bed (Hebrews 13:4). This is crucial in rebuilding the relationship. This will also aid in the forgiveness process of his wife and his children as they literally watch him demonstrate over and over his commitment to his purity before God and them.

A Personal Response

Dear Heavenly Father,

    I recognize you are my sovereign Lord. As I was reading this chapter, I realized that I have not completely forgiven myself for the sins I have committed toward you and (add name). I am so sorry. Please help me forgive myself as You have already fully forgiven me. Help me to constantly honor and glorify You in my relationship with (add name). Give to me Your wisdom as I set up safeguards to prevent me from falling into this sin again. I pray this in the name of Jesus. Amen.

HEALING RELATIONSHIPS THROUGH FORGIVENESS

Instructor's Notes

AN INSTRUCTOR'S MANUAL

Chapter 5

Forgive Yourself All

Now, we must fully forgive ourselves. Though this may be difficult at times, God does not desire His children to feel guilty for their sins after confessing them.

In the section, "A Typical Scenario," the author describes an encounter with someone who had not forgiven himself for a sin he had committed in a relationship.

What is the scenario about?

A Christian had been asked how he was and initially told the person he was fine and then blurted out his shame over a sin.

What did the conflict concern?

He was conflicted within himself, God, and the one he transgressed.

What was the relationship between the parties?

It could have been a friend, parent, sibling, child, acquaintance, co-worker, or fellow student.

Have you had a similar experience?

(Various answers should be shared including yours.)

HEALING RELATIONSHIPS THROUGH FORGIVENESS

In the section, "A Scriptural Principle" the author presents an important biblical principle in the forgiveness process which concerns forgiving ourselves.

How would you express this principle in your own words?

The fifth principle is "we must forgive ourselves for our sin as God has forgiven us."

(Various answers should be shared including yours.)

How would you rewrite this principle to make it even more personal to your life (using your name and situation)?

(Various answers should be shared including yours.)

Why do you think this principle might be important in your life right now?

(Various answers should be shared including yours.)

How would you rate yourself on the percentage of times you followed this principle in the past when you did something wrong in a relationship?

(Various answers should be shared including yours.)

Directions: Put a horizontal mark and your name where you see yourself on the percentage line.

| 0% | 25% | 50% | 75% | 100% |

In the section, "A Biblical Explanation," the author explains the reasons why we are to forgive ourselves for the sins we commit against others in a relationship and how to do it.

According to Romans 7:20, what is inside us which keeps us from forgiving ourselves?

To unchain ourselves from the bonds of our own lack of forgiveness, we must understand the source of the shame, guilt, and humiliation we feel. This does not originate from the Lord Jesus Christ. Once we confess the sins and accept our forgiveness by faith, it should all flow away. If it does not, then the flesh is the culprit.

According to 2 Corinthians 10:5, what must we do with the false concept that our sin is too great or sins too numerous for us to forgive ourselves?

This is a simple concept when examined carefully. Every single idea or thought should be examined. Those thoughts that are contrary to the Scriptures should be discarded and those consistent should be embraced. In Romans 12, Paul explains how Christians can resist conforming themselves to the world, and it involves their minds. In verse 2, Paul states this, "Don't be conformed to this world, but be transformed by the renewing of your mind."

According to Romans 12:2, how can we subdue these guilt-filled thoughts that condemn?

Our mind is renewed in God's Word by discarding worldly thoughts and embracing God's thoughts. This then transforms us into His image. Christians forgive themselves and do not carry around guilt, shame, and humiliation. They continually discard thoughts that condemn and embrace thoughts that forgive.

According to Philippians 4:6–7, what must we do to guard our hearts and minds from these unforgiving thoughts?

Our minds must dwell on honorable, just, pure, lovely, virtuous, reputable, praise-worthy things, while we behave in a way that is consistent with Paul and the apostles (righteous ways). The result will be peace in our hearts and souls. This is a godly peace which will surpass any comprehension.

When a memory of a sin against another returns, how are we to handle it?

We will need to rehearse what was learned and recommit to our new behavior. These are reminders to be careful.

I will thank the Lord Jesus Christ for His forgiveness and rejoice in my relationship with Him always.

In what ways might these truths impact your relationships?

(Various answers should be shared including yours.)

AN INSTRUCTOR'S MANUAL

In the section, "An Ancient Portrait," the author describes how Peter handled his grievous sin against the Lord and the guilt which must have accompanied it.

What was Peter's attitude when Jesus told him that he would deny him three times that night?

In the Garden of Gethsemane, Jesus told His disciples that He was about to be betrayed, and all of them would fall away. Peter declared that he would never fall away. Jesus looked at Peter and told him directly that this very night before the cock crowed, Peter would deny Him three times.

The apostle declared that he would die before he ever denied the Lord. Aren't we exactly the same way? At first, we think that we could never do some of the sins that others have done. Later, we find we have done the very same or similar thing.

How did Peter actually deny Christ?

After he entered, a slave girl walked up to him and asked if he were one of the disciples of Jesus.

He was joined by some of the servants and officials. Again, he was asked if he knew Jesus. Again, Peter denied knowing Him.

Finally, a servant of one of the officials noticed his accent. The servant proclaimed that not only did Peter have a Galilean accent, but he had actually seen him with Jesus.

Peter responded by cursing, swearing, and proclaiming loudly that he did not know the man. Peter had the accent and was seen with Jesus by an eyewitness, but He still lied.

What was Peter's response after he had denied Christ?

After this, Peter was so distraught that he went out and wept bitterly. He was genuinely repentant and sorrowful for this wicked deed. I am sure he confessed it to God.

What were the consequences of Peter's denial?

When he was restored by Jesus in John 21:15, it is never brought up again.

This does not mean there were no consequences to Peter's denial. It is written in all four gospels as a testimony to what Peter did. The greater testimony was the courage and boldness Peter displayed after his fall. He went on to achieve great things for God.

Why do you think Peter was silent about his sin in his letters (1 and 2 Peter)?

It is never mentioned in his letters or in the book of Acts. Peter was a joy-filled, peace-filled, and thankful saint. He had accepted by faith his forgiveness and did not beat himself up over and over or churn it over and over in his mind. Peter had found joy after his confessions. We can find the same.... Peter never dwelt on his colossal failure, nor did he forget it because he never denied the Lord again. In fact, on many occasions he stood boldly for the Lord Jesus. In his letters, he spoke of the courage of the other men of faith to encourage his brothers and sisters to remain strong.

Have you ever been in a situation like Peter's in which you knew God forgave your sin against another, but you could not forgive yourself? How was it different and how was it the same?

(Various answers should be shared including yours.)

In the section, "A Modern Anecdote," the author describes a deep struggle a husband had to forgive himself for the sin of adultery.

What did the husband mean when he said, "I am that guy?"

I asked him to explain what he meant by that comment. He told me that he was now "the guy that everyone in his community, church, job, and neighborhood, will stare at, talk about, and avoid." Unfortunately, this situation could and does actually occur, but it is a sin and transgression that can be forgiven (1 John 1:7; Colossians 2:13).

What does a healthy fear in a relationship involve?

The issue is not trust, it is a healthy fear of the flesh, the world (society and their values), and the Devil, and the devastation one can experience when these enemies of our righteousness are left unguarded and unchecked.

Why was the husband filled with anxiety?

He was filled with anxiety because he felt like he was wearing a large sign that read "Adulterer!" which everyone could see. He began to think every conversation was about him, and every look was a look of condemnation.

According to Romans 7:20, where did the condemning voice inside his head come from?

In Romans 7:20, Paul calls our sinful flesh the "sin which dwells in me." The sin principle resides in our physical bodies. The flesh (common word for this principle) desires to wallow in its own sin.

What might be some safeguards the family could set up to rebuild the trust and keep this sin from occurring again?

The setting up of various safeguards (Philippians 3:1) will preserve his purity and the sanctity of their marriage bed (Hebrews 13:4). This is crucial in rebuilding the relationship. This will also aid in the forgiveness process of his wife and his children as they literally watch him demonstrate over and over his commitment to his purity before God and them.

Based on the truths learned in this chapter, how would you have reacted to your sin if you were the husband? How would you have acted if you were the wife?

(Various answers should be shared including yours.)

AN INSTRUCTOR'S MANUAL

In the section, "A Personal Response," the author provides a model you may use for prayer if you find it necessary after discovering the truths in this chapter.

Are you presently in a relationship where you have sinned against another and have not asked God for forgiveness? If not, is there one from the past that still needs this prayer to be prayed?

(Various answers should be shared including yours.)

Based on the truths you have just learned, what will you continue doing in your current relationships and what will you do differently?

(Various answers should be shared including yours.)

What additional thoughts would you like to share with the others?

(Various answers should be shared including yours.)

Instructor's Notes

AN INSTRUCTOR'S MANUAL

Conclusion to Group Study and Workbook Part 1

As we conclude this book, I would like to leave us with some final thoughts about our God of forgiveness and what His Son did on the cross for us. First, if we understand the full extent of what was wrought for us on that cursed tree in order to forgive us, it will become so much easier to do the same thing for others. Second, if you read this entire book and realized that you do not understand salvation or have never received Christ as Lord and Savior, then I would like to provide that opportunity. Please do not skip this section; it may be the most important in your life.

From all outward appearances, humans seem "good" and attempt to live decent lives. This is man's concept of himself. This is not God's concept. The Almighty's view is that people all over the world and throughout the ages sin, sin, and sin again (Romans 3:23). This is a terrible and utterly destructive condition. Yet, they have ramifications that are far worse. These sins condemn us to everlasting divine retribution.

Though described briefly in the Old Testament, the Lord Jesus Christ clearly announced and proclaimed the future punishment to come. Contrary to popular belief, Jesus did not only speak of love, grace, and mercy, He also spoke of the coming judgment for sin. He declared that the judgment of sin would be everlasting punishment in a place He called "Hell." The Lord portrayed this place as an eternal inferno (Matthew 18:8) where there would be the weeping (from the sorrow) and gnashing of teeth (from the agony and anguish of suffering) continually into eternity (Matthew 8:12; 13:42, 50; 22:13; 24:51; 25:30; Luke 13:28).

HEALING RELATIONSHIPS THROUGH FORGIVENESS

Why must people face this horrific punishment? Though God is a God of love, grace, and mercy, He is also a God of great holiness, righteousness, and justice (Psalm 89:14,18). These attributes are just as much a part of His divine nature as His love, grace, and mercy. You have broken God's law as we all have, and the penalty must be paid. This began with the first man Adam (Genesis 3:1-7). When this occurred, His love, grace, and mercy surfaced, and a provision was made. Someone else would have to take man's place and pay the penalty. Someone who had never transgressed Him, who would never deserve punishment, and would fulfill all of God's Laws, would be substituted in man's place. This was the Son of God, Jesus Christ.

As the God-Man, He would pay the penalty for our sins in His death on the cross. Once done, the Lord God made only one provision for people to appropriate what His Son had done on the cross for them. This provision is receiving Jesus Christ as Savior and Lord. Though I cannot possibly share with you this good news in the confines of this book, I would love for you to consider purchasing my book entitled, *Finding The Light: The Kingdom of Heaven and How To Enter It*. It can be found for sale on Amazon.com. It is inexpensive and contains the full gospel message for your consideration. This message is so important and extensive that it cannot adequately be contained in a few pages at the end of a book.

If you are a believer, you must go out into the world and forgive as you are forgiven. These principles are to be lived and shared with others. You now have the tools to make your relationships last a lifetime. Go live them out and share them with others!

AN INSTRUCTOR'S MANUAL

PART 2

*REQUESTING GOD'S GRACE
FROM OTHERS*

THE GROUP STUDY BOOK WITH ADDITIONAL NOTES

AND THE WORKBOOK QUESTIONS WITH SUGGESTED ANSWERS

FOR EACH CHAPTER

AN INSTRUCTOR'S MANUAL

CONTENTS

Introduction to Group Study Part 2   169
Introduction to the Workbook Part 2   173

Chapter - 1. Ask Others Next (Study)   175
Chapter - 1. Ask Others Next (Workbook)   193

Chapter - 2. Humbly Make Restitution (Study)   203
Chapter - 2. Humbly Make Restitution (Workbook)   219

Chapter - 3. Accept the Consequences (Study)   229
Chapter - 3. Accept the Consequences (Workbook)   247

Chapter - 4. Gently Confront Sin (Study)   257
Chapter - 4. Gently Confront Sin (Workbook)   273

Conclusion to Group Study and Workbook Part 2   283

AN INSTRUCTOR'S MANUAL

Introduction to Group Study Part 2

This series of three books (Part 1,2,3) grew out of a desire to put the material in my main book on healing relationship through forgiveness into a format for small group study. As a result, the introductions are the same in all three books. This is primarily due to the essential nature of the content in our understanding of the truths found in each one. It also allows the books to be read and studied one after the other or to be studied independent of the other two. This provides more flexibility to the various individuals, groups, churches, and organizations who wish to use it.

After Moses had received the Ten Commandments, the prophet and leader requested that God show him His glory. The Almighty explained to Moses that no human could see Him and live. Nevertheless, God would grant his request by allowing His servant Moses to experience the passing of His "goodness" by him and the actual viewing of the "backside of His glory." On the next morning, he stood upon a rock and called upon the name of the Lord. The Lord God descended in the form of a cloud, shielded Moses in the cleft of the rock, and covered him with His divine hand. As God displayed His divine glory visibly, He declared the many attributes of His supernatural, divine character.

In Exodus 34:6-7, Moses described this amazing moment and the words that he heard the Lord declare about Himself. The prophet recorded, "Yahweh [I AM THAT I AM] passed by before him...he proclaimed, 'Yahweh! Yahweh, a merciful and gracious God, slow to anger...abundant in His loving kindness and truth, keeping loving kindness for thousands, forgiving iniquity and disobedience and sin.'" A book that is written on healing relationships through forgiveness by its nature must begin with the proclamation that the God of the

universe is not only the merciful, gracious, patient, loving, kind, truth-filled, just, and righteous Lord but an Almighty deity who "forgives iniquity, transgressions, and sin." This Lord God announced that He is a "forgiving" God.

This by no means negates the fact that He is also a just and righteous one; therefore, this forgiveness comes with a price that had to be paid. So, He sent His Son to die to pay the penalty for our sins in order to pour out His forgiveness upon all mankind. Through faith in Jesus Christ, men and women experience the full extent of His forgiveness that was proclaimed to Moses many years ago on that mountain top. Once this has occurred in our lives, we are to live for Him. We are to act like Him, and we are to obey Him. One of the critical ways in which God desires His forgiven people to live for, act like, and obey Him is *to forgive others as we are forgiven*. This is the key point of these books. As the Lord God has forgiven us and healed our relationship with Him, He requires us to forgive and heal our relationships with others. This is found in several passages in the Scriptures. Two of them are mentioned by our Lord and one from the apostle Paul. All three clearly explain the important truth that relationships are to be "reconciled" and "restored" to "gain back" one's brother, sister, or neighbor. This is done primarily through forgiveness.

In Matthew 5, the Lord Jesus discusses the heart attitudes people in His kingdom should possess. After speaking of anger, the Lord presents a general principle of living in His kingdom on earth. In verses 23-24, He explains, "If therefore you are offering your gift at the altar, and there remember that your brother has anything against you, leave your gift there before the altar, and go your way. First be reconciled to your brother, and then come and offer your gift." The Greek word translated "reconciled" means "to make changes." It originates from a Greek root word that was a banking term

meaning "to render accounts the same." There would be a discrepancy between two bank ledgers, and all the mistakes would have to be found and corrected in order for them to agree. We express this between people as "being on the same page." The Lord Jesus indicates that the Father desires His people to come to Him fully reconciled with each other. If we, as Christians, know that someone harbors something against us, we are to take the initiative and go to them and reconcile with them. We should not wait for them to come to us. We take our responsibility and go to them. We must once again "settle accounts." They have the same responsibility.

In Matthew 18, Jesus discusses those who are sinning in the church and what all believers should do. In verse 15, the Lord commands, "If your brother sins against you, go, show him his fault between you and him alone. If he listens to you, you have gained back your brother." The Greek word translated "gain" refers "to obtaining or securing something." When a relationship is restored, we gain back everything that the other parties contributed. In this particular case, we have something against our brother, rather than the reverse. If this does happen, we are to take the initiative and confront our brother or sister to gain him or her back and restore the relationship. So, whether someone has something against us or we have something against someone else, the procedure is essentially the same. Christians must take the initiative and reconcile with them.

The third passage involves the restoration of a sinning brother in the church. In Galatians 6, Paul opens the chapter with an explanation of how to help a sinning saint. In verse one, Paul asserts, "Brothers, even if a man is caught in some fault, you who are spiritual must restore such a one." The Greek word translated "restore" means "to render fit, sound, or complete; to mend or repair what has been broken." The word is used of a physically broken fishing net. In Mark 1:19

and Matthew 4:21, when Jesus called James and John into ministry with Him, they were in the process of "mending" their fishing nets. They were mending the holes in their net so the fish would not fall through. This restoration could easily involve a conflict between two people. The holes in their relationship need to be mended. This process involves healing relationships through forgiveness. These passages will be referred to as you read.

These books are my original works on reconciliation and forgiveness. It is not based on other books that I have read and simply collated. To produce this work, I carefully read through the entire New Testament verse by verse. Then, I meticulously perused the Old Testament paying particular attention to the Psalms and Proverbs. As I read, categories were built from the individual passages, rather than a set of preconceived notions. These numerous categories became the individual biblical principles found in every chapter. Each passage was studied in its historical, grammatical, and scriptural contexts. After this, I compared my interpretations with those of past and present scholars. After this study, I have attempted to follow these biblical principles in my own personal life and also utilize them in my pastoral counseling practice. I have seen the Holy Spirit use them to transform relationships of all kinds.

One last thought. At the end of each chapter, I discuss a counseling experience. Due to confidentiality, none of these are based on one particular counseling situation. Instead, I have mixed together common elements I have seen, details from books and films, bits from my own life and the lives of people I have known, and thoughts from my imagination to create a situation where the biblical principles discussed in the chapters can fully be applied. These are composites of real-life situations. Read, learn, and apply. I commend you to the Lord and His Word (Acts 20:32).

AN INSTRUCTOR'S MANUAL

Introduction to the Workbook Part 2

This workbook is designed to aid in the comprehension and application of the truths from the Scriptures which are found in the book of the same name. It has a question-and-answer format because asking questions was a powerful teaching method that the Lord used to reveal God's divine truth. Jesus asked over one hundred and thirty questions as He instructed the people of God and others. These are only the recorded ones. We can only speculate as to how many questions He might have actually asked. The Lord used His questioning techniques to prompt His listeners to focus, understand, analyze, evaluate, and apply the principles He was proclaiming to them. The same has been done in this workbook.

In Matthew 17, Jesus enters the town of Capernaum after a long absence. This was a perfect opportunity for the tax-collectors to make some money and see if Jesus was paying his share of the taxes. These were Jewish tax collectors who obtained money for the support of the temple. The people of the town would have known Jesus and His disciples well since Peter's home and the town functioned as their base of operations. When they saw Peter, they approached him and asked if Jesus had paid the temple taxes. It was the drachma which was two days wages. Peter responded with a "yes." Then, Peter went into the house to ask the Lord if they actually had paid them. He was perplexed. He may have been thinking, "Do we pay taxes or not?" Or, he may have thought "Why do we have to pay taxes when we are citizens of heaven?"

Matthew states that Jesus knew exactly what was on his mind. As a result, Jesus asked one of His defining questions to direct Peter to the correct answer. At the end of verse 25,

HEALING RELATIONSHIPS THROUGH FORGIVENESS

Matthew records this, "When he came into the house, Jesus anticipated him, saying, "What do you think, Simon? From whom do the kings of the earth receive toll or tribute? From their children or from strangers?" To assist Peter, Jesus asks Peter if a king has his own sons (family members) pay taxes or does he have strangers do it. The answer is obvious the king receives taxes from strangers for his sons. So, Peter responds, "Strangers." Then, at the end of verse 26, Jesus explains, "Therefore the children are exempt."

Here Jesus is referring to God the Father as the king of the temple and He as His Son. Therefore, as His Son, He does not have to pay taxes because the King (God) collects taxes for His Son (Jesus). Jesus is exempt. Yet, the Lord will pay it anyway. Why? He doesn't want to offend them. He doesn't want the gospel hindered in the eyes of the tax-collectors and the people. At the beginning of verse 27, the Lord says, "But, lest we cause them to stumble."

Here is a perfect opportunity to teach a truth and perform a miracle. At the end of the verse 27, Jesus commands Peter, "Go to the sea, cast a hook, and take up the first fish that comes up. When you have opened its mouth, you will find a stater [different coin, same amount] coin. Take that and give it to them for me and you." This is exactly what happened. The taxes were miraculously paid. Jesus used a question to aid Peter in his thinking process concerning the tax. As Jesus used questions, so shall we. May the questions in this book help you focus, understand, analyze, evaluate, and apply these biblical principles.

Chapter 1

Ask Others Next

When we have sinned against others, one of the most difficult things to do is to ask for forgiveness. Perhaps, we are too proud to humble ourselves. Maybe, we are fearful of their response. We could even be simply too ashamed to face them. This is a step that is often ignored, and we may even pretend the sin never happened. We simply go about our business as if everything is fine when it is not. Herein lies the problem: if we cannot do this with God, our Father, then we cannot do this with others. The Scriptures do not allow it. Whether the other person requests it or not, the Lord does.

A Typical Scenario

Have you ever had or perhaps heard a conversation like this concerning a father and his teenage daughter? He says, "I am not going to ask for forgiveness. (Wife responds.) Yes, I know I accused her and punished her for the dent in the car. (Wife responds.) I know now that the neighbor did it and not her, but I do not like her attitude. (Wife responds.) No! I will not ask her for forgiveness. Period!" Even though this typical father was wrong, he does not want to admit it. He refuses to ask his daughter for forgiveness. Have you ever felt that way about someone you know or love? Have you refused to ask for forgiveness from someone you have wronged?

The answer is obvious, we all have experienced this. Since he is a Christian, we know it will not be long before the Holy Spirit convicts him, and he will reconcile with his daughter.

If he does not, this will create a wall in their relationship. As he does this over and over again, this wall will grow taller and taller. Eventually, there will no longer be a relationship. All our relationships can fall victim to our unwillingness to ask for forgiveness and to reconcile. In the introduction to this book, I referred to three important passages indicating that God has only one way to restore relationships, and it is through forgiveness (Matthew 5:23-24; 18:15; Galatians 6:1).

A Scriptural Principle

The first principle is both obvious and natural. It is "we must reconcile our relationship (see Introduction) with those we have sinned against by asking for forgiveness." This next important step simply involves asking for and then receiving forgiveness. This will occur first with God, then with the others involved. This was described in 1 John 1:9, "If we confess our sins, he is faithful and righteous to forgive us the sins, and to cleanse us from all unrighteousness with God." These Greek verbs are in the present tense which indicates continuous action in present time. In our relationship to the Father through Jesus Christ, we are continually confessing our sins, and the Lord God is continually forgiving our sins. This describes the life of a believer with God: confessing and forgiving. This does not describe the full forgiveness on the cross (Romans 8:1); instead, it explains relational forgiveness people bestow on each other as they fellowship together.

A Biblical Explanation

As Christians, we are constantly confessing, and God is constantly forgiving. It is the same way in our relationships with others. We are to behave in our relationship with others as we do with God: confessing and forgiving. In Luke 17:3-4, this is exactly what Jesus affirms when He says, "Be careful. If your brother sins against you, rebuke him. If he repents [confesses and asks for forgiveness], forgive him. If he sins against you seven times in the day, and seven times returns, saying, 'I repent,' you shall forgive him." This confessing is the admitting of what we specifically did wrong. Then there is a mourning and sorrow over the sin. This leads to the final stage which involves turning in the opposite direction from what we did. We do this with God, and then we do the same with others.

This asking for forgiveness of those we have wronged is so obvious and is such a normal part of life. It is woven into our very fabric as human beings. When we are transgressed, we expect the person to come to us and ask for forgiveness. In Romans 2, Paul is discussing the conscience, and its place in the judgment of man. He explains that within people is a law God puts within their hearts, and they will be judged according to that law. In verse 15, Paul describes it, "In that they show the work of the law written in their hearts, their conscience testifying with them, and their thoughts among themselves accusing or else excusing them." When we hurt, or harm a person, we will have a natural desire to ask for forgiveness because it is written on our hearts.

Additional Notes: If asked about the conscience, here is the Bible reference I cite:

Romans 2:11-15
For there is no partiality with God. For as many as have sinned without law will also perish without the law. As many as have sinned under the law will be judged by the law. For it isn't the hearers of the law who are righteous before God, but the doers of the law will be justified (for when Gentiles who don't have the law do by nature the things of the law, these, not having the law, are a law to themselves, in that they show the work of the law written in

their hearts...conscience testifying with them, and their thoughts among themselves accusing or else excusing them).

When people sin against others, their consciences begin to condemn them for the transgression and exhort them to ask for forgiveness. Why? It is in their nature. In verse 14, Paul asserts, "For when Gentiles who don't have the law do by nature the things of the law, these, not having the law, are a law to themselves." Asking for forgiveness is one of those natural things inside us. It is a law or rule within our nature. When we wrong people, we know innately that we must ask them for their forgiveness. When people wrong us, then we expect them to ask for forgiveness. This is so obvious that it barely needs discussion.

This concept of "sinning against" someone is found in several places in the Bible. One example is found in the life of Abraham. While living in the land of Gerar, he was afraid that the king would be attracted to his wife and kill him to take her for himself. Abraham asked Sarah to tell the king that he was her brother which she did. When the king took Sarah, as Abraham had predicted, his life was spared. Then God stepped in and stopped the king before he could violate her. The Lord told the king the truth about Abraham and closed the wombs of Abimelech's wife and female servants until he rectified the situation. In Genesis 20:9, Moses writes, "Then Abimelech [the king] called Abraham, and said to him, 'What have you done to us? How have I sinned against you, that you have brought on me and on my kingdom a great sin? You have done deeds to me that ought not to be done!'" Abimelech questioned Abraham as to how the king had "sinned against" him. Notice, this concept of "sinning against" others was a truth that was natural to all people.

Additional Notes: If asked about the details of this story, here is the Bible reference I cite:

AN INSTRUCTOR'S MANUAL

Genesis 20:1-18

Abraham traveled from there toward the land of the South and lived between Kadesh and Shur. He lived as a foreigner in Gerar. Abraham said about Sarah his wife, "She is my sister." Abimelech king of Gerar sent, and took Sarah. But God came to Abimelech in a dream of the night, and said to him, "Behold, you are a dead man, because of the woman whom you have taken. For she is a man's wife."

Now Abimelech had not come near her. He said, "Lord, will you kill even a righteous nation? Didn't he tell me, 'She is my sister?' She, even she herself, said, 'He is my brother.' In the integrity of my heart and the innocence of my hands have I done this."

God said to him in the dream, "Yes, I know that in the integrity of your heart you have done this, and I also withheld you from sinning against me. Therefore, I didn't allow you to touch her. Now therefore, restore the man's wife. For he is a prophet, and he will pray for you, and you will live. If you don't restore her, know for sure that you will die, you, and all who are yours."

Abimelech rose early in the morning, and called all his servants [subjects], and told all these things in their ear. The men were very scared. Then Abimelech called Abraham, and said to him, "What have you done to us? How have I sinned against you, that you have brought on me and on my kingdom a great sin? You have done deeds to me that ought not to be done!" Abimelech said to Abraham, "What did you see, that you have done this thing?"

Abraham said, "Because I thought, surely the fear of God is not in this place. They will kill me for my wife's sake.' Besides, she is indeed my sister, the daughter of my father, but not the daughter of my mother; and she became my wife. When God caused me to wander from my father's house, I said to her, "This is your kindness which you shall show to me. Everywhere that we go, say of me, 'He is my brother.'"

HEALING RELATIONSHIPS THROUGH FORGIVENESS

Abimelech took sheep and cattle, male servants and female servants, and gave them to Abraham, and restored Sarah, his wife, to him. Abimelech said, "Behold, my land is before you. Dwell where it pleases you." To Sarah he said," Behold, I have given your brother a thousand pieces of silver. Behold, it is for you a covering of the eyes to all...with you. In front of all you are vindicated."

Abraham prayed to God. God healed Abimelech, and his wife, and his female servants, and they bore children. For Yahweh had closed up tight all the wombs of the house of Abimelech, because of Sarah, Abraham's wife."

Another example is found in the life of Jeremiah. When the Chaldeans were about to defeat Judah, King Zedekiah asked the prophet to inquire of the Lord and find out if the nation would be defeated. Some of his princes thought the prophet was a Chaldean sympathizer, and so they arrested him and imprisoned him. When the king called for Jeremiah, he asked the king what he had done wrong which deserved imprisonment. Jeremiah 37:18 describes the incident in these words, "Moreover Jeremiah said to king Zedekiah, 'Wherein have I sinned against you, or against your servants, or against this people, that you have put me in prison?'" The prophet attempts to ascertain exactly what he had done to this king. Notice again, Jeremiah calls it "sinning against" him, his servants, or people. Neither of these men needed to ask for forgiveness because they had done nothing wrong. Yet, both examples describe this concept of "sinning against" someone.

This companion concept of "asking for forgiveness" once someone is sinned against is also found in Scripture. After Pharaoh had refused to listen to Moses and let God's people go, the land was overtaken by swarms of locusts. Pharaoh responded immediately by repenting of his rash actions. In Exodus 10:16-17, Moses described it in these words, "Then

Pharaoh called for Moses and Aaron in haste, and he said, 'I have sinned against Yahweh your God, and against you. Now therefore please forgive my sin again, and pray to Yahweh your God, that he may also take away from me this death.'" Here is a clear example of what this "asking for forgiveness" looks like, though it is from such a hard-hearted man. Pharaoh admits his transgression against God first and then Moses.

In 1 Samuel 25, David encounters a foolish man named Nabal who refused to be hospitable toward David and his men while they were on a journey. David had been careful to make sure his men had treated Nabal's men properly and then asked for some provisions for their travels. This was an important cultural practice, since there were very few inns and places to eat on the road. Nabal, though very wealthy, refused to even acknowledge David. This was an offensive act on Nabal's part, and David was extremely offended. He immediately commanded his men to take up their swords to defend their honor.

When Nabal's wife, Abigail, discovered this humiliation of David, she quickly took action to protect her husband. She went out to meet David and took full responsibility for her husband's actions. She pleaded for forgiveness for the both of them. In 1 Samuel 25:23-24, the author describes their encounter, "When Abigail saw David, she hurried and got off of her donkey, and fell before David on her face, and bowed herself to the ground. She fell at his feet, and said, 'On me, my lord, on me be the blame! Please let your servant speak in your ears. Hear the words of your servant.'" Abigail admitted the transgression and displayed her sorrow over the whole incident. Then she provided David with all the rations that they needed for their journey. What gifts! This demonstrated her repentance as she turned in the opposite direction from what had been done. Ultimately, God judged foolish Nabal by taking his life, and this righteous woman became David's wife.

The parables of Jesus were made-up stories of the many common life experiences of the people. Jesus utilized them to teach particular truths about the kingdom of God. We can learn what life was like at the time merely by observing the interactions of the many characters in these parables. In the parable known as "The Parable of the Prodigal Son," we have an example of this principle of "asking for forgiveness" when one transgresses another. After the son had taken his portion of his inheritance and squandered it all, he repents of this sin. He returns to his father to beg him for forgiveness. He explained that he no longer deserved treatment as a son and requested he be hired as a day laborer, so he could pay back all he had wasted.

In Luke 15:21, Jesus described the meeting of the father and son in these words, "He arose, and came to his father. But while he was still far off, his father saw him, and was moved with compassion, and ran, and fell on his neck, and kissed him." The father showed his son great compassion, mercy, and grace. His arms were open to him. Then Jesus speaks of the repentant son's urgent request for his father's full forgiveness, "The son said to him, 'Father, I have sinned against heaven, and in your sight. I am no longer worthy to be called your son.'" This wayward son recognized that he had sinned both against God and against his father. He then asks his father for forgiveness. We are to do the same when we transgress others.

Paul himself alludes to this practice when he rebukes the Corinthians for accusing him of preaching to them in order to ascertain money. It was exactly the opposite. He was so concerned that they might think this that he worked in his tent-making trade and used the funds from other churches to support himself. Then he shared the gospel with them. In 2 Corinthians 12:13, he sarcastically questions, "For what is there in which you were made inferior to the rest of the assemblies, unless it is that I myself was not a burden to you? Forgive me this wrong." He requests them to forgive him for a wrong which he did not do, but they had thought he had done. Though he is using sarcasm to make his point, we have a simple example of this principle of "asking for forgiveness" when someone has been wronged by us.

At times, people are afraid to ask for forgiveness because they might not receive a kind and gracious reaction from the person they transgressed. This does not matter. The reaction he or she has is entirely up to the Lord God. It only matters that we accept the responsibility for the sins we committed. Be forewarned, it may take some time to prepare ourselves fully for the confessing and repenting, and it may take time for the person we have wronged to forgive.

That's fine! This is one of the many reasons the Christian life is called a walk because it involves one step at a time (Galatians 5:16).

Additional Notes: If asked about the Christian life as a walk, here is the Bible reference I cite:

Galatians 5:16
But I say, walk by the Spirit, and you won't fulfill the lust of the flesh.

Why? The sin principle within all believers is strong and influential (Romans 7:14).

Additional Notes: If asked about the sin principle in our bodies, here is the Bible reference I cite:

Romans 7:14
For we know that the law is spiritual, but I am fleshly, sold under sin.

If we are the ones who have wronged someone, our flesh may want to pretend it never happened and move on. It may require some serious time in the word and prayer to ask for forgiveness. If we do engage in this process, we can expect a slow and meticulous decline in every aspect of our relationship. How do people live with others who can never utter these important and necessary words, "I am sorry?" The other will feel that they are always taking the blame which will wear them out.

An Ancient Portrait

This process is so aptly demonstrated in the life of Joseph. His brothers were reluctant to ask for forgiveness when they sinned against Joseph. This story is found in Genesis 37-50. Joseph was hated by his brothers because he was the favored son and had two disturbing dreams. These dreams indicated that his brothers would bow down, honor, and serve him one day. As a result, they sold him into slavery and Joseph was then purchased by Potiphar, the captain of Pharaoh's bodyguard.

Additional Notes: While in Potiphar's household, God continually blessed Joseph, and he was given authority over Potiphar's whole household. Yet, his master's wife desired to lie with him. So, she propositioned him over and over again, but he always refused. Then one day, she finally had enough of his refusals and grabbed his garment. When he fled, she accused him of attempting to rape her. Without investigation, his master threw him into prison. Joseph remained there for two years. While incarcerated, he met a cupbearer and a baker who had been imprisoned by the Pharaoh.

They both had dreams and Joseph interpreted them successfully. The cupbearer's dream foretold his restoration to Pharaoh's court. The baker's dream was more ominous. He would be put to death. Joseph asked the cupbearer to please remember him when he was eventually reinstated. Once this man was returned to Pharaoh's court, the Pharaoh himself had two powerful and disturbing dreams. None of his officials could interpret them. Suddenly, the cupbearer remembered the man who accurately interpreted his dream and the dream of the baker. Pharaoh immediately summoned Joseph.

After being accused of rape and being thrown in prison, Joseph interpreted the dreams of two Egyptians. One was restored to Pharaoh's court and informed him of Joseph's gift when the emperor wanted two dreams interpreted. The Pharaoh explained the dreams to Joseph and begged him for the interpretations from his God. This favored son of Jacob predicted that there would be seven years of plenty and seven years of famine in the land. He recommended that Pharaoh assign someone to gather grain into storehouses during the time of plenty and then distribute it during the time of famine. Pharaoh took his advice and appointed him over the entire kingdom at the age of thirty.

Several years later, his father Jacob began to experience the famine back in the land of Canaan. Jacob sent his sons to Pharaoh's court to buy grain. All went except Benjamin who was Joseph's blood brother. When his brothers arrived to purchase grain from Joseph, they did not recognize him. Yet, Joseph realized that he was in the presence of his brothers. He had to excuse himself to weep in private. Though Moses does not explain the tears, they appeared to be tears of joy. Though they had sold him into slavery, Joseph knew God's higher purpose for allowing it to happen. He had already forgiven his brothers for what they had done; even though, they had not asked for forgiveness. Isn't this what God does continually in our lives, since the entire debt of our sins were nailed to the cross (Colossians 2:14)?

Additional Notes: If asked about the debt that has been forgiven, here is the Bible reference I cite:

Colossians 2:14
Wiping out the handwriting in ordinances which was against us; and he has taken it out of the way, nailing it to the cross.

Through a series of schemes, Joseph forced his brothers to bring Benjamin and eventually their father Jacob to Egypt. Finally, Joseph revealed himself.

Additional Notes: In Genesis 45:5, Moses records what happened in these words, "Now don't be grieved, nor angry with yourselves, that you sold me here, for God sent me before you to preserve life." Notice Joseph mentions both anger and grief. This is what happens when Christians are unwilling to forgive themselves. They either become angry at themselves or grieve over the sin continuously. They will relive the sin over and over in anger or grief. Yet, in Joseph's statement is the secret to dealing with the anger or grief. God is in control and had a plan. Christians are not victims of evil doers, but servants of a real Living God. God is always in control working out His purposes (Ephesians 1:3-14).

Additional Notes: If asked about the sovereignty of God, here is the full Bible reference:

Ephesians 1:3-14
Blessed be the God and Father of our Lord Jesus Christ, who has blessed us with every spiritual blessing in the heavenly places in Christ; even as he chose us in him before the foundation of the world, that we would be holy and without defect before him in love; having predestined us for adoption as children through Jesus Christ to himself, according to the good pleasure of his desire, to

the praise of the glory of his grace, by which he freely gave us favor in the Beloved, in whom we have our redemption through his blood, the forgiveness of our trespasses, according to the riches of his grace, which he made to abound toward us in all wisdom and prudence, making known to us the mystery of his will, according to his good pleasure [what pleases Him] which he purposed in him to an administration of the fullness of the times, to sum up all things in Christ, the things in the heavens, and...on the earth, in him; in whom also we were assigned an inheritance, having been foreordained according to the purpose of him who does all things after the counsel of his will; to the end that we should be to the praise of his glory, we who had before hoped in Christ: in whom you also, having heard the word of the truth, the Good News of your salvation — in whom, having also believed, you were sealed with the promised Holy Spirit, who is a pledge of our inheritance, to the redemption of God's own possession, to the praise of his glory.

After this, Jacob was brought to Egypt. His family was given a choice piece of land, and life in Egypt began. After a long period of time, Jacob eventually died. Now the brothers became fearful because they had not reconciled with Joseph. They had never acknowledged their evil before him, nor had they asked him for forgiveness. In Genesis 50:15, Moses describes it in this way, "When Joseph's brothers saw that their father was dead, they said, 'It may be that Joseph will hate us, and will fully pay us back for all of the evil which we did to him.'" They were scared of Joseph, so they sent a message asking for forgiveness. In verse 16 and the first part of 17, they claim that their father Jacob had wanted them to tell Joseph to forgive them. We do not know whether Jacob had actually said this, but it seems obvious that they were fearful that their brother was going to put them to death.

Then the brothers finally did what they should have done from the beginning - ask for forgiveness. Moses continues,

"'Now please forgive the disobedience of your brothers, and their sin, because they did evil to you. Now, please forgive the disobedience of the servants of the God of your father." Here they bring God into the picture and beg for forgiveness which is what He would want them to do. After this, they both wept in each other's presence, Joseph granted them his forgiveness and explained God's purpose in it all. Joseph had to experience all of this to bring him to a position that he could save the entire nation of Israel who was not yet born but still in his and his brother's loins. He also could save many others on earth who came to buy grain from Egypt. We don't know if Jacob had actually requested Joseph to forgive them or whether they lied to appease Joseph's anger. However, we do know that they did ask for forgiveness and humble themselves in confession, repentance, and sorrow before their brother Joseph.

Sometimes, the confession and repentance of people can be less than perfect but real and genuine. Again, we are all battling the flesh. Notice, they sent a message. There are times we have difficulty asking for forgiveness face to face. This is perfectly fine. A card, a letter, or even a text asking for forgiveness is very appropriate. Remember, much of the New Testament was written as letters. What could be better confirmation of the appropriateness of writing letters than this? Though I would like to give a caution, some people we have wronged may desire a face-to-face reconciliation. This should be granted, if possible.

Additional Notes: His brothers were worried that Joseph would bear a grudge. This can and does happen, if we do not reconcile with someone we have wronged. They will carry a grudge against us which will feel like a dark cloud following us. The relationship becomes awkward and often the person will be avoided. This never works. God's method is always the best: confession and repentance to the person transgressed. Then their brother Joseph gave the divine perspective. God is in control, even when evil is perpetrated against us.

What a great illustration of our principle of asking someone for forgiveness. So, if we have a broken relationship with our spouse, partner, parent, child, friend, neighbor, co-worker, fellow student, or even an acquaintance, then we must go to them, ask for forgiveness, and reconcile. This is God's only process for restoration.

A Modern Anecdote

Sometime ago, a man entered my office in an angry rage. He wanted equal custody of his children, but his ex-wife had moved them to another city. This would not allow them to share custody on a rotating weekly basis. I inquired as to the salvation of both him and his ex-wife. He indicated that they were both saved but not living the Christian life the way they knew God had wanted. They divorced, and both found someone else and just as quickly married. There were four children involved of various ages, and they were having a myriad of problems with them at home and in school. He wanted more access to them so he could be the father they needed, and the ex-wife was angry at him over the marriage and didn't want to give him any more time.

After several sessions, it was obvious to all of us that they had no biblical reason to end the marriage. They realized that they divorced over insignificant issues which had never been resolved. They let these simply built up over time until they claimed they were no longer "in love." This led to all the other problems including the custody issues. Since they were already married to someone else, they could not reconcile the relationship. Yet, they still had a relationship as mother and father. Their children needed a stable environment in both homes. This stability must come by aligning their new lives as close to the Lord's biblical blueprint for the family as possible. I asked each individually if they thought the other ex-spouse was a good parent. Each agreed.

As a result, the first aspect of their lives which must align more fully with the Scriptures was the children's access to both parents. Numerous times in the book of Proverbs and elsewhere, the inspired writers mention the teaching and training of both mother and father (Proverbs 1:8; 4:3; 6:20; 10:1; 15:20; 23:25; 30:17).

Additional Notes: If asked about this teaching, here are the Bible references I cite:

Proverbs 1:8
My son, listen to your father's instruction, and don't forsake your mother's teaching.

Proverbs 4:3
For I was a son to my father, tender and an only child in the sight of my mother.

Proverbs 6:20
My son, keeps your father's commandment, and don't forsake your mother's teaching.

Proverbs 10:1
A wise son makes a glad father; but a foolish son brings grief to his mother.

Proverbs 15:20
A wise son makes a father glad, but a foolish man despises his mother.

AN INSTRUCTOR'S MANUAL

Proverbs 23:25
Let your father and your mother be glad! Let her who bore you rejoice!

Proverbs 30:17
The eye that mocks at his father, and scorns obedience to his mother: the ravens of the valley shall pick it out, the young eagles shall eat it.

So, the custody was legally changed to rotating weeks. Since discipline is the critical issue in the lives of children, they should together establish four or five general rules with similar consequences for both homes. We worked on other parts of this new custody agreement and living plan that would stabilize both environments for these children. Children do not stop being children, when parent's divorce. They must still be trained and disciplined.

The next step in the process would require the greatest power from the Holy Spirit. They must reconcile with each other and the children. This could only be accomplished by each of them asking for forgiveness of the other and then the children. Both of them had sinned in the marriage, both had agreed to the divorce, and both had disrupted the lives of all their children by being unwilling to follow God's biblical blueprint. They must let the children know that the way they are living was not God's blueprint, but through His grace and His mercy He would work in spite of it. This way they would not add this broken model to their own repertoire of the many actions they could take when they had difficulties in their marriages. This healing process would also lessen the children's own wounds from the divorce as they entered their adolescent and adult lives. After asking forgiveness of each other, each parent sat in my office with each individual child. The father went first and then the mother.

It was a beautiful and supernatural experience for all involved. Both parents humbled themselves and asked for forgiveness from each child individually. Each one lovingly responded in their own way, "Yes, Daddy, I forgive you" and "Yes, Mommy, I forgive you." Then each was asked if they had something to confess to the parents concerning the wrong responses they may have made at home or in school in response to their parent's divorce (according to their age and understanding).

Each admitted that they were misbehaving and asked them for forgiveness and made a commitment "to be better." As each one spoke, I was praying and prompting them as necessary. Then we met together with the children and the new stepparents and explained the new stable living plan they would have. The joy on their faces was so rewarding. They looked at both parents and thanked them for trying so hard to make things right again for them. These new families had finally been reconciled through God's forgiveness. It was wonderful to watch God's Holy Spirit bring much joy, peace, and unity to the families. Of course, this was just the beginning of the work that needed to be done.

A Personal Response

Dear Heavenly Father,

While I was learning the biblical principles in this chapter, I recognize that I have not asked (add name) for forgiveness for the transgressions I have committed against (add name). First, I am so sorry for (list transgressions) that I committed against (add name). Please help me have the courage to go to him (her) and ask him for forgiveness. Help me to honor and glorify You in my relationship with (add name) and follow your Word. I pray this in the name of Jesus. Amen.

AN INSTRUCTOR'S MANUAL

Chapter 1

Ask Others Next

We constantly ask God for forgiveness and are forgiven by Him and He desires that we do the same toward others. This pattern of confessing and forgiving is His blueprint.

In the section, "A Typical Scenario," the author describes an encounter with a father who has wrongfully accused his own daughter of denting the car and will not ask her for forgiveness.

What is the scenario about?

A father discovered that he had a dent in his car and blamed his daughter.

What did the conflict concern?

He had blamed and punished his daughter when his neighbor had done it and was unwilling to ask for forgiveness.

What was the relationship between the parties?

They were father and daughter.

Have you had a similar experience?

(Various answers should be shared including yours.)

HEALING RELATIONSHIPS THROUGH FORGIVENESS

In the section, "A Scriptural Principle" the author presents an important biblical principle in the forgiveness process which concerns asking others for forgiveness.

How would you express this principle in your own words?

The first principle is "we must reconcile our relationship with those we have sinned against by asking for forgiveness."

(Various answers should be shared including yours.)

How would you rewrite this principle to make it even more personal to your life (using your name and situation)?

(Various answers should be shared including yours.)

Why do you think this principle might be important in your life right now?

(Various answers should be shared including yours.)

How would you rate yourself on the percentage of times you followed this principle in the past when you did something wrong in a relationship?

(Various answers should be shared including yours.)

Directions: Put a horizontal mark and your name where you see yourself on the percentage line.

0%   25%   50%   75%   100%

In the section, "A Biblical Explanation," the author explains the reasons why we are to ask for forgiveness when we sin against others in a relationship and how to do it.

What is the Lord God's usual pattern of dealing with sin in our relationship with Him?

As Christians, we are constantly confessing, and God is constantly forgiving. It is the same way in our relationships with others. We are to behave in our relationship with others as we do with God: confessing and forgiving.

According to Romans 2:15, what is inside all people which instinctively prompts them to ask others for forgiveness?

In Romans 2, Paul is discussing the conscience, and its place in the judgment of man. He explains that within people is a law God puts within their hearts, and they will be judged according to that law.

When we hurt, or harm a person, we will have a natural desire to ask for forgiveness because it is written on our hearts.

In the incident between Abimelech and Abraham, who was the one who asked for forgiveness and why?

In Genesis 20:9, Moses writes, "Then Abimelech [the king] called Abraham, and said to him, 'What have you done to us? How have I sinned against you, that you have brought on me and on my kingdom a great sin? You have done deeds to me that ought not to be done!'"

Notice, this concept of "sinning against" others was a truth that was natural to all people.

HEALING RELATIONSHIPS THROUGH FORGIVENESS

In incident between Pharaoh and Moses, who was the one who asked for forgiveness and why?

After Pharaoh had refused to listen to Moses and let God's people go, the land was overtaken by swarms of locusts. Pharaoh responded immediately by repenting of his rash actions.

Here is a clear example of what this "asking for forgiveness" looks like, though it is from such a hard-hearted man. Pharaoh admits his transgression against God first and then Moses.

In the incident between Nabal and David, who was the one who asked for forgiveness and why?

When Nabal's wife, Abigail, discovered this humiliation of David, she quickly took action to protect her husband. She went out to meet David and took full responsibility for her husband's actions.

In what ways might these truths impact your relationships?

(Various answers should be shared including yours.)

In the section, "An Ancient Portrait," the author describes the sin of Joseph's brothers against him and the circumstances that led them to ask him for forgiveness.

What was the brothers' sin against Joseph and why did they do it?

Joseph was hated by his brothers because he was the favored son and had two disturbing dreams. These dreams indicated that his brothers would bow down, honor, and serve him one day. As a result, they sold him into slavery and Joseph was then purchased by Potiphar, the captain of Pharaoh's bodyguard.

When Joseph met his brothers many years later, how did he demonstrate that he had already forgiven them?

When his brothers arrived to purchase grain from Joseph, they did not recognize him. Yet, Joseph realized that he was in the presence of his brothers. He had to excuse himself to weep in private.

What happened to make his brothers fearful that Joseph may have not forgiven them and would retaliate?

In Genesis 50:15, Moses describes it in this way, "When Joseph's brothers saw that their father was dead, they said, 'It may be that Joseph will hate us, and will fully pay us back for all of the evil which we did to him.'"

Since the brothers were fearful of facing Joseph directly, how did they ask him for forgiveness?

They were scared of Joseph, so they sent a message asking for forgiveness.

What was Joseph's response to their gesture?

Here they bring God into the picture and beg for forgiveness which is what He would want them to do. After this, they both wept in each other's presence, Joseph granted them his forgiveness and explained the Lord's purpose in it all.

Have you ever been in a situation that was comparable to either Joseph having to forgive a harsh sin or his brothers who needed to ask for forgiveness? How was it different and how was it the same?

(Various answers should be shared including yours.)

AN INSTRUCTOR'S MANUAL

In the section, "A Modern Anecdote," the author explains how two parents impulsively divorced and discovered that they had to ask for forgiveness from their children.

According to Proverbs, what was the initial step the parents had to take to resolve their divorce issues?

As a result, the first aspect of their lives which must align more fully with the Scriptures was the children's access to both parents. Numerous times in the book of Proverbs and elsewhere, the inspired writers mention the teaching and training of both mother and father (Proverbs 1:8; 4:3; 6:20; 10:1; 15:20; 23:25; 30:17). So, the custody was legally changed to rotating weeks.

Why was it so important for each spouse to ask the other for forgiveness?

They must reconcile with each other and the children. This could only be accomplished by each of them asking for forgiveness of the other and then the children. Both of them had sinned in the marriage, both had agreed to the divorce, and both had disrupted the lives of all their children by being unwilling to follow God's biblical blueprint.

Why was it important for the parents ask their children for forgiveness?

They must let the children know that the way they are living was not God's blueprint, but through His grace and His mercy He would work in spite of it.

How would the asking of forgiveness by the parents affect their children's future?

This way they would not add this broken model to their own repertoire of the many actions they could take when they had difficulties in their marriages. This healing process would also lessen the children's own wounds from the divorce as they entered their adolescent and adult lives.

After the parents asked the children for forgiveness what did the children have to do and why?

Each admitted that they were misbehaving and asked them for forgiveness and made a commitment "to be better." As each one spoke, I was praying and prompting them as necessary.

Based on the truths learned in this chapter, what would you have done differently if you were one of the parents or one of the children?

(Various answers should be shared including yours.)

AN INSTRUCTOR'S MANUAL

In the section, "A Personal Response," the author provides a model you may use for prayer if you find it necessary after discovering the truths in this chapter.

Are you presently in a relationship where you have sinned against another and have not asked God for forgiveness? If not, is there one from the past that still needs this prayer to be prayed?

(Various answers should be shared including yours.)

Based on the truths you have just learned, what will you continue doing in your current relationships and what will you do differently?

(Various answers should be shared including yours.)

What additional thoughts would you like to share with the others?

(Various answers should be shared including yours.)

Instructor's Notes

Chapter 2

Humbly Make Restitution

Once we have asked others for forgiveness, we should consider another important step which is to make restitution if necessary. Though it is quite intuitive, often it is neglected. Why? We think this step is a part of forgiveness, rather than repentance. We suppose that we should make restitution to somehow influence or persuade them to forgive us. We also expect others to make restitution to us before we will truly forgive them. Yet, the Scriptures teach that we should simply forgive. Nothing is added to that anywhere in the Bible. So, restitution is really a way of demonstrating true repentance and may also be a part of our consequences.

A Typical Scenario

Have you ever had or heard a conversation with someone that went something like this? You or they are mopping the floor and commenting to someone, "This is difficult. I never realized how hard housework can be. Yesterday was a house cleaning day for my wife (husband) and me. To be honest, I really did not want to clean up. So, I got up late and took a really long time getting ready, but that didn't work. When she (he) told me to come and help, we got into an argument. It wasn't long before the conviction of the Holy Spirit came."

"First, I went to God and asked for His forgiveness; then I went to my wife (husband) and humbly asked for her (his) forgiveness, but I couldn't stop there. I felt so sorry, I had to make restitution. So, I am doing yesterday's housework, and then I realized how poorly I had behaved. So, I decided that

I would add some extra cleaning to what she (he) wanted me to do, so I am adding two additional things."

A Scriptural Principle

Now we come to the second principle. It is "we should demonstrate repentance by making restitution." The concept of restitution involves primarily doing something we should have done, or maybe replacing something we took or broke, perhaps retracting something we should not have said, or redoing something we should not have done in the first place. Restitution is not penance to make-up for any of our transgressions, so someone we wronged will forgive us. God does not require this from us because that it is considered "works." As a result, forgiveness is based on His grace, not any works. We should forgive someone who transgresses us based on God's grace. Then, someone we transgress forgives us based also on God's grace. This is God's way.

A Biblical Explanation

Restitution is not a part of the forgiveness process of the person wronged but a part of the repentance process of the person who did the wrong. It is to demonstrate repentance to the wronged party and ourselves. This process may also be a part of the consequences of our wrongdoing and will definitely aid in the repair of a broken relationship. For us to forgive or be forgiven, it is not biblically required. Christians are to forgive whether restitution comes or not. When we are sorry for what we did, it is natural to want to fix the wrong.

In the Old Testament, as the people of Israel journeyed through the wilderness, the Lord was preparing them to be a nation devoted to Him and to His will. He set certain laws that He wanted Israel to follow as His nation and people. These laws were either moral, legal, ceremonial, or even a combination of two or all three. The Lord also determined that different misdeeds, both intentional and unintentional, would have different consequences which depended on the specific actions. Most of these misdeeds involved making restitution to the one transgressed. This was to be done as a manner of life, whether a judgment (legal actions) was given or not (personal actions). In either case, since God was also transgressed a sacrifice had to be made to the priest.

In Leviticus 6:4, God declares, "Then it shall be, if he has sinned, and is guilty, he shall restore that which he took by robbery, or the thing which he has gotten by oppression, or the deposit which was committed to him, or the lost thing which he found."

Additional Notes: In the wilderness, Moses was commanded to build the Tent of Meeting or Tabernacle and set up a system of sacrifice for various sins of the people. As the Lord explained what sacrifices should be given for which sins, He reiterates in summary form the various laws He had given to Moses when he delivered to him the Ten Commandments. At this time, the Lord reiterated his laws, explained what sacrifice should be made, and described the restitution that should be made to those who were wronged. This is the second time the laws were given.

The Lord begins with a list of wrongdoing that needs to be recompensed. The most important issue is that it actually occurred. Since these are national laws, then the person needs to be found guilty. If it is a personal act, then the person must admit he did it. This is the confession step we have discussed. Then the Lord lists robbery which is stealing something that one does not own. He mentions extortion which is forcing someone to give you something that he owns. The third is keeping a deposit wrongfully which means one made a commitment to do something if another put a deposit down, but he did not do it. He must return the deposit. Another grievance may involve someone borrowing something, losing it, and never replacing it.

In the beginning of verse 5, the Lord continues with the last one, "Or anything about which he has sworn falsely." This is a person who was a false witness, or who lied and committed slander or libel. Then God explains exactly what He desires to be done to make restitution, "He shall restore it even in full, and shall add a fifth part more to it." The person who must make restitution should give the same amount back plus twenty percent more. Then God provides the exact timetable for this to occur, "To him to whom it belongs he shall give it, in the day of his being found guilty." As soon as people are found guilty of the transgression or in a personal case admit it, they should begin the restitution process. This demonstrates repentance, acceptance of the consequences and the desire to restore the relationship.

In Numbers 5:6-7, the Lord God reiterates His commands concerning restitution again.

Additional Notes: During the second year, God established how He wanted the tribes to set themselves up around the Tent of Meeting as they traveled through the wilderness toward the Promised Land. On this occasion, the Lord delivered His laws through Moses with the promises that would follow as a reminder to His people. This was the third time that the laws were given.

Here God summarizes this important truth. In verse 6, God commands, "Speak to the children of Israel: 'When a man or woman commits any sin that men commit, so as to trespass against Yahweh, and that soul is guilty." God speaks of any transgression that involves another person in anyway which is also a transgression against God. Then He explains what they are to do. In verse seven, God explains, "Then he shall confess his sin which he has done, and he shall make restitution for his guilt in full, and add to it the fifth part of it, and give it to him in respect of whom he has been guilty." God's people were to give back what they took or lost, tell the truth if they lied, and add a fifth part. They would add twenty percent more, if possible.

Previously, God had indicated other situations that may require more than twenty percent plus the replacement or replacement amount. In Exodus 22:1-14 the restitution can double or quadruple for certain actions.

Additional Notes: After God's people left Egypt and entered the wilderness, the Lord desired to establish how he wanted His people to behave as a nation. This was not only the Ten Commandments, but a long series of detailed laws which Moses was to deliver to the people. This portion of the laws which concerned restitution was given to Moses at this point. I mention it out of chronological sequence due to this important detail not mentioned in the other passages. This was the first time the laws were given.

The point is that the nation of Israel *(God's people)* was bound by restitution. This was their national law *(given by God)* and their everyday practice. Today, numerous governments may require restitution for certain acts. If they do, then we make restitution as we obey the government as servants of God (Romans 13:1-4).

So, the Old Testament not only required restitution in its laws but also provides several examples of this. One is an incident involving Abimelech and Abraham. Though this king did not actually violate Sarah, he did take the wife of a prophet of God into his own household with the intention of doing so. As the king or not, Abimelech had no right to take multiple women into his household for his own pleasure.

Abraham was in such fear of Abimelech's evil and lecherous methods, he lied about his wife. The Lord God punished his household until Abimelech made restitution.

In Genesis 20:14-16, Moses describes it, "Abimelech took sheep and cattle, male servants and female servants, and gave them to Abraham, and restored Sarah, his wife, to him. Abimelech said, 'Behold, my land is before you. Dwell where it pleases you.' To Sarah he said, 'Behold, I have given your brother a thousand pieces of silver. Behold, it is for you a covering of the eyes to all that are with you. In front of all you are vindicated.'" The restitution was to demonstrate his repentance and to show the world that Sarah had never been violated by Him. It was also consequences from God that he would have to accept. Then Abraham prayed for Abimelech and God once again opened the wombs of his wife and his female servants.

Another illustration of this restitution is found in another story from the Bible. This was the spurning of David by Nabal when he would not provide the hospitality that the culture at the time demanded of him. When Abigail asked for forgiveness, she provided restitution. In 1 Samuel 25:27, the author records, "Now this present which your servant has brought to my lord, let it be given to the young men who follow my lord." We discover from 1 Samuel 25:18 what this "present" was, "Then Abigail hurried and took two hundred loaves of bread, two bottles of wine, five sheep ready dressed, five seahs of parched grain, one hundred clusters of raisins, and two hundred cakes of figs, and laid them on donkeys." This restitution would have more than provided for all their needs. Also, this restitution built a relationship between Abigail and David that would later blossom into a marriage when she became a widow at God's hand. In 1 Samuel 25:32-33, David responded with this blessing, "David said to Abigail, 'Blessed is Yahweh, the God of Israel, who sent you today to meet me!'" He gives tribute to the Lord God then to Abigail. He adds, "Blessed is your discretion, and blessed are you, who have kept me today from blood guiltiness, and from avenging myself with my own hand."

When God's people were released from captivity, they returned to the land under the leadership of Nehemiah. Sometime later, Nehemiah discovered that the Jewish people left behind were charging huge amounts of interest (called usury) to loan people money to eat and supply some basic needs. As a result, they even took some of their own people as slaves who could not pay them back. Nehemiah was livid and called the people together and rebuked them strongly. As they repented, they then made restitution. In Nehemiah 5:10-13, the author communicates, "'I likewise, my brothers and my servants, lend them money and grain. Please let us stop this usury."

First, Nehemiah rebukes them. Then he cries out, "Please restore to them, even today, their fields, their vineyards, their olive groves, and their houses, also the hundredth part of the money, and of the grain, the new wine, and the oil, that you are charging them." After he entreats them to make restitution, they responded, "Then they said, 'We will restore them, and will require nothing of them; so, will we do, even as you say.'"

To make sure this occurred, he demanded an oath, "Then I called the priests, and took an oath of them, that they would do according to this promise. Also, I shook out my lap, and said, 'So may God shake out every man from his house, and from his labor, that doesn't perform this promise; even thus be he shaken out and emptied.'" With this oath, Nehemiah proclaimed a curse, and the people answered, "All the assembly said, 'Amen,' and praised Yahweh. The people did according to this promise." After their repentance for the usury, Nehemiah required them to make restitution in full by returning everything they had taken. The account doesn't mention whether he required an additional amount or not.

When we come to the New Testament, Rome ruled over the Jewish nation. The Jews were allowed to enforce certain of their laws, and the Romans the more serious ones. Both Jewish law and Roman law had elements of restitution. For Jews, it was still a powerful cultural mandate and expected. There is no specific command by Jesus or the other inspired writers to make restitution in every instance. Yet, it certainly appears to be a practice in normal Jewish life. The story of the two debtors in Matthew 18:23-35, both offered to make restitution for their debts, though neither was able to.

Many are familiar with the story of the repentance of the prodigal son. After this son had consumed his portion of the inheritance, even before his father had died, he experienced great remorse. He then decided that he would return to his loving father and beg for forgiveness. As he did this, he asked his father for a job as a day laborer. Why? He desired to pay back all he had taken. He wanted to make restitution for the squandered money. Jesus describes the son's desire to make this restitution in Luke 15:19. He says, "I am no more worthy to be called your son. Make me as one of your hired servants." Yet, the prodigal son was not required to make any restitution because the father did not desire it. This was a picture of God, the Father, who does not require restitution from us, since Christ paid for the debt of our sins on the cross. Next, Jesus accepted it from Zacchaeus as a sign of his repentance. He did not hinder his restitution attempt.

Additional Notes: The making of restitution is an important part of the repentance process. Those who are transgressed must forgive either way. They do not wait for this action to occur first.

An Ancient Portrait

The classic biblical example of making restitution is the tax-collector Zacchaeus when he meets Jesus, repents, and receives the Lord. The story of Zacchaeus is found in Luke 19:1-10. Jesus Christ entered the town of Jericho on His way to Jerusalem for the yearly Passover with a large crowd. This important city was on the main route to Jerusalem, and all the pilgrims would be traveling through this town also. The citizens of Jericho would have heard that Jesus had raised Lazarus from the dead and would have come out to see Him. The town would have been teeming with people.

Additional Notes: The city of Jericho was the first city conquered when Joshua and the Israelites entered the Promised Land. It was a city that was enclosed by walls wide enough and strong enough to allow dwellings inside it. Rahab lived in one of these dwellings and helped the Israelite spies escape from the king of the city. As a result of her faith in the true God, she and her family were saved from destruction (Joshua 2:1-21). The city is mentioned again as having been rebuilt by Hiel the Bethelite (1 Kings 16:34). Years later, Herod the Great had fortified it and built a number of new palaces and it grew in influence. It was here the announcement of this king's death occurred. Soon after the town was burnt and plundered. By the time of Jesus Christ, Archelaus had rebuilt it and planted palm trees; thus it was known as the "city of palms." It was here that Jesus restored sight to Blind Bartimaeus and his fellow beggar (Matthew 20:30; Mark 10:46; Luke 18:35).

Amid this crowd, a rich and powerful tax collector named Zacchaeus entered the scene. It was the law that once these officials charged the people what Rome had designated, they could then charge any fee they desired. As a result, these men gouged the people and became rich. If they did not pay, the tax collectors would try and intimidate them into paying through threats or physical force. He was one of the "chief" tax collectors, so he also received a percentage of the amount of taxes collected by every tax collector under him. This made him even richer. These people were hated by the Jews. Why? They extorted the Jewish people and worked for the Romans. The Hebrews called them "sinners." This was the lowest class of people in their country. They were unclean, defiled, and outcasts. These evil ones were to be completely avoided and not allowed to enter the home of any Jew or the synagogue. Zacchaeus was a member of this group. He had heard that the Lord Jesus was in town and wanted to see Him. Why? We can discern this from what happened.

This hated man was honestly seeking true salvation as the Holy Spirit was working powerfully in his heart. The Spirit was convicting Him of His sin and leading Him to the Jesus, the Savior. He had one "big" problem. He was small, a little man vying for a place to see in a large crowd. So, Zacchaeus decided to run ahead of Jesus and find himself a place to see this extraordinary man. He climbed up into a sycamore or perhaps a mulberry tree because these had short trunks and long branches which made them easy to climb. When the Messiah came to the place where Zacchaeus was located, something remarkable happened.

The Lord stopped, looked him straight in the eyes, and called him by his name. Jesus knew Zacchaeus, who he was and all that he had done. He said, "Come down, I will stay with you today." Jesus decided to lodge with him overnight. This tax collector hurried down and received the Lord Jesus joyfully into his home. Zacchaeus stood before Jesus and repented saying, "Behold, Lord, half of my goods I will give to the poor." The Lord Christ's recognition of Zacchaeus was miraculous and obviously the final action that convinced this searching but scorned man that Jesus was the Christ. It obviously led to his act of repentance. In his repentance, we see a very dramatic reaction to receiving Christ as Savior and Lord. Zacchaeus first declares he will give half of his money away. Why? Money had been his idol. Now, Jesus was His Lord, and he wouldn't serve money any longer.

Then Zacchaeus committed himself to making restitution. This tax collector had essentially stolen and cheated so many people out of so much money that he declared, "If I have wrongfully exacted anything of anyone, I restore four times as much." He saw the awfulness of his greed which had led him to oppress many innocent people and absolutely had to compensate them even more than required. The Lord saw this dramatic response and declared, "Today, salvation has come to this house." This was a true son of Abraham in the Spirit now not one of the flesh alone. The Lord Jesus doesn't correct Zacchaeus regarding the restitution but affirms it as a demonstration of his strong repentance. Does not restitution make sense in not only displaying one's true repentance but also in rebuilding the broken relationship?

In every way, it is a typical occurrence in our lives. If we break someone's stuff, we have it fixed. If we eat someone's pie by mistake, then we replace it. The conscience demands a proper demonstration of repentance through restitution, and this humble action should aid in the crucial process of restoring relationships. It is not commanded in the New Testament, but it was definitely an Old Testament law and pattern. Also, it makes good sense. Sometimes, it is hard to take the many necessary steps to make restitution, but we will never be disappointed by its supernatural effects. More importantly, it always demonstrates repentance and honors our glorious Lord.

Additional Notes: Though this is an argument of silence rather than a direct command, it has validity given the other evidence.

A Modern Anecdote

We live in a world of credit cards and personal loans. If we so desire, we can simply purchase anything by sliding a card into a machine, and it is ours. Unfortunately, the money must be paid back with interest, and this is a source of much conflict between couples in their marriages. One such couple came to my counseling office to speak about this very issue. From the start, the couple had decided that the wife ought to be a "stay at home mom" and handle the actual payment of the bills while her husband worked. The problem started when her only child, a daughter, entered high school. Before that time, mom was quite involved with her school. When the high school years began, her daughter simply did not want her mother around. The wife suddenly had a large amount of time on her hands. To fill the time, she developed a practice of going shopping. At first, she merely window shopped, but it was not very long before she was noticing the many sales she was missing out on.

In fact, she felt like the family was losing money as she perused the sales but did not buy. So, she decided to utilize the family's credit cards to make the purchases that they needed in order to take advantage of the numerous sales and save money. It soon turned into the things she wanted for herself. Within months, their credit cards were maxed out.

Additional Notes: If asked about the Bible's teaching on debt, here are some references:

Romans 13:8
Owe no one anything, except to love one another; for he who loves his neighbor has fulfilled the law.

Psalm 37:21
The wicked borrow, and don't pay back, but the righteous give generously.

Proverbs 3:28
Don't say to your neighbor, "Go, and come again; tomorrow I will give it to you," when you have it by you.

Proverbs 22:7
The rich rule over the poor. The borrower is servant to the lender.

At first, she was panicked. Then an idea came to her. She would borrow money from the college savings account earmarked for their daughter and then quickly and quietly pay it back. At first, it started with small withdrawals. Then, she did not have enough to pay for all the minimum credit card payments, and so the wife had to leave the deficit in the savings.

This happened more often than she had anticipated. Over a matter of time, the savings account was depleted, and her daughter's future at college was in jeopardy. It finally came to a head when the daughter asked her father if she could use her college money to hire a tutor to help her prepare for her college entrance exams. Since she would be taking these exams in another year, she wanted to be ready. When her father went to the bank to make the appropriate withdrawal, the teller explained to him that he had insufficient funds.

He could not believe what he had just heard. This was impossible, so he demanded to see the bank manager. As she showed him the many withdrawals his wife had made over the past months, the husband squirmed in his seat. After humbly apologizing, the husband drove home furious with his "out of control" wife. He stomped in the house, shouted a series of unflattering and unholy words at her, and then he demanded an explanation.

A huge argument ensued. When their teenage daughter found out what her mother had done, she ran into her room and cried about her now grim future. Finally, the wife and mother confessed all that she had done. The hard part was over, she regretted her actions and desired reconciliation as did her husband and daughter.

Additional Notes: If asked about the teaching of the Scriptures on contentment, here are some references:

Romans 13:8
Owe no one anything, except to love one another; for he who loves his neighbor has fulfilled the law.

Psalm 37:21
The wicked borrow, and don't pay back, but the righteous give generously.

Proverbs 3:28
Don't say to your neighbor, "Go, and come again; tomorrow I will give it to you," when you have it by you.

Proverbs 22:7
The rich rule over the poor. The borrower is servant to the lender.

As we finished up the wife suddenly said, "I want to get a job and pay the entire college fund back before my daughter needs the money. I want to make restitution for what I have done!" The husband and daughter responded with their own desire to help by taking on extra hours and paying off the credit card debt. After some time, everything was restored. Then, I encouraged the mother to take her extra time and use her spiritual gifts to minster to the saints and share the gospel. She now happily works at her church with young mothers (Titus 2:3-4).

A Personal Response

Dear Heavenly Father,

Your Holy Spirit has shown me that I have not fully made restitution for the transgressions I have committed toward (add name). I am truly sorry. Please give me the wisdom to discern what restitution would be appropriate and provide the commitment and courage to do it. I do desire to reconcile my relationship with (add name) for your honor and glory. I pray this in the name of Jesus. Amen.

Chapter 2

Humbly Make Restitution

There may be times when we should make restitution to those we have wronged. This is not a part of forgiveness on their part, but a part of repentance on ours.

In the section, "A Typical Scenario," the author describes an incident where a husband and wife disagree and may need to reconcile.

What is the scenario about?

A Christian husband tried to avoid helping his wife with the housework and they got into an argument.

What did the conflict concern?

To avoid the housework, the husband slept in late and then took a long time getting ready which led to a confrontation.

What was the relationship between the parties?

They were spouses.

Have you had a similar experience?

(Various answers should be shared including yours.)

HEALING RELATIONSHIPS THROUGH FORGIVENESS

In the section, "A Scriptural Principle" the author presents an important biblical principle in the forgiveness process which concerns making restitution toward those we have wronged.

How would you express this principle in your own words?

The second principle is "we should demonstrate repentance by making restitution."

(Various answers should be shared including yours.)

How would you rewrite this principle to make it even more personal to your life (using your name and situation)?

(Various answers should be shared including yours.)

Why do you think this principle might be important in your life right now?

(Various answers should be shared including yours.)

How would you rate yourself on the percentage of times you followed this principle in the past when you did something wrong in a relationship?

(Various answers should be shared including yours.)

Directions: Put a horizontal mark and your name where you see yourself on the percentage line.

0%   25%   50%   75%   100%

In the section, "A Biblical Explanation," the author explains the reasons why we should demonstrate repentance through restitution when we sin against others and how to do it.

What is the relationship of restitution to our repentance and forgiveness?

Restitution is not a part of the forgiveness process of the person wronged but a part of the repentance process of the person who did the wrong. It is to demonstrate repentance to the wronged party and ourselves.

According to Leviticus 6:5, how much restitution should be made and when?

The person who must make restitution should give the same amount back plus twenty percent more. Then God provides the exact timetable for this to occur, "To him to whom it belongs he shall give it, in the day of his being found guilty." As soon as people are found guilty of the transgression or in a personal case admit it. At this point, they should begin the restitution process. This demonstrates repentance, acceptance of the consequences and the desire to restore the relationship.

According to 1 Samuel 25, how did Abigail make restitution to David for the foolishness of her husband Nabal?

When Abigail asked for forgiveness, she provided restitution.

What was David's response to her actions?

In 1 Samuel 25:32-33, David responded with this blessing, "David said to Abigail, 'Blessed is Yahweh, the God of Israel, who sent you today to meet me!'" He gives tribute to the Lord God then to Abigail. He adds, "Blessed is your discretion, and blessed are you,

who have kept me today from blood guiltiness, and from avenging myself with my own hand."

In what two parables is restitution presented by Jesus?

The story of the two debtors in Matthew 18:23-35, both offered to make restitution for their debts, though neither was able to.

In Luke 15:19. He says, "I am no more worthy to be called your son. Make me as one of your hired servants." Yet, the prodigal son was not required to make any restitution because the father did not desire it.

In what ways might these truths impact your relationships?

(Various answers should be shared including yours.)

In the section, "An Ancient Portrait," the author shares the story of the salvation of Zacchaeus and his great desire to make restitution to those he had cheated.

How did tax-collectors get paid?

Amid this crowd, a rich and powerful tax collector named Zacchaeus entered the scene. It was the law that once these officials charged the people what Rome had designated, they could then charge any fee they desired.

How did tax-collectors usually mistreat people?

As a result, these men gouged the people and became rich. If they did not pay, the tax collectors would try and intimidate them into paying through threats or physical force.

What were the reactions of the people who were cheated?

These people were hated by the Jews. Why? They extorted the Jewish people and worked for the Romans. The Hebrews called them "sinners." This was the lowest class of people in their country. They were unclean, defiled, and outcasts.

When Zacchaeus believed in the Lord Jesus, what restitution did he desire to make?

In his repentance, we see a very dramatic reaction to receiving Christ as Savior and Lord. Zacchaeus first declares he will give half of his money away. Why? Money had been his idol. Now, Jesus was His Lord, and he wouldn't serve money any longer.

Then Zacchaeus committed himself to making restitution. This tax collector had essentially stolen and cheated so many people out of so much money that he declared, "If I have wrongfully exacted anything of anyone, I restore four times as much."

How might restitution affect our relationship with those we have wronged?

The Lord Jesus doesn't correct Zacchaeus regarding the restitution but affirms it as a demonstration of his strong repentance.

Does not restitution make sense in not only displaying one's true repentance but also in rebuilding the broken relationship?

In every way, it is a typical occurrence in our lives. If we break someone's stuff, we have it fixed. If we eat someone's pie by mistake, then we replace it.

Have you ever been in a situation comparable to Zacchaeus or those he wronged? How was it different and how was it the same?

(Various answers should be shared including yours.)

AN INSTRUCTOR'S MANUAL

In the section, "A Modern Anecdote," the author describes how a mother wronged her daughter and wanted to make restitution.

What was the mother's problem and how did she get herself into it?

The problem started when her only child, a daughter, entered high school. Before that time, mom was quite involved with her school. When the high school years began, her daughter simply did not want her mother around.

What were the consequences of the mother's wrongdoing?

He stomped in the house, shouted a series of unflattering and unholy words at her, and then he demanded an explanation.

A huge argument ensued. When their teenage daughter found out what her mother had done, she ran into her room and cried about her now grim future.

After her repentance, how did the mother want to make the necessary restitution?

After each had asked the Lord for forgiveness, they turned toward each other and requested forgiveness. As we finished up, the wife suddenly said, "I want to get a job and pay the entire college fund back before my daughter needs the money. I want to make restitution for what I have done!"

Why did the husband want to make restitution to his wife and how was he going to do it?

I gently confronted her husband for not watching over her as Christ does His church. He was too preoccupied with his work schedule to notice even what she had purchased.

The husband responded with their own desire to help by taking on extra hours and paying off the credit card debt. After some time, everything was restored.

Why did the daughter want to make restitution to her mom and how was she going to do it?

Her daughter also felt badly because she wouldn't let her mom around the school when that was such an important part of her mom's life.

The daughter responded with their own desire to help by taking on extra hours and paying off the credit card debt. After some time, everything was restored.

Based on the truths learned in this chapter, what would you have done differently if you were the husband, mother, or daughter?

(*Various answers should be shared including yours.*)

In the section, "A Personal Response," the author provides a model you may use for prayer if you find it necessary after discovering the truths in this chapter.

Are you presently in a relationship where you have sinned against another and have not asked God for forgiveness? If not, is there one from the past that still needs this prayer to be prayed?

(Various answers should be shared including yours.)

Based on the truths you have just learned, what will you continue doing in your current relationships and what will you do differently?

(Various answers should be shared including yours.)

What additional thoughts would you like to share with the others?

(Various answers should be shared including yours.)

Instructor's Notes

Chapter 3

Accept the Consequences

Another step involves the willingness to accept all the consequences for what we have done. This truth can be seen in various relationships we have. Children living at home will have consequences for violating their parent's rules. At times, our spouses may desire to set up boundaries for some habitual sinful behavior we may have developed during the marriage (drunkenness, drug use, gambling, etc.). They may require us to seek help or take the risk of a break-up of the marriage. These are consequences of our sins.

The church is required to discipline its many members for unrepentant sins against the brethren (Matthew 18:17). We always find that our employers have rules and consequences for breaking them. Every society has a government which creates its laws and punishes its citizens for violating them. Even our friends may have to help us get back in line with them by providing consequences for our behavior towards them. In fact, every healthy relationship has boundaries and rules set up formally or informally with consequences for ones who refuse to respect the other member or members. God may intervene and have consequences of His own since we have also violated His laws. This chapter involves the discussion of these consequences and their importance.

A Typical Scenario

Imagine yourself involved in an intense time-consuming activity. You suddenly look at your clock, gasp, and scream, "Oh no, I forgot to pick up (insert name) at their activity. He (she) is going to be so angry at me. I came into the family room to retrieve my keys and had just a few extra minutes. Then I got started, and those minutes turned into an hour. I totally forgot to pick (insert name) up!" Suddenly, your flesh begins to flare up, and you think, "I'm in trouble, but I don't care. That is not my problem! Everybody makes mistakes. If I get the silent treatment or yelled at, then I will give it back to him (her)" Has this ever happened to you? It has to me. Sometimes, we do something wrong, but we refuse to accept the consequences. This is not what God desires.

A Scriptural Principle

We now come to principle number three. This principle is "we should accept whatever consequences that may result from our sin against God and others." Sin leads to a variety of consequences. When we travel back to the garden, God told Adam that if he disobeyed Him and ate of a particular tree, he would die. That is a consequence of sin. When Adam ate of the fruit, he died, not physically but spiritually and set in motion a myriad of consequences for that one act.

A Biblical Explanation

Why must there be consequences to almost everything we do? Scientists describe it as a simple case of cause and effect. To every action there is some kind of reaction or effect. The Bible describes it as a law of God set forth in His universe. In Galatians 5, Paul had just contrasted the fruits of the Spirit with the deeds of the flesh. In Galatians 6, to encourage the saints at Galatia to remain diligent in producing these fruits (doing good), he explains that the spiritual realm functions according to this cause-and-effect relationship. In verses 7-8, he utilizes a farming analogy to explain it. He writes, "Don't be deceived. God is not mocked, for whatever a man sows, that he will also reap. For he who sows to his own flesh will from the flesh reap corruption. But he who sows to the Spirit will from the Spirit reap eternal life."

Here the apostle describes a general principle of farming. If a farmer sows with good seeds, he will reap good crops; if he sows using bad seeds, he will reap bad crops. Whatever he sows, he will reap. Then Paul explains how this physical analogy applies to supernatural things. When Christians sin by sowing to the flesh, they reap corruption. When believers live righteously and sow to the Spirit, they reap eternal life. When we follow our lusts, they lead us to corrupt activities, not activities of eternal life. When we follow the Spirit, He leads us to activities having to do with eternal life.

The general principle is the same spiritually or physically: whatever we sow, we reap. Then he issues a strong entreaty in verse nine. He asserts, "Let us not be weary in doing good, for we will reap in due season, if we don't give up." True Christians can never give up in their striving for good. The reaping of blessings will come at the right time not only in this life but more importantly in the life to come. After Paul exhorted the Thessalonians to work hard as he did and not to depend on others for their livelihood, Paul entreats them with the same principle. In 2 Thessalonians 3:13, the apostle proclaims, "But you, brothers, don't be weary in doing well." This includes all relationships. Why? When we grow weary, the flesh becomes active and corrupt activities occur in our relationships.

How does this principle of sowing and reaping actually work in relationships? First, if we sow good seeds in our relationships, it will reap blessings. If we sow bad seeds in our relationships, it will reap corruption. Sowing the fruits of the Spirit (love, joy, peace, patience, kindness, goodness, faith, gentleness, and self-control), will produce a thriving relationship. Sowing the deeds of the flesh (hatred, strife, immorality, jealousy, anger), will produce a deteriorating relationship. In our seeking forgiveness context, we have sown bad seeds into our relationships with people, and now we must reconcile with them. Since we sowed bad seed into the relationship, there will come some bad consequences. When we repent of the sin, we should still expect some of those consequences. This is often in the form of restitution. We may have to retract something we should not have said, do something we did not do, undo something we did, fix what we broke or even replace what we lost. Accepting these consequences demonstrates our repentance also. So, restitution could be one of the many ways we accept the consequences for our sins against others.

Another way we might have to accept the consequences for our sin is to allow the people transgressed to deal with our sin in the manner and time frame they may require, not the manner and time frame we may require. For example, if we make our spouses, parents, friends, neighbors, children, fellow students, or co-workers angry and they ignore us for a few days, we must accept this consequence for our action. They could need time to work out their responses to our sinful actions. If we violate a trust of our parents or spouses, we may have to check in with them more often. Perhaps, they will want everything we say to be verified for a while. These consequences ought to be accepted. It might not be something we would need to rebuild the trust, but they do. It is critical that they receive this assurance.

If we promised to do something that is important to a friend and we fail to do it, he or she may not rely on us for a while. They might even need for us to demonstrate we are reliable by proceeding through a series of steps so they may finally trust us again. It may differ completely from how we would handle the same issue, but it is part of accepting every one of the consequences. Often times, once believers have repented, they think no consequences are really necessary. A spouse will say to the other, "I told you I was sorry. You have to forgive me and drop it!" We will not allow people to be human and to experience all the feelings humans may feel when something evil is done against them. People need time to deal with the issue in a spiritual way themselves. They may react sinfully and need to deal with the Lord. If our sinful actions set into motion a wide range of sinful and non-sinful reactions to them from those we have transgressed, the consequences may be to allow them time to process all of it. This is the second reason that this acceptance is important.

The third reason accepting consequences is so critical to a relationship is that this is God's basic strategy to train us. If we refuse to accept the consequences for our sins, we are circumventing our learning process. Because God is a loving Father, He trains and disciplines us to act like Him and live in a holy way. This is called "sanctification." Accepting the many consequences for our actions will assist in the training process. In Hebrews 12:7, speaking of the numerous trials in the life of believers, the author declares, "It is for discipline that you endure. God deals with you as with children, for what son is there whom his father doesn't discipline?"

God brings trials into the lives of His children (some self-imposed) to train them. This is what a loving father will do. The Greek word translated "discipline" means "instruction, learning, teaching, or training." In Ephesians 6:4, it is used to speak of the training of a child for godly living. In Titus 2:12, the verb form was used to speak of instruction for denying ungodliness and worldly lusts in our Christian lives. In 1 Corinthians 11:32, Paul uses the word to refer to the Lord's discipline of the Christians who were receiving communion improperly. As a result, some had become sick or even died.

The word refers to God's process of training to make us holy (wholly different from the world).

Additional Notes: Here are the Bible references I cite:

Ephesians 6:4
You fathers, don't provoke your children to wrath, but nurture them in the discipline and instruction of the Lord.

Titus 2:12
Instructing us to the intent that, denying ungodliness and worldly lusts, we would live soberly, righteously, and godly in this present world.

1 Corinthians 11:32
But when we are judged, we are punished by the Lord, that we may not be condemned with the world.

In verse 8, the author continues, "But if you are without discipline, of which all have been made partakers, then are you illegitimate, and not children." True believers are always disciplined by their Father. People who claim that they are Christians but are never disciplined for their sin cannot be true children of God. Then in verse 10, the author says, "For they indeed, for a few days, punished us as seemed good to them." Earthly fathers discipline us for a few days to help us be good in this life, but God has something greater in mind. He adds, "But he for our profit, that we may be partakers of his holiness." God trains His children to partake of His own holiness. We are provided a chance through God's training process to experience what He experiences - His holiness.

In verse 11, the inspired writer asserts, "All chastening seems for the present to be not joyous, but grievous." We do not like God's discipline. It can be extremely unpleasant. Yet, the results are so powerful. He finishes, "Yet afterward it yields the peaceful fruit of righteousness to those who have been exercised thereby." The training is for righteous living which brings forth peace. In our context, it is the peace we will have in our relationships. How do the consequences of our actions fit into God's discipline? The consequences for actions are often the very discipline God uses to keep us on the right path. The consequences make us say to ourselves, "I better not do that again. That was too painful! I never ever want to experience that again!"

Consequences built into our relationships that we have to accept for sinful actions are there to train us not to do them again. When we accept the consequences and bear the brunt of what we did, it lessens the likelihood we will repeat what we did. This will then cause us to be far more righteous and experience peace in our relationships. Attempting to dodge the bad consequences, to guilt others into removing difficult consequences, or to brow beat them into rescinding painful consequences is a direct action against God, our Father, and His sanctification process instituted for our holiness.

Believers often do this because they mix up in their minds God's punishment process with His discipline training. We tend to think consequences are punishment, but believers no longer receive punishment (Romans 8:1). Christians receive the consequences of what they do to teach them to remain in the righteous path. To repeat Paul's farming analogy, if we discover that sowing good seeds reap the fruits of eternal life, this will encourage us to continue sowing good seeds. If we are sowing bad seeds and poor crops (bad consequences) are produced, this will discourage us from sowing the bad seeds. This cause and effect (sowing and reaping) will teach and train us to live righteously, especially when it entails our relationships. We must have these consequences.

HEALING RELATIONSHIPS THROUGH FORGIVENESS

Additional Notes: Often times, when we lose relationships due to our own poor behavior, we blame the other person and never learn from our own mistakes. This happens regularly in divorce. Spouses divorce, blame the other person for all their woes, and then take their poor behavior into the next relationship. The divorce occurs again, and this time they become fearful of another messy break up or broken heart. Then they begin looking at their own behavior and discover that both the ex-spouse and current spouse are making the same complaints.

As with restitution, the accepting of every consequence is a part of the repentance process and not forgiveness. People we have wronged should forgive us whether we decide to accept the consequences or not. But like restitution, it does demonstrate to them our repentance. Also, it helps to rebuild the relationship. It is not penance for sin nor is it works for our forgiveness. This is an important difference.

At times, God will use the government to intervene in our dispute. When a wrong is done to another and is against the law, whether we repent or not, there may be consequences. In Romans 13:1-4, Paul indicates that the government is the arm of God to provide consequences for grievous sins. In verse four Paul explains, "For he is a servant of God to you for good. But if you do that which is evil, be afraid, for he doesn't bear the sword in vain; for he is a servant of God, an avenger for wrath to him who does evil." To learn from their mistakes, the saints must take the punishment that the law demands. This again demonstrates their true repentance. If someone acts as if he or she has done nothing wrong and resists the law, how can this portray sorrow over his or her sin?

It is important to understand that sometimes God will not use natural consequences for sin but deal directly with His children. There are numerous examples of this in both the

Old and New Testaments. For example, Moses, the leader of Israel, was not allowed to enter the Promised Land because of his disobedience to the Lord. In the wilderness of Zin, He told Moses to speak to the rock so it would pour forth water, and Moses struck the rock two times while he rebuked the people in anger (Numbers 20:9-12). David lost his son from his adulterous relationship with Bathsheba and his murder of her husband Uriah (2 Samuel 12). There were many saints at Corinth who were sick due to their improper observance of communion (1 Corinthians 11:30).

Additional Notes: Here is another Bible reference if needed.

James 5:15
And the prayer of faith will heal him who is sick, and the Lord will raise him up. If he has committed sins, he will be forgiven.

Here James, the half-brother of Jesus, mentions that among his readers were those who were ill due to their sins.

Since God does not speak to us directly any longer, He may bring a trial from some kind of odd *(unusual)* circumstances or perhaps one that seems like it came out of nowhere to get our attention.

Additional Notes: These previous examples would have seemed like they were out of nowhere had the inspired writers or God Himself not commented on them. If this occurs, we may ask ourselves if God is trying to get our attention and we are not listening to Him through His Word. If Christians will not listen to His Word by either not reading it regularly or ignoring it, then God will bring another believer to confront us or a trial to get our attention. Often people do not ask this question and must.

When this occurs, we should ask ourselves if we are in the midst of committing *(practicing)* sins which the Lord God wants stopped. So, it is important to accept the consequences of sin. We learn from them.

An Ancient Portrait

A great example of the acceptance of the consequences for one's sins in a relationship is found in a parable told by our Lord in Luke 15:17-31. This is the tale of the Prodigal Son. In this story a son rebels against his father, repents, and is then restored based on the father's love and grace, not the son's works. The Pharisees saw God as accepting only those who had a righteousness from good works, rather than faith. It did not matter the evil that was in their hearts. Jesus told this tale to demonstrate that God will seek out even the outcasts of this world, call them, forgive them, and accept them into His kingdom apart from works. The heart is what matters. Though this is the key intent of this story, it also teaches other principles of forgiveness as well. One is the accepting of every consequence when one sins against another.

A certain man had two sons. The younger son demanded from his father all of his inheritance. In that culture, he was essentially saying that he wished his dad was dead, so he could cash him out. The father should have slapped him in the face, dismissed him from the family, and treated him as dead. The town would then rebuke, scorn, and shun him for such disrespectful behavior. This would have been a typical Jewish response. Instead, the father breaks with all forms of tradition and gives him one-third of all he had. This was the younger son's portion (Deuteronomy 21:17).

Additional Notes: If asked about this law of God, here is the Bible reference I cite:

Deuteronomy 21:17
But he shall acknowledge the firstborn, the son of the hated, by giving him a double portion of all...he has; for he is the beginning of his strength. The right of the firstborn is his.

The father would remain in the full management of the property until his death. His son could sell his portion, but the buyer would have to wait until the owner (father) died to collect. It would be a future investment for a buyer. The first-born son would manage the property and then retain the rights to the remaining two-thirds which were not sold. This was the ancient custom for handling inheritance and property.

The son cashed out and took off to a very distant Gentile country. It was a place where he would not be known, and it would be inhabited by citizens who would not even know his traditions or customs of behavior. Also, these non-Jewish citizens would be very unfamiliar with either His God or His God's laws. This way, he was absolutely free to behave any way that he desired. He proceeded to waste all of his money. He squandered assets that had been passed down from one generation to another in his family on riotous living. He had committed all the sins that money could buy. He spent and spent while he partied and partied until it was all gone. He consumed everything until he was left with nothing.

For the first time in his life, he became virtually penniless and utterly destitute. Then a famine came, and there was no food in the land. Everyone was starving, including him. So, this impoverished son decided to attach himself (Jesus uses the word "glued") to a citizen of the land. This term "citizen" would have meant that he was a man of means, and yet he did not have much interest in helping him. This is why the son ended up in the rich man's field feeding the pigs. A good

Jewish boy could not eat or even touch the carcass of such an unclean animal (Deuteronomy 14:8; Leviticus 11:7).

Additional Notes: If asked about this law of God, here are the Bible references I cite:

Deuteronomy 14:8
The pig, because...has a split hoof...doesn't chew the cud, is unclean to you. You shall not eat their flesh, and you shall not touch their carcasses.

Leviticus 11:7
The pig, because...has a split hoof, and is cloven-footed, but doesn't chew the cud, he is unclean to you.

This was a fitting place to end such an epic episode of one man's rebellion. Yet, Jesus describes how he found God. It is often out of some deep desperation that we turn back to God. He truly welcomes us just as this father did with his son.

As he was feeding the pigs, he began to desire the pods that the pigs were eating. He was so hungry that this now crazed son literally fought the pigs for their left-over food. No one was available to help him get it. In the midst of this terrible condition of chaos and dying of starvation, he came to his senses. He woke up from his sinful stupor and took a hard look at his predicament. He had gotten himself into a huge mess. Then his heart changed, and the son completely repented. Obviously, he confessed his wickedness, mourned over the evil he had done, and turned from his sins; this is implied. The rebellious son decided that he ought to return home and declare to his father that he had sinned against heaven and him. He knew that he was not worthy to be his father's son; instead, he would beg to be a day-laborer.

The point of requesting to be a day-laborer indicated the son's intent to pay back the entire amount he had spent, no matter how long it took. Not only was he willing to make restitution but willing to accept the consequences of his sin, even if it meant holding the lowest position on the estate. Even the slaves had shelter and food. All he would receive was perhaps a job every day, if there was work available.

To return, this wayward son would also have to face the consequences of shame and humiliation from so many. This would include the townspeople, his father, and his older brother. He did not care. He would accept and bare it all. He would not attempt to dodge, guilt his father into removing, or brow beat him into rescinding the humiliating outcome of his foolish actions. He had to learn from his mistakes. As he approached the town, the father had been waiting for him. He ran swiftly to his son and hugged him, kissed him, and also forgave him.

Most know the rest of the story. The son was not required to do restitution or bare any of the consequences of his sin except for the starvation of the famine. This was solved by his loving father who provided a magnificent feast for him. Perhaps, if Jesus Christ was teaching on the importance of accepting the consequences of his sin, the outcome might have been quite different. Jesus is teaching the Pharisees the absolute free gift of eternal life without works, so the father had to offer all to the son because that is what God does at salvation.

We will look at the rest of this story in another part of the book. As can be clearly seen from the son's poor behavior, accepting the consequences is a part of repentance. Whether we must make the restitution or suffer the consequences is up to the person wronged, the governing authorities, or even God. Yet, we must accept every consequence that may arise.

A Modern Anecdote

One day, two male friends came into my office obviously upset with one another. They explained that normally they would not think this was a matter for counseling, but their college pastor referred them to me. He knew that they had been best friends since the first grade, and he did not want them to lose the relationship they had. Everyone watched them grow up together in the church and wanted them to reconcile. After a few sessions, I discovered that they were attending college together and shared an apartment. Since Steve's parents were willing to co-sign on the apartment, it was in his name alone.

Every month, John would pay his friend Steve half of the rent and utilities in cash, and Steve would pay the bills. Then one day, John came home to see a sign posted on the front door indicating that they were being evicted. This occurred because Steve had not paid three month's rent. Of course, John blew up and started shouting at Steve. He demanded to know exactly what had happened. His roommate could not understand how Steve could not have paid the rent since his parents were supporting him, while John had to work. Steve began with a long list of pathetic excuses, but none of them were adequate to explain why the rent wasn't paid.

Additional Notes: If asked about a believer's responsibility to pay debts, here are some Bible references:

Romans 13:8
Owe no one anything, except to love one another; for he who loves his neighbor has fulfilled the law.

Psalm 37:21
The wicked borrow, and don't pay back, but the righteous give generously.

AN INSTRUCTOR'S MANUAL

Proverbs 3:28
Don't say to your neighbor, "Go, and come again; tomorrow I will give it to you," when you have it by you.

Proverbs 22:7
The rich rule over the poor. The borrower is servant to the lender.

Finally, John gave up and went downstairs and paid the three month's rent. Six months later, the same thing occurred again. Steve had the same litany of excuses with no real reason for not paying the rent. He had now had enough and was going to move out and never speak to Steve again. It was time for a closer examination of the facts. It turns out that Steve had always been irresponsible. Since John liked Steve so much, he simply ignored it for so long that John almost became unaware of it. Steve had low grades, was always fooling around in his classes, missed his SAT's three times, couldn't hold down a decent job, and finally got into college because his dad knew someone who knew someone.

When they were younger, every time they went over to Steve's house, his parents would complain about his poor grades and lazy behavior but never did anything. He had never been disciplined, and John knew that one day Steve's nonsense would catch up to him too. What John did not anticipate (and really should have) was that Steve would be involved when it finally happened. I explained to John that it was time for Steve to accept consequences for his actions or he would never learn to take responsibility. This did not mean the drastic measure of destroying their friendship over it. It did mean that John would have to move out and find another roommate, and let Steve learn from his mistakes.

Before he did that, John thought he should give Steve one more chance, by having him put three month's rent in a savings account with John's name on it in case this were to happen again. In the Old Testament, the Lord gave Israel so many warnings and opportunities, before He judged them. As a result, John should give Steve one final chance. If it happens again, he should close the savings account, pay the back rent and move out. All of the other aspects of their relationship could remain in place; they simply could not become financially dependent on one another again.

I told him, he should sit Steve down and explain all of this to him in a very calm manner.

Additional Notes: If asked about the principles that apply to this situation, one of them would involve gently confronting people who have wronged you.

Matthew 18:15
If your brother sins against you, go, show him his fault between you and him alone. If he listens to you, you have gained back your brother.

2 Timothy 2:25
In gentleness correcting those who oppose him: perhaps God may give them repentance leading to a full knowledge of the truth.

2 Timothy 3:16
Every Scripture is God-breathed and profitable for teaching, for reproof, for correction, and for instruction in righteousness [a purpose of the Bible].

The Lord God has set consequences into place to help define relationships and build them. Once the pressure was off John, he could finally enjoy the friendship they had as kids. It is so important that we do not constantly bail people out of their self-imposed problems because we love them. Believers should allow all people to accept the consequences of their mistakes and sins in order for them to learn from them.

Additional Notes: If asked about another principle that applies to this situation, it would be warning others of the consequences of their actions (admonish primarily means warn).

Romans 15:14
I myself am also persuaded about you, my brothers, that you yourselves are full of goodness, filled with all knowledge, able also to admonish others.

1 Corinthians 4:14
I don't write these things to shame you, but to admonish you as my beloved children.

Colossians 1:28
Whom we proclaim, admonishing every man and teaching every man in all wisdom, that we may present every man perfect in Christ Jesus.

Colossians 3:16
Let the word of Christ dwell in you richly; in all wisdom teaching and admonishing one another with psalms, hymns, and spiritual songs, singing with grace in your heart to the Lord.

This is the way of the Lord *(Jesus)*. This is one of the loving methods our Father uses to discipline us as His children. This is even the way a loving human father behaves. It is the basic blueprint for the raising of human children and the raising of God's children.

A Personal Response

Dear Heavenly Father,

I recognize you are present everywhere I go and view everything I do. While I was reading this chapter, I realized that I have not fully accepted the consequences for the sins I have committed towards (add name). I am so sorry. Please help me accept the consequences and do what I am required to do in order to reconcile the relationship. Help me to honor and glorify You in my relationship with (add name) and follow your Word. I pray this in the name of Jesus. Amen.

AN INSTRUCTOR'S MANUAL

Chapter 3

Accept the Consequences

When we sin in relationships, we accept the consequences as God trains us to be more like Him. These may come from God, parents, spouses, friends, bosses, churches, or the law.

In the section, "A Typical Scenario," the author describes an incident where someone forgot a task and refused to accept the consequences.

What is the scenario about?

A Christian got involved in an activity and forgot to pick someone up and would not accept the consequences.

What did the conflict concern?

The Christian should have been willing to accept the consequences which came from their mistake and not get angry.

What was the relationship between the parties?

It appears as if it is two parents.

Have you had a similar experience?

(Various answers should be shared including yours.)

HEALING RELATIONSHIPS THROUGH FORGIVENESS

In the section, "A Scriptural Principle" the author presents an important biblical principle in the forgiveness process which concerns our acceptance of the consequences for our sin.

How would you express this principle in your own words?

The third principle is "we should accept whatever consequences that may result from our sin against God and others."

(Various answers should be shared including yours.)

How would you rewrite this principle to make it even more personal to your life (using your name and situation)?

(Various answers should be shared including yours.)

Why do you think this principle might be important in your life right now?

(Various answers should be shared including yours.)

How would you rate yourself on the percentage of times you followed this principle in the past when you did something wrong in a relationship?

(Various answers should be shared including yours.)

Directions: Put a horizontal mark and your name where you see yourself on the percentage line.

0%   25%   50%   75%   100%

AN INSTRUCTOR'S MANUAL

In the section, "A Biblical Explanation," the author explains the reasons why we should demonstrate repentance through accepting the consequences when we sin against others.

How is restitution related to accepting the consequences for our actions?

Accepting these consequences demonstrates our repentance also. So, restitution could be one of the many ways we accept the consequences for our sins against others.

If someone has difficulty forgiving us, could this problem be a consequence for our wrongdoing in the relationship and why?

Another way we might have to accept the consequences for our sin is to allow the people transgressed to deal with our sin in the manner and time frame they may require, not the manner and time frame we may require.

We will not allow people to be human and to experience all the feelings humans may feel when something evil is done against them. People need time to deal with the issue in a spiritual way themselves.

How does God use consequences to train us to have stronger relationships?

You have to forgive me and drop it!" We will not allow people to be human and to experience all the feelings humans may feel when something evil is done against them. People need time to deal with the issue in a spiritual way themselves.

People need time to deal with the issue in a spiritual way themselves.

When we accept the consequences and bear the brunt of what we did, it lessens the likelihood we will repeat what we did. This will then cause us to be far more righteous and experience peace in our relationships.

How would the government become involved in providing consequences for actions in a relationship?

At times, God will use the government to intervene in our dispute. When a wrong is done to another and is against the law, whether we repent or not, there may be consequences.

What are two Biblical examples of God directly providing the consequences for sin?

For example, Moses, the leader of Israel, was not allowed to enter the Promised Land because of his disobedience to the Lord. In the wilderness of Zin, He told Moses to speak to the rock so it would pour forth water, and Moses struck the rock two times while he rebuked the people in anger (Numbers 20:9-12).

David lost his son from his adulterous relationship with Bathsheba and his murder of her husband Uriah (2 Samuel 12).

There were many saints at Corinth who were sick due to their improper observance of communion (1 Corinthians 11:30).

In what ways might these truths impact your relationships?

(Various answers should be shared including yours.)

AN INSTRUCTOR'S MANUAL

In the section, "An Ancient Portrait," the author describes the prodigal son's desire to accept the consequences for his sin.

In what way did the younger son transgress his father and then his older brother?

A certain man had two sons. The younger son demanded from his father all of his inheritance.

Instead, the father breaks with all forms of tradition and gives him one-third of all he had. This was the younger son's portion (Deuteronomy 21:17).

He spent and spent while he partied and partied until it was all gone. He consumed everything until he was left with nothing.

How did the father respond in love?

For the first time in his life, he became virtually penniless and utterly destitute. Then a famine came, and there was no food in the land. Everyone was starving, including him. So, this impoverished son decided to attach himself (Jesus uses the word "glued") to a citizen of the land.

As he was feeding the pigs, he began to desire the pods that the pigs were eating. He was so hungry that this now crazed son literally fought the pigs for their left-over food. No one was available to help him get it. In the midst of this terrible condition of chaos and dying of starvation, he came to his senses.

What critical event drove the prodigal son to finally repent?

As he approached the town, the father had been waiting for him. He ran swiftly to his son and hugged him, kissed him, and also forgave him.

What action did the prodigal son want to take in order to accept the consequences for his sin?

The point of requesting to be a day-laborer indicated the son's intent to pay back the entire amount he had spent, no matter how long it took. Not only was he willing to make restitution but willing to accept the consequences of his sin, even if it meant holding the lowest position on the estate. Even the slaves had shelter and food. All he would receive was perhaps a job every day, if there was work available.

Do you think the prodigal son received back all the money he had spent and why?

No, he had spent his inheritance. Forgiveness does not remove all consequences.

Have you ever been in a situation comparable to the son's desire to accept the consequences or the father's willingness to forgive?

(Various answers should be shared including yours.)

AN INSTRUCTOR'S MANUAL

In the section, "A Modern Anecdote," the author discusses a situation where one roommate needed to set consequences for another who was being irresponsible.

What two words might characterize the kind of relationship John and Steve had?

He knew that they had been best friends since the first grade, and he did not want them to lose the relationship they had.

What did Steve do to break his relationship with John?

This occurred because Steve had not paid three month's rent. Of course, John blew up and started shouting at Steve. He demanded to know exactly what had happened. His roommate could not understand how Steve could not have paid the rent since his parents were supporting him, while John had to work. Steve began with a long list of pathetic excuses, but none of them were adequate to explain why the rent wasn't paid.

How did Steve display over and over his irresponsibility to John when they were growing up?

Steve had low grades, was always fooling around in his classes, missed his SAT's three times, couldn't hold down a decent job, and finally got into college because his dad knew someone who knew someone.

What plan did John put into place for Steve to become more responsible for his actions?

Before he did that, John thought he should give Steve one more chance, by having him put three month's rent in a savings account with John's name on it in case this were to happen again.

HEALING RELATIONSHIPS THROUGH FORGIVENESS

Once John had initiated the plan, what was he now free to do?

Once the pressure was off John, he could finally enjoy the friendship they had as kids. It is so important that we do not constantly bail people out of their self-imposed problems because we love them.

Based on the truths learned in this chapter, what would you have done differently if you were John or Steve?

(Various answers should be shared including yours.)

AN INSTRUCTOR'S MANUAL

In the section, "A Personal Response," the author provides a model you may use for prayer if you find it necessary after discovering the truths in this chapter.

Are you presently in a relationship where you have sinned against another and have not asked God for forgiveness? If not, is there one from the past that still needs this prayer to be prayed?

(Various answers should be shared including yours.)

Based on the truths you have just learned, what will you continue doing in your current relationships and what will you do differently?

(Various answers should be shared including yours.)

What additional thoughts would you like to share with the others?

(Various answers should be shared including yours.)

Instructor's Notes

Chapter 4

Gently Confront Sin

Once we have asked both God and the others involved for their forgiveness, it is time to consider the responsibility of the others. They may have played a part in the destruction of or break up of the relationship. If they did, then we must gently confront them. This is the last step we take when we ask others for forgiveness. It is also the first step we take when others have sinned against us.

As a result, this becomes the last step in our transgressing of others (Part 2) and the first step in others transgressing us (Part 3). This is such an important point. Even if others started the conflict and bear more responsibility, we must take ours first. Once we have owned up to what we did, no matter how great or small, then and only then, can we gently confront others for what they did. Both of these processes involve gently confronting sin. As a result, this one principle will be studied in both contexts.

A Typical Scenario

Have you ever had or heard a conversation with a spouse, parent, or friend about your neighbor that went something like this? You say or hear (holding a torn dress shirt in your hand), "I have had it with that neighbor! Every discussion we have gets ugly. There will be no more arguments about who was the greatest president ever to serve. We both got angry, I threw a soda in his face, and he ripped this shirt. I am going over there right now to give him a large piece of my mind for ruining my good clothes. (Pause for a thought.)

Wait! I cannot possibly behave that way. It will utterly ruin my relationship with him. He is a neighbor and a friend after all. Besides, I now realize that I bear responsibility for what happened too. I am now going to have to go over there and apologize."

In this simple illustration both parties bear responsibility for transgressing their relationship. Usually, one will begin a problem with a sinful word or action, then another responds sinfully and then they go back and forth. This destroys many relationships. Both are required to ask for forgiveness for the sins they committed. They must leave the response of the other to God. We ask and leave it up to God to prompt the other to ask also. We also depend on God for the other to graciously accept the request.

A Scriptural Principle

The next principle that must guide our reconciliation with others will address both of these common occurrences (final step and the first step) which demand a gentle confrontation. Principle four is "we must gently confront those who have sinned against us." The definition that I will use for the word "confront" in our discussion will be this: to face people and explain exactly what they did wrong. It will not include its usual negative connotation of hostility.

This is a time of mutual information exchange, not a time of bitter and angry confrontation. We explain our motives and reasons for what we did and give them a chance to explain theirs. We may describe what we think are their transgressions, and they may add our own transgressions to the discussion. We try and discover what actually happened, not what we think occurred. This will help in the important process of clearing things up.

Additional Notes: Our feelings reveal inner reactions that we may not have been expressed in our words. They may also communicate messages we may have received from the words or actions of others which were not intended by them. This is a time that is devoted to clearing things up. Sometimes, we want to omit this critical step because it may lead to additional tension between the parties. This does not have to be the case.

A Biblical Explanation

To gently confront sin is the final step in reconciling with those we have transgressed. It is the first step in reconciling with others who have transgressed us. Let's face it, in most conflicts we both will bear responsibility for the many evil words spoken and actions taken. We may have more or less responsibility, or an equal amount. At times, one party may have no responsibility. In any of these cases, we are required by our Lord to go and reconcile the relationship. If we have sinned in any way, we must ask for forgiveness. Once it is granted, then we should gently confront them concerning their part in the problem. If we do not feel we have sinned, then we must approach them with a gentle confrontation. This step will also allow them to confront us, in case we are unaware of our sin.

When a transgression occurs, people usually wait for the other to approach them. Jesus does not provide this option for the people of His kingdom. Instead, in Matthew 5:23-24, Jesus proclaimed, "If therefore you are offering your gift at the altar, and there remember that your brother has anything against you, leave your gift there before the altar, and go your way. First be reconciled to your brother, and then come and offer your gift." Notice, the Lord Jesus said that if others have something against us, we are to go to them, not if we have something against them. Notice also, the Lord does not say that if someone has something against us and we bear most of the responsibility for what happened, then we ought to go. He did not assign any weight of responsibility or guilt to the person who was to go. If we have any responsibility, we are to go.

On certain occasions, we may actually think that we bear no responsibility for any sin in the conflict; then, we should go to them and gently confront their sin against us. This is the first step in handling all who transgress us. In Matthew 18:15. Jesus declares, "If your brother sins against you, go, show him his fault between you and him alone. If he listens to you, you have gained back your brother." If we do not go to confront them, they may not know there is a problem.

Often times, we think that others should be able to figure out on their own what they did to us. We will say, "If they knew me, they would know what they did or if they weren't so selfish they would know what they did." This assumes that either they are able to read our minds or know what is deep inside our hearts. Only one man (God-Man) could do this and that person was Jesus. They are not the Lord, so we should allow them to be human and explain to them what they did. Both of these biblical passages imply that even if we think we carry no responsibility for what happened, we must go anyway. The fact that a problem occurred between us is enough reason to approach someone to reconcile.

This confrontation has several critical purposes. First, it provides an opportunity to discuss the facts and come to an agreement as to what actually happened. Sometimes, the message we send in our words and actions are not really what we may have intended. Other times, we think we said something that may have been in our minds but was not actually spoken. Often, in the heat of the moment we think someone said or did something when they did not. We are fallible and get things mixed up. This process allows a time for figuring out exactly what was said and done.

We can discern what message was sent and how each felt about it. This provides a great opportunity to share feelings. When feelings are aroused, they cannot simply be dismissed. Also, we are a product of all of our various experiences. Therefore, a word or action may mean one thing to us and a very different thing to others. These meanings produce very powerful emotions. Because they are not our feelings, we may dismiss them. This destroys relationships. Our lives, views, values, and feelings are not the only valid ones. Our partners have lives, views, values, and feelings that are also valid. These must be communicated and acknowledged by both parties, especially when they are different. This gentle confrontation process will allow this kind of communication to occur.

The second purpose is that it allows us to repent of our sins. Once the facts are clearly seen, responsibility can be taken, and repentance will follow. Third, it allows others to repent of their sins. God desires this repentance. Fourth, it provides the opportunity to reconcile and "gain back" the relationship with a fellow believer. In the end of Matthew 18:15, Jesus explains the purpose, "If he listens to you, you have gained back your brother." The relationship will be rebuilt and restored. Fifth, it allows an unbeliever to repent of the sin and perhaps receive Jesus as Savior and Lord. Is not the confrontation of sin an essential part of the gospel message (Romans 1:18; 3:23)?

Additional Notes: If asked about this truth, here are the Bible references I cite:

HEALING RELATIONSHIPS THROUGH FORGIVENESS

Romans 1:18
For the wrath [anger] of God is revealed from heaven against all ungodliness and unrighteousness of men, who suppress the truth in unrighteousness.

Romans 3:23
For all have sinned, and fall short of the glory of God.

Is it supposed to be sort of a generic sin message or can it deal with specific sins? In Acts 2:23, Peter indicted the Jews for crucifying Jesus. That is very specific. In Acts 7:52-53, Stephen spoke specifically of the transgressions of the Jewish leaders: killing the prophets, the Righteous One (Jesus), and refusing to obey God's law.

Additional Notes: If asked about this truth, here is the Bible references I cite (notice the details of their sin):

Acts 7:52-53
Which of the prophets didn't your fathers persecute? They killed those who foretold the coming of the Righteous One, of whom you have now become betrayers and murderers. You received the law as it was ordained by angels, and didn't keep it!"

Sixth, it helps Christians escape from the snare of the Devil. In 2 Timothy 2:24-26, Paul writes, "The Lord's servant must not quarrel, but be gentle towards all, able to teach, patient, in gentleness correcting those who oppose him." Here, Timothy is encouraged to correct those who oppose him. Then, Paul explains the reason for this, "Perhaps God may give them repentance leading to a full knowledge of the truth, and they may recover themselves [come to their senses and escape] out of the devil's snare [trap], having been taken captive by him to do his will." Notice, the apostle explains to Timothy that his correction will lead to these true believers escaping the snare and trap that the Devil had them in. The

Devil can capture Christians into a wrong kind of thinking which can destroy many of their relationships.

This is exactly what happened in the church at Corinth and Galatia, among others. Certain false prophets had risen up against Paul and opposed Him. Both of these examples are studied in length elsewhere in this book. Suffice it to say, the Serpent of Old was at work attempting to destroy his relationship with these saints. Seventh, it allows the church to become involved if we cannot work out the differences between us. In Matthew 18:17, the Lord Jesus describes the involvement of the church in these words, "If he refuses to listen to them, tell it to the assembly." This is an important truth to consider.

This confrontation must be done in gentleness. It is not an angry or bitter engagement. I have frequently heard people say, "We like to fight things out." This is not God's way. As Paul mentioned to Timothy, there is no quarreling; instead, there is gentleness and patience. In Galatians 6:1, the apostle describes turning a fellow Christian back from sin, "Brothers, even if a man is caught in some fault, you who are spiritual must restore such a one in a spirit of gentleness; looking to yourself so that you also aren't tempted." We must be gentle because we could fall at any time and may find ourselves in the same situation. Also, it is important to be gentle because the other person may point out a sin or sins, we could have committed or a fact or assumption that we may have wrong.

There is no actual time frame or statute of limitations for this process of gentle confrontation. If someone has wronged us in the past, we can still go years later and gently confront them or ask for forgiveness to heal the wounds in our own life and theirs. As a counselor, I often suggest that my clients work out issues with parents or children even though the transgressions may have occurred years before. The wounds are still there and cannot fully be healed or the relationships reconciled without a gentle confrontation. It is God's way! What a beautiful pattern the Lord God has established for His children: repent, confront, repent and then forgive. This is God's blueprint for living and cannot be circumvented. At times, we might not want to confront unbelievers because we think they will be driven away from the good news, or believers will turn away from God. As believers, we must obey God, and let God through His Son and Spirit handle the other people's reaction.

An Ancient Portrait

The proper and improper steps of this gentle confronting of sin are illustrated through the interaction of two sisters, Martha and Mary with Jesus. This is found in Luke 10:38-42.

Additional Notes: Most people know about Martha and Mary from Jesus' raising of their brother Lazarus from the dead. This story occurs before this incident, but after they had both received Him as their Savior and Lord. We know this because they address Jesus in the story as Lord (master). The story occurs in Bethany. Here the sisters live with their brother, though Lazarus is not specifically mentioned.

While Jesus was out preaching the gospel, He decided to stay the night at their house. You can imagine how excited the sisters would be, but both had very different reactions. Once Martha welcomed Jesus into her home, Mary parked herself right next to Jesus and began to listen to Him teach.

Additional Notes: Martha was most likely a widow because she is called the mistress of the house. This indicates that she was alone and owned the home. Luke asserts that Martha "received Him into her house." The Greek word that is translated "received" means "to welcome as a guest." It comes from a root word which is used for welcoming the teaching of someone or to reaching out the hand to learn from someone. We can assume Martha welcomed Jesus into her home in order to be hospitable, but Mary wanted to learn from Him.

Luke recorded that Mary sat at the feet of Jesus and heard His word. Sitting at a person's feet was an expression that meant to get as close as you can to hear them as they spoke. The Greek word translated "heard" means more than just hearing someone speak, but it would include "attending to, attempting to understand, and considering what is being said." In the Greek, the tense of this verb is in the imperfect active indicative demonstrating a continuous action in past time. Mary was listening as the Lord was speaking. This was the Lord of All teaching truth, and she was learning.

But where was Mary's sister? Why wasn't she also sitting at the feet of our Lord Jesus? What was Martha doing? She was attempting to serve the Lord by preparing a fine meal for him. Unlike Mary, Martha was working in the kitchen. Luke described her as "distracted with much serving." The Greek word translated "serving" is the word for "ministry" in the New Testament. Martha was ministering to the Lord in a different way. Mary's sister was ministering to the Lord by handling all the preparations for His stay. What a selfless and wonderful act of kindness. Then she got "distracted" by it. The Greek word which is translated "distracted" means "dragged away with, over-occupied, too busy with." She got dragged away with the work, and it suddenly had become overwhelming. Why? Luke explains that there were "much" preparations. Perhaps, she intended to put something nice together but not too elaborate. Then she got carried away, and suddenly there seemed to be so much to do. So, the task got bigger and bigger in her mind. Allowing Mary to sit and listen to the Lord seemed fine at first, but now the entire thing became too much for one human being to handle.

Additional Notes: She must have felt that a whole crew would be necessary. She really was trying to follow the Lord and serve Him with all her heart. The Bible says Christians are to be hospitable and to serve others.

Romans 12:13
Contributing to the needs of the saints; given to hospitality.

Here Paul describes the characteristics of the saints. She desired to serve the Lord with gladness, but things got out of hand. Ever been there? We all have.

Then she had really had enough. Martha was in the other room while Mary was enjoying the time with Jesus, and she was missing out! Luke writes that she "came up" to Jesus. The Greek word translated "came up" means "to come up and stand over." The Lord would have been seated in a place of honor outside in the home's courtyard (like our backyard patio). Mary would have been seated in front of Him, rather than to the side. She was listening. There most likely would have been other guests who had come to hear Jesus. In the midst of this, Martha just marches right in and would have stopped any conversation that might have been going on among the people with Jesus.

Standing over the both of them, obviously like an enraged mother whose children had made a mess, they needed to clean up; she began to let the Lord have it! She doesn't even talk to Mary but goes right to the top. She chastises the Lord for allowing Mary to get out of all the work and leave her stuck with the preparations. Martha scolds, "Lord, don't you care that my sister left me to serve alone?" Martha accuses the Lord of being insensitive to her problems and showing favoritism to her sister. This is the Master of the universe. Couldn't Jesus see how stressed, upset, and overwhelmed she was with everything? Doesn't He care about her?

Additional Notes: It is interesting that Jesus is accused of the same thing by His disciples when he was asleep on the boat in the storm.

Mark 4:38
He...was in the stern, asleep on the cushion, and they woke him up, and told him, "Teacher, don't you care that we are dying?"

Of course, Jesus did care and was in control even when asleep. It was the disciples' lack of faith which led to this question. It is the same in Martha's case.

Here Martha accuses her sister Mary indirectly of leaving her alone to serve Jesus. The Greek word translated "left" means "to leave or to abandon." Martha felt abandoned by her sibling Mary and completely alone. Then after accusing Jesus of such an insensitive act, her audaciousness continues. Then Martha directs, "Ask her therefore to help me." This sister of Mary basically demanded the Lord to command Mary to help her. Actually, Martha does the right thing, only in the wrong way. The woman felt wronged, and according to Matthew 18:15, what should she have done? She should have gently confronted the sins.

Additional Notes: Here is the Bible reference I cite:

Matthew 18:15
If your brother sins against you, go, show him his fault between you and him alone. If he listens to you, you have gained back your brother.

So that part *(confrontation)* was righteous and according to biblical principles. Unfortunately, all the rest went terribly wrong.

First, a gentle confrontation implies that one is not angry. We cannot be gentle and angry at the same time. Remember our use of the word "confront." Martha was not "facing the person and dealing with the issue;" but rather, she dealt with the problem in a very argumentative and hostile manner. Second, we are to go to them privately, not in front of others or to the authority over them. Third, we're to go with the intention of restoring a relationship, not to incite more anger and destroy what we have. Martha should have come up to her sister and excused herself. Then, she should have asked to speak to Mary in private having a gentle smile of an intent which would encourage restoration. This is not how Martha had behaved, but it is how the Lord behaved in his response to her. Since she had made a public remark, here was a great learning opportunity for all from the master teacher.

Then Jesus responds with a gentle confrontation to restore the relationship with Him first, "Martha, Martha, you are anxious and troubled about so many things." He repeats her name to indicate the utter importance of what He was about to say. He does recognize how upset she is. The language Jesus utilizes indicates that Martha was not just anxious but overly concerned about this problem. Martha was not only troubled but in an uproar.

There was turbulence and great noise in her declaration. Martha's mind had become completely flooded, She had so many thoughts that she was just acting on impulse. Ever been that way? Then Jesus calmly says, "But one thing is needed. Mary has chosen the good part, which will not be taken away from her." The Lord told her that Mary was not going to enter the kitchen. Martha's service was appreciated, but her sister's learning from the Lord was much more important. It would last into eternity.

The Lord Jesus makes a simple point: learning Bible truth is more important than Christian service. We need the truth because it lasts. The word translated "good" here means "the most excellent part, the best part." Service is great also, but it doesn't last. Both are essential, but truth comes first. What a beautiful story of a struggle to confront sin in a gentle way. This is not easy to do as Martha experienced and will require supernatural strength from the Holy Spirit. At times, we may want to confront sin in an argumentative and angry way as Martha did, even using the Bible as a weapon (as Martha wanted to use Jesus). Instead, we need to make our confrontation of sin gentle as Jesus did when He gave His response to Martha. It must also be in private.

A Modern Anecdote

One of the issues people have been dealing with in recent years has been an issue around their consumption of food. I received a phone call from a woman who claimed that her daughter was a Christian and needed help quickly. She had lost a lot of weight and was disappearing right before her eyes. Finally, she noticed that her daughter would eat and then immediately use the bathroom. One day, this mother listened through the door and heard the purging. She was frantic. The young lady came into my office looking gaunt and tired. I discovered that her older sister had criticized her from the time she could remember. It was always the same subject: her weight. She would constantly tell her she needed to lose weight. This produced so much anxiety in her life that she ate even more to relieve it.

She explained that her parents were always working, and so her older sister became her "mother." When she was about seventeen, she became very sick and lost a large amount of weight. The "plump" had finally left her. Suddenly, the boys began to notice her and were calling and texting her all the time. Even some of the girls in her school, who would never even look at her, started talking to her. She became popular and happy. Then the unexpected happened, she began to worry about her weight for the first time in her life. Once her appetite returned, she fell into her old eating habit that put the weight on in the first place: fast food. She adored it.

Rather than give up the fast food, she simply ate as much as she wanted and then went into the restroom and threw it up. She got the idea from a movie she had seen. At first it was disgusting, but she quickly got used to it. She thought this would be the best of both worlds. She could eat as much as she wanted and still remain slim. Eventually, the more she ate, the more she worried about getting fat. The more she worried about getting fat, the more she ate. Now, fast food was all that she thought about, and she was constantly tired.

This went on for quite some time. Now she was almost twenty-two, living at home, working for her favorite fast-food restaurant, dating boys, and being tired. She felt stuck in this dilemma. In this situation we took a two-pronged approach. First, we would work on her self-esteem and food problems. To do this, we would begin with her sister whose criticism started this whole issue in the first place.

I told her that it was time that she let Jesus be her Lord (Master) and not herself, her sister, fast food, fatigue, or boys. She needed to begin to see herself, not as her sister or the society at large saw her, but how God saw her.

Additional Notes: If asked about the details of this truth, I usually cite this Bible reference:

Psalm 139:13-15
For you formed my inmost being. You knit me together in my mother's womb. I will give thanks to you, for I am fearfully and wonderfully made. Your works are wonderful. My soul knows that very well. My frame wasn't hidden from you, when I was made in secret, woven together in the depths of the earth.

Then she had to put away these old habits and put on the utterly new habits that Christ desired. It took many sessions and hard work to get her back on the road to good health and a life that glorified Jesus Christ. Her joy and sense of purpose returned.

The final task was to reconcile the relationships with her family. She called her older sister and asked to meet. When they met, she explained what had been happening to her and how God was working miraculously in her life. The next time they met, she explained what her older sister had done and its contribution to the weight problem.

The older sister sat there utterly speechless. She had been so young herself and had so much responsibility. The older sister told her that she did not even realize she had hurt her. She sobbed and told her younger sister how sorry she was. She was so glad that this was shared with her so she could repent. Then they hugged and looked forward to a closer relationship.

After this, the younger sister also gently confronted her parents who had given so much responsibility to her older sister. They had forced a young girl into being a mother far too early making her words far too important. Of course, they repented. Finally, the younger daughter was confronted for not handling the situation in a healthy, righteous, and holy way. This too was met with confession, sorrow, and repentance by the daughter. This becomes such a beautiful example of a gentle confrontation and how it can reconcile and restore relationships. After this, the young lady was able to move out and begin her future with her relationships in her family now rebuilt. What a powerful testimony of God's power and the importance of a gentle confrontation.

A Personal Response

Dear Heavenly Father,

Now I know that the gentle confrontation of sin is critical in the forgiveness process, and I have not done this. I have been sinned against by (add name) and have not confronted him (her). Give me the strength, boldness, and wisdom to do this. If I have also sinned against him (her), open my heart to be receptive to it. Please help me to restore my relationship with (add name). I want to honor and glorify you through this. I pray this in the name of Jesus. Amen.

AN INSTRUCTOR'S MANUAL

Chapter 4

Gently Confront Sin

If others sin against us or we sin against them, we are to take our responsibility first for what we have done and then gently confront them.

In the section, "A Typical Scenario," the author describes an encounter between neighbors that resulted in a torn dress shirt and would require a reconciliation.

What is the scenario about?

Two neighbors get into an argument, and one threw a soda and the other torn a shirt.

What did the conflict concern?

Two neighbors argued over who was the greatest president.

What was the relationship between the parties?

They were neighbors and friends.

Have you had a similar experience?

(Various answers should be shared including yours.)

HEALING RELATIONSHIPS THROUGH FORGIVENESS

In the section, "A Scriptural Principle" the author presents an important biblical principle in the forgiveness process which concerns gently confronting others for their sin.

How would you express this principle in your own words?

The fourth principle is "we must gently confront those who have sinned against us."

(*Various answers should be shared including yours.*)

How would you rewrite this principle to make it even more personal to your life (using your name and situation)?

(*Various answers should be shared including yours.*)

Why do you think this principle might be important in your life right now?

(*Various answers should be shared including yours.*)

How would you rate yourself on the percentage of times you followed this principle in the past when you did something wrong in a relationship?

(*Various answers should be shared including yours.*)

Directions: Put a horizontal mark and your name where you see yourself on the percentage line.

| 0% | 25% | 50% | 75% | 100% |

AN INSTRUCTOR'S MANUAL

In the section, "A Biblical Explanation," the author explains the reasons why we are to gently confront those who have sinned against us in a relationship and how to do it.

What is the primary and most important purpose of gently confronting others?

This is a time of mutual information exchange, not a time of bitter and angry confrontation.

In the discussion of the second and third purposes, once we know the facts, what does each party do?

We try and discover what actually happened, not what we think occurred. This will help in the important process of clearing things up.

The fourth purpose is to gain back your brother. What does this mean?

The relationship will be rebuilt and restored.

According to the fifth purpose, what positive result could arise from the gentle confrontation of an unbeliever?

Fifth, it allows an unbeliever to repent of the sin and perhaps receive Jesus as Savior and Lord. Is not the confrontation of sin an essential part of the gospel message (Romans 1:18; 3:23)?

According to the sixth purpose, what is the Devil's snare of an unbeliever that gentle confrontation can eliminate?

The Devil can capture Christians into a wrong kind of thinking which can destroy many of their relationships.

In what ways might these truths impact your relationships?

(Various answers should be shared including yours.)

AN INSTRUCTOR'S MANUAL

In the section, "An Ancient Portrait," the author describes the confrontation of the Lord Jesus by Martha concerning Mary and His response.

What was the conflict between Mary and Martha?

Mary was listening as the Lord was speaking. This was the Lord of All teaching truth, and she was learning.

What was Martha doing? She was attempting to serve the Lord by preparing a fine meal for him. Unlike Mary, Martha was working in the kitchen. Luke described her as "distracted with much serving." The Greek word translated "serving" is the word for "ministry" in the New Testament. Martha was ministering to the Lord in a different way. Mary's sister was ministering to the Lord by handling all the preparations for His stay.

In what three ways did Martha improperly confront Mary?

First, a gentle confrontation implies that one is not angry. We cannot be gentle and angry at the same time. Remember our use of the word "confront." Martha was not "facing the person and dealing with the issue;" but rather, she dealt with the problem in a very argumentative and hostile manner. Second, we are to go to them privately, not in front of others or to the authority over them. Third, we're to go with the intention of restoring a relationship, not to incite more anger and destroy what we have.

Why had Martha become so upset about the tasks that she had taken on?

Here Martha accuses her sister Mary indirectly of leaving her alone to serve Jesus. The Greek word translated "left" means "to leave or to abandon." Martha felt abandoned by her sibling Mary and completely alone. Then after accusing Jesus of such an insensitive act, her audaciousness continues. Then Martha directs, "Ask her therefore to help me."

How did the Lord Jesus properly confront Martha after she had improperly confronted Him?

Then Jesus responds with a gentle confrontation to restore the relationship with Him first, "Martha, Martha, you are anxious and troubled about so many things." He repeats her name to indicate the utter importance of what He was about to say.

Then Jesus calmly says, "But one thing is needed. Mary has chosen the good part, which will not be taken away from her." The Lord told her that Mary was not going to enter the kitchen. Martha's service was appreciated, but her sister's learning from the Lord was much more important. It would last into eternity.

Why did the Lord Jesus take a stand against Martha rather than simply surrender to her demands?

The Lord Jesus makes a simple point: learning Bible truth is more important than Christian service. We need the truth because it lasts. The word translated "good" here means "the most excellent part, the best part."

Have you ever been in a situation comparable to Martha's demands, Mary's choice, or Jesus' stand and how was it the same and how was it different?

(Various answers should be shared including yours.)

AN INSTRUCTOR'S MANUAL

In the section, "A Modern Anecdote," the author discusses a situation in which a young woman developed unhealthy eating habits in response to her sister's criticism.

How did the young lady's eating problems begin?

I discovered that her older sister had criticized her from the time she could remember. It was always the same subject: her weight. She would constantly tell her she needed to lose weight. This produced so much anxiety in her life that she ate even more to relieve it.

How did the author immediately deal with her self-esteem problem?

I told her that it was time that she let Jesus be her Lord (Master) and not herself, her sister, fast food, fatigue, or boys. She needed to begin to see herself, not as her sister or the society at large saw her, but how God saw her. Then she had to put away these old habits and put on the utterly new habits that Christ desired.

Why did her older sister have to be gently confronted and what was the result?

The next time they met, she explained what her older sister had done and its contribution to the weight problem.

The older sister sat there utterly speechless. She had been so young herself and had so much responsibility. The older sister told her that she did not even realize she had hurt her. She sobbed and told her younger sister how sorry she was.

Why did her parents have to be gently confronted and what was the result?

After this, the younger sister also gently confronted her parents who had given so much responsibility to her older sister. They had forced a young girl into being a mother far too early making her words far too important. Of course, they repented.

Why did the young lady have to be gently confronted by her parents and what was the result?

Finally, the younger daughter was confronted for not handling the situation in a healthy, righteous, and holy way. This too was met with confession, sorrow, and repentance by the daughter.

Based on the truths learned in this chapter, what would you have done differently if you were young lady who was being criticized, the older sister with all the responsibility, or the parents who were so concerned?

(Various answers should be shared including yours.)

AN INSTRUCTOR'S MANUAL

In the section, "A Personal Response," the author provides a model you may use for prayer if you find it necessary after discovering the truths in this chapter.

Are you presently in a relationship where you have sinned against another and have not asked God for forgiveness? If not, is there one from the past that still needs this prayer to be prayed?

(Various answers should be shared including yours.)

Based on the truths you have just learned, what will you continue doing in your current relationships and what will you do differently?

(Various answers should be shared including yours.)

What additional thoughts would you like to share with the others?

(Various answers should be shared including yours.)

Instructor's Notes

Conclusion to Group Study and Workbook Part 2

As we conclude this book, I would like to leave us with some final thoughts about our God of forgiveness and what His Son did on the cross for us. First, if we understand the full extent of what was wrought for us on that cursed tree in order to forgive us, it will become so much easier to do the same thing for others. Second, if you read this entire book and realized that you do not understand salvation or have never received Christ as Lord and Savior, then I would like to provide that opportunity. Please do not skip this section; it may be the most important in your life.

From all outward appearances, humans seem "good" and attempt to live decent lives. This is man's concept of himself. This is not God's concept. The Almighty's view is that people all over the world and throughout the ages sin, sin, and sin again (Romans 3:23). This is a terrible and utterly destructive condition. Yet, they have ramifications that are far worse. These sins condemn us to everlasting divine retribution.

Though described briefly in the Old Testament, the Lord Jesus Christ clearly announced and proclaimed the future punishment to come. Contrary to popular belief, Jesus did not only speak of love, grace, and mercy, He also spoke of the coming judgment for sin. He declared that the judgment of sin would be everlasting punishment in a place He called "Hell." The Lord portrayed this place as an eternal inferno (Matthew 18:8) where there would be the weeping (from the sorrow) and gnashing of teeth (from the agony and anguish of suffering) continually into eternity (Matthew 8:12; 13:42, 50; 22:13; 24:51; 25:30; Luke 13:28).

Why must people face this horrific punishment? Though God is a God of love, grace, and mercy, He is also a God of great holiness, righteousness, and justice (Psalm 89:14,18). These attributes are just as much a part of His divine nature as His love, grace, and mercy. You have broken God's law as we all have, and the penalty must be paid. This began with the first man Adam (Genesis 3:1-7). When this occurred, His love, grace, and mercy surfaced, and a provision was made. Someone else would have to take man's place and pay the penalty. Someone who had never transgressed Him, who would never deserve punishment, and would fulfill all of God's Laws, would be substituted in man's place. This was the Son of God, Jesus Christ.

As the God-Man, He would pay the penalty for our sins in His death on the cross. Once done, the Lord God made only one provision for people to appropriate what His Son had done on the cross for them. This provision is receiving Jesus Christ as Savior and Lord. Though I cannot possibly share with you this good news in the confines of this book, I would love for you to consider purchasing my book entitled, *Finding The Light: The Kingdom of Heaven and How To Enter It*. It can be found for sale on Amazon.com. It is inexpensive and contains the full gospel message for your consideration. This message is so important and extensive that it cannot adequately be contained in a few pages at the end of a book.

If you are a believer, you must go out into the world and forgive as you are forgiven. These principles are to be lived and shared with others. You now have the tools to make your relationships last a lifetime. Go live them out and share them with others!

AN INSTRUCTOR'S MANUAL

PART 3

*DISPLAYING GOD'S GRACE
TO OTHERS*

THE GROUP STUDY BOOK
WITH ADDITIONAL NOTES

AND THE WORKBOOK QUESTIONS
WITH SUGGESTED ANSWERS

FOR EACH CHAPTER

CONTENTS

Introduction to Group Study Part 3	287
Introduction to the Workbook Part 3	291
Chapter - 1. Forgive as Forgiven (Study)	293
Chapter - 1. Forgive as Forgiven (Workbook)	311
Chapter - 2. Forgive the Forgiven (Study)	321
Chapter - 2. Forgive the Forgiven (Workbook)	337
Chapter - 3. Forgive the Lost (Study)	347
Chapter - 3. Forgive the Lost (Workbook)	369
Chapter - 4. Keep No Records (Study)	379
Chapter - 4. Keep No Records (Workbook)	395
Chapter - 5. Restore Through Action (Study)	405
Chapter - 5. Restore Through Action (Workbook)	427
Conclusion to Group Study and Workbook Part 3	437

Introduction to Group Study Part 3

This series of three books (Part 1,2,3) grew out of a desire to put the material in my main book on healing relationship through forgiveness into a format for small group study. As a result, the introductions are the same in all three books. This is primarily due to the essential nature of the content in our understanding of the truths found in each one. It also allows the books to be read and studied one after the other or to be studied independent of the other two. This provides more flexibility to the various individuals, groups, churches, and organizations who wish to use it.

After Moses had received the Ten Commandments, the prophet and leader requested that God show him His glory. The Almighty explained to Moses that no human could see Him and live. Nevertheless, God would grant his request by allowing His servant Moses to experience the passing of His "goodness" by him and the actual viewing of the "backside of His glory." On the next morning, he stood upon a rock and called upon the name of the Lord. The Lord God descended in the form of a cloud, shielded Moses in the cleft of the rock, and covered him with His divine hand. As God displayed His divine glory visibly, He declared the many attributes of His supernatural, divine character.

In Exodus 34:6-7, Moses described this amazing moment and the words that he heard the Lord declare about Himself. The prophet recorded, "Yahweh [I AM THAT I AM] passed by before him...he proclaimed, 'Yahweh! Yahweh, a merciful and gracious God, slow to anger...abundant in His loving kindness and truth, keeping loving kindness for thousands, forgiving iniquity and disobedience and sin.'" A book that is written on healing relationships through forgiveness by its nature must begin with the proclamation that the God of the

universe is not only the merciful, gracious, patient, loving, kind, truth-filled, just, and righteous Lord but an Almighty deity who "forgives iniquity, transgressions, and sin." This Lord God announced that He is a "forgiving" God.

This by no means negates the fact that He is also a just and righteous one; therefore, this forgiveness comes with a price that had to be paid. So, He sent His Son to die to pay the penalty for our sins in order to pour out His forgiveness upon all mankind. Through faith in Jesus Christ, men and women experience the full extent of His forgiveness that was proclaimed to Moses many years ago on that mountain top. Once this has occurred in our lives, we are to live for Him. We are to act like Him, and we are to obey Him. One of the critical ways in which God desires His forgiven people to live for, act like, and obey Him is *to forgive others as we are forgiven*. This is the key point of these books. As the Lord God has forgiven us and healed our relationship with Him, He requires us to forgive and heal our relationships with others. This is found in several passages in the Scriptures. Two of them are mentioned by our Lord and one from the apostle Paul. All three clearly explain the important truth that relationships are to be "reconciled" and "restored" to "gain back" one's brother, sister, or neighbor. This is done primarily through forgiveness.

In Matthew 5, the Lord Jesus discusses the heart attitudes people in His kingdom should possess. After speaking of anger, the Lord presents a general principle of living in His kingdom on earth. In verses 23-24, He explains, "If therefore you are offering your gift at the altar, and there remember that your brother has anything against you, leave your gift there before the altar, and go your way. First be reconciled to your brother, and then come and offer your gift." The Greek word translated "reconciled" means "to make changes." It originates from a Greek root word that was a banking term

meaning "to render accounts the same." There would be a discrepancy between two bank ledgers, and all the mistakes would have to be found and corrected in order for them to agree. We express this between people as "being on the same page." The Lord Jesus indicates that the Father desires His people to come to Him fully reconciled with each other. If we, as Christians, know that someone harbors something against us, we are to take the initiative and go to them and reconcile with them. We should not wait for them to come to us. We take our responsibility and go to them. We must once again "settle accounts." They have the same responsibility.

In Matthew 18, Jesus discusses those who are sinning in the church and what all believers should do. In verse 15, the Lord commands, "If your brother sins against you, go, show him his fault between you and him alone. If he listens to you, you have gained back your brother." The Greek word translated "gain" refers "to obtaining or securing something." When a relationship is restored, we gain back everything that the other parties contributed. In this particular case, we have something against our brother, rather than the reverse. If this does happen, we are to take the initiative and confront our brother or sister to gain him or her back and restore the relationship. So, whether someone has something against us, or we have something against someone else, the procedure is essentially the same. Christians must take the initiative and reconcile with them.

The third passage involves the restoration of a sinning brother in the church. In Galatians 6, Paul opens the chapter with an explanation of how to help a sinning saint. In verse one, Paul asserts, "Brothers, even if a man is caught in some fault, you who are spiritual must restore such a one." The Greek word translated "restore" means "to render fit, sound, or complete; to mend or repair what has been broken." The word is used of a physically broken fishing net. In Mark 1:19

and Matthew 4:21, when Jesus called James and John into ministry with Him, they were in the process of "mending" their fishing nets. They were mending the holes in their net so the fish would not fall through. This restoration could easily involve a conflict between two people. The holes in their relationship need to be mended. This process involves healing relationships through forgiveness. These passages will be referred to as you read.

These books are my original works on reconciliation and forgiveness. It is not based on other books that I have read and simply collated. To produce this work, I carefully read through the entire New Testament verse by verse. Then, I meticulously perused the Old Testament paying particular attention to the Psalms and Proverbs. As I read, categories were built from the individual passages, rather than a set of preconceived notions. These numerous categories became the individual biblical principles found in every chapter. Each passage was studied in its historical, grammatical, and scriptural contexts. After this, I compared my interpretations with those of past and present scholars. After this study, I have attempted to follow these biblical principles in my own personal life and also utilize them in my pastoral counseling practice. I have seen the Holy Spirit use them to transform relationships of all kinds.

One last thought. At the end of each chapter, I discuss a counseling experience. Due to confidentiality, none of these are based on one particular counseling situation. Instead, I have mixed together common elements I have seen, details from books and films, bits from my own life and the lives of people I have known, and thoughts from my imagination to create a situation where the biblical principles discussed in the chapters can fully be applied. These are composites of real-life situations. Read, learn, and apply. I commend you to the Lord and His Word (Acts 20:32).

Introduction to the Workbook Part 3

This workbook is designed to aid in the comprehension and application of the truths from the Scriptures which are found in the book of the same name. It has a question-and-answer format because asking questions was a powerful teaching method that the Lord used to reveal God's divine truth. Jesus asked over one hundred and thirty questions as He instructed the people of God and others. These are only the recorded ones. We can only speculate as to how many questions He might have actually asked. The Lord used His questioning techniques to prompt His listeners to focus, understand, analyze, evaluate, and apply the principles He was proclaiming to them. The same has been done in this workbook.

In Luke chapter 24, the Lord had already resurrected but had only appeared to the women who had gone to His tomb. Many of His followers did not understand why Jesus had died. He was supposed to be the Savior and now He was gone. Two on the road to Emmaus (Cleopas and another) were traveling to the town and discussing this perplexing state of affairs when Jesus appeared. Luke states that their eyes were supernaturally prevented from recognizing Him. The Lord approached them and inquired as to what they were discussing. Here Jesus uses a question to draw out the information He needs to provide the context for His time of instruction. Cleopas could not believe what he had asked. It was all anyone was talking about. He asked Jesus why He did not know the thing that had just occurred in Jerusalem. In verse 19, Luke describes the Lord's simple response, "He said to them, 'What things?'" Our Savior utilizes another question to get to crux of what they knew. This was not for His sake (since He knew their minds) but to display their ignorance of the Scriptures and its prophecies of Him.

HEALING RELATIONSHIPS THROUGH FORGIVENESS

The two men explained that a prophet named Jesus from Nazareth who had done miraculous deeds was killed by the chief priests. They had hoped that He would redeem Israel. The women who had gone to His tomb claimed that angels had appeared, and His body was gone. Yet, it had been three days of silence, and they were discouraged. The veiled Lord responds with a strong rebuke and another key question. In verse 25-26, the apostle writes, "He said to them, 'Foolish men, and slow of heart to believe in all that the prophets have spoken! Didn't the Christ have to suffer these things and to enter into his glory?'"

Here again, the Messiah asks a rhetorical question. This time it is to assist them in understanding the connection between Jesus of Nazareth and the words of the prophets. Without waiting for an answer, the Lord launches into His teaching concerning all the Messianic prophecies and other truths about Him in the Scriptures. He stayed with them that night. As they were having a meal together, the traveler's eyes were opened, and they saw that it was Jesus who had been speaking to them the entire time. Then, Christ vanished into thin air. Each looked at the other and described how their hearts were burning inside of them as Jesus spoke of Himself in all the Scriptures. As Jesus used questions, so shall we. May these questions help you focus, understand, analyze, evaluate, and apply these critical biblical principles.

Chapter 1

Forgive as Forgiven

In part two of this three-part series of books, we discussed the gentle confrontation of sin. We must confront those who have sinned against us. This would occur after we had asked them for forgiveness even if they started the conflict. This was the last step in that process. We also viewed the gentle confrontation of sin as the initial step to take when others have transgressed us. After this, the action that should be taken by Christians should be to forgive as they are forgiven. This will not be easy and is a divine act. It is important to note that this forgiveness is not dependent on others asking for our forgiveness first. It is not a result of their acceptance of the consequences either. True believers simply forgive as God has forgiven them when the Holy Spirit convicts them. This will not be easy because it requires a supernatural, divine act.

A Typical Scenario

Have you ever had or heard a conversation with a spouse, parent, or friend about a co-worker that went something like this? You say, "I cannot believe he stole my idea at work. I came up with the basic concept of the new company logo and showed it to him. He went to our boss and said it was his. I am so angry. If he ever comes to me and begs for my forgiveness, I'm not forgiving him. He can crawl on his hands and knees, but it will not do any good." This simple scenario illustrates the fact that sometimes, we do not want to forgive others for what they have done to us. Sometimes the transgression is so hurtful that it becomes difficult to overcome. Other times, we will not forgive out of pure pride or stubbornness. This does not sit well with our Lord. He forgives us all that we do each and every day, and He requires His children to act like Him and do the same.

A Scriptural Principle

The first principle in the forgiveness process is "we must forgive others as we have been forgiven." This principle encompasses has several important aspects. First, we must forgive all transgressions, nothing can be held back. Second, we must forgive all people, no one can be excluded. Third, we must forgive all the sins of all the people because we have been forgiven all our sins. Why are we to do this? The primary reason is that God expects His children to behave like Him. Since He has forgiven all the transgressions of believers, so they are to do the same.

A Biblical Explanation

Our God is a God that forgives. It is a part of His divine nature. In Micah 7:18-19 the prophet makes this declaration, "Who is a God like you, who pardons iniquity, and passes over the disobedience of the remnant of his heritage?" God, our Father, pardons all our transgressions and passes over all our disobedience. Then Micah adds, "He doesn't retain his anger forever, because he delights in loving kindness." When His anger is kindled toward our sin, it subsides in the light of his love and kindness. The prophet asserts, "He will again have compassion on us. He will tread our iniquities under foot; and you will cast all their sins into the depths of the sea." In God's compassion all our sins are cast away and tread under his foot. We studied numerous passages in the Scripture that teach the full and total forgiveness of all sins.

This occurred at the cross and was appropriated to us when we received Christ as Savior and Lord. We were declared righteous (justified) before God for all eternity (Romans 3:24, 28; 4:5).

Additional Notes: If asked about our "total justification," here are the Bible references I cite:

Romans 3:24
Being justified freely by his grace through the redemption that is in Christ Jesus.

Romans 3:28
We maintain therefore that a man is justified by faith apart from the works of the law.

Romans 4:5
But to him who doesn't work, but believes in him who justifies the ungodly, his faith is accounted for righteousness.

When we sin on earth as we await our eternal dwelling place, we maintain a relationship with the Lord. At times, our flesh gets control, and we sin (James 1:14). That sin must be dealt with through confession (1 John 1:9). When we confess our sins, God is faithful to forgive us all our sins. This is a relational forgiveness. In our relationship with Him, His love, grace, and compassion proceed from Him and cover over all our sins that are against Him. He desires that same compassion, love, and grace to cover over the sins of others against us in forgiveness. He wants His people to tread the transgressions of others under their feet and cast them in their minds as far away as the depths of the sea!

Next, God does not make any distinctions in forgiveness when it comes to His people. All are forgiven. One of the issues, Paul encountered in the churches was a distinction the Christians were making among themselves. Since the Jews were originally God's people, they thought they were above the Gentiles. Paul spent so much time explaining to both groups, God does not make distinctions among people when it comes to His forgiveness and blessings. In Ephesians 3:6, Paul discloses, "That the Gentiles are fellow heirs, and fellow members of the body, and fellow partakers of his promise in Christ Jesus through the Good News." Then in Galatians 3:28, the apostle speaks against other distinctions, "There is neither Jew nor Greek, there is neither slave nor free man, there is neither male nor female; for you are all one in Christ Jesus." All people are forgiven no matter what differences they may have. Though this may seem obvious, it is not always practiced. Instead, we tend to want to forgive some and not others who have wronged us.

In Corinth, the church made distinctions based on which leader one followed or who had what gifts of the Spirit. In 1 Corinthians 1:13, Paul asks the powerful question, "Is Christ divided?" The answer to this rhetorical question was no. As a result, we also may not divide Him by making distinctions. In 1 Corinthians 12:13, Paul says, "For in one Spirit we were all baptized into one body, whether Jews or Greeks, whether bond or free; and were all given to drink into one Spirit." We cannot make distinctions in our forgiveness of others. Why? The Lord makes no distinctions in His forgiveness of us. This means we can make no distinctions in our forgiveness of other believers. We cannot say, "I do not like him, and I will not forgive him." The flesh can create in our minds some of the most ridiculous excuses for why we shouldn't forgive. We cannot succumb to its seemingly rational reasons which are utterly sinful. All believers are to be forgiven all sins without distinctions.

If all believers should be forgiven their sins without any distinctions made, what about unbelievers? Should we make any distinctions among those who do not know Jesus Christ concerning forgiveness? The answer is found in the answer to another question, "Does God call all people to salvation and forgiveness?" In 1 Timothy 2:3, Paul entreated Timothy, his son in the faith, to pray for the salvation of all people, He wrote, "For this is good and acceptable in the sight of God our Savior." Then in verse four, Paul provided the important reason, "Who desires all people to be saved and come to full knowledge of the truth." So, we must forgive all people.

There were some people mocking believers because they were claiming that Christ was coming back, and He had not yet come. In 2 Peter 3:9, Peter proclaimed, "The Lord is not slow concerning his promise, as some count slowness; but is patient with us, not wishing that any should perish, but that all should come to repentance." Our God desires all people to find forgiveness in His only Son. He does not make any distinctions. This means that the Father desires His children in the same way to also forgive people their transgressions. We cannot say, "He's an unbeliever or (insert some criticism here), and I will not forgive him."

The Lord taught the following principle throughout His ministry. If God forgives the sins of all of us against Him, then we are to forgive the sins against us. In Matthew 6:12, during the Sermon on the Mount, Jesus explained that the prayers of God's kingdom people should conclude with these words, "Forgive us our debts, as we also forgive our debtors." In Mark 11:25, on His way to Jerusalem, Jesus told His disciples, "Whenever you stand praying, forgive, if you have anything against anyone." In Luke 11:4, when He was asked how to pray, Jesus Christ delivered the Lord's Prayer for a second time which included the forgiveness of others. He said, "Forgive us our sins, for we ourselves also forgive everyone who is indebted to us." Notice, the Lord makes no distinction between believers and unbelievers in His words.

HEALING RELATIONSHIPS THROUGH FORGIVENESS

The Lord Jesus uses the inclusive terms "debtors," "anyone," and "everyone." Forgiveness is extended to all.

In Ephesians 4:31-32, concerning believers, Paul exhorted, "Let all bitterness, wrath, anger, outcry, and slander, be put away from you, with all malice." Here is a list of terrible sins and transgressions believers may commit toward us and us toward them. They may become angry, bitter, hot-tempered and then yell, scream, lie, plot, and gossip about us. We may do the same to them. He commands us to stop this sin and behave in a wholly different way. Paul continues, "And be kind to one another, tenderhearted, forgiving each other, just as God also in Christ forgave you." When these harsh and cold transgressions occur against us, we should not respond in the same way. Instead, we must be kind, compassionate, tender, and then forgive them fully as God did us.

This was such an issue in the churches that Paul had to speak of it again in his letter to the church in Colossae. This inspired writer in Colossians 3:12-13 explained what their "wholly different" behavior should be, "Put on therefore, as God's chosen ones, holy and beloved, a heart of compassion, kindness, lowliness, humility, and perseverance." These are the divine qualities of our Father. When transgressed, he continues with these words, "Bearing with one another, and forgiving each other, if any man has a complaint against any; even as Christ forgave you, so you also do." As our God is pouring out His forgiveness upon us every day of our lives, we, as His people, are to be pouring out our forgiveness on others every day.

Jesus also delineated the consequences if God's kingdom people did not forgive. In these same passages, Jesus warns His followers. In Matthew 6:14-15, He beseeches, "For if you forgive men their trespasses, your heavenly Father will also forgive you. But if you don't forgive men their trespasses, neither will your Father forgive your trespasses." In Mark 11:25, He declares, "Whenever you stand praying, forgive, if you have anything against anyone; so that your Father, who is in heaven, may also forgive you your transgressions." The Lord is not talking about eternal forgiveness, but here again relational forgiveness on this earth. This is the kingdom life of believers on this earth with their God. God forgives them, and they forgive others. If we want things to be right with God in our lives, we need to be behaving towards others as He behaves towards us. We need to act just like Him. If not, we should expect the process of discipline and training to begin in order that we become more like His Son in this area.

Now, how does this work in real life? When we become filled with anger and bitterness and unwilling to forgive, we must consider the amount and extent of the transgressions we have committed against God.

Additional Notes: It might help us to remember the punishment we would have received had God not forgiven us. We could consider the passage on the Great White Throne we would have endured:

Revelation 20:11-15
I saw a great white throne, and him who sat on it, from whose face the earth and the heaven fled away. There was found no place for them. I saw the dead, the great and the small, standing before the throne, and they opened books. Another book was opened, which is the book of life. The dead were judged out of the things which were written in the books, according to their works. The sea gave up the dead who were in it. Death and Hades gave up the dead who were in them. They were judged, each one according to his works. Death and Hades were thrown into the lake of fire. This is the second death, the lake of fire. If anyone was not found written in the book of life, he was cast into the lake of fire.

He has made absolutely no distinctions in forgiving us. Then we will discover that the sins against us will look so much smaller in comparison to our large number of sins against God. After this, our hearts will be opened to His Spirit through this biblical truth. Then God's mercy, grace, and love that was shown and is shown every day to us in forgiveness, will pour forth into our own love, grace, and mercy in forgiveness toward others. People struggle with forgiveness when they forget how much they have been forgiven. Sometimes, they may be too proud to realize what horrible sinners they are!

When believers are continually coming before the throne of God begging God for forgiveness, they will understand be able to forgive in a greater way whether the transgressors are believers or not. One of the primary ways Christians can have growing relationships with spouses, parents, children, friends, church members, co-workers, fellow students, and acquaintances is through this constant confession process. We admit our sins, accept His forgiveness, and then provide the same toward all others. The Lord does not desire that we make any distinctions between people when it comes to the forgiveness toward others. Forgiveness for all believers and unbelievers should pour from our hearts.

Also, the forgiveness of others does not necessarily occur after we gently confront them with their sin, and they ask for forgiveness. It could happen as the sin is occurring or even immediately afterward. Every sin someone commits against us cannot possibly be confronted. There are simply too many annoyances and little sins. God certainly does not confront us on every sin we commit, nor does He discipline us. We cannot wait for those who have sinned against us to ask for forgiveness because often they do not or will not. Forgiving others is not dependent on their response but only on God's forgiveness of us. If our forgiveness was solely dependent on waiting for them to ask, then we would be full of bitterness.

An Ancient Portrait

This principle is beautifully illustrated in the "Parable of the Unforgiving Debtor" in Matthew 18:23-35. Peter had just inquired of the Lord as to whether seven times is enough to forgive someone who had sinned against us. To him that seemed pretty reasonable. To Jesus, it was absurd. Instead, Jesus told him it was more like "seventy times seven." This meant as many times as needed. Then to help His disciples understand the absolute importance of forgiving others as many times as they sin against them, He tells this powerful story that speaks directly to the issue.

Additional Notes: It is important to observe that this story does not have to do with all of the consequences for the sins of others against us, but simply forgiving someone in the heart. The Lord forgives believers, but as we have seen previously there are still consequences for sin. When our children lie to us, we may forgive them, but they might also be grounded for some time. Forgiveness removes all eternal punishment but has nothing ultimately to do with discipline. The main purpose of discipline is to train someone to be righteous. This is an entirely different issue. In this parable, Jesus Christ was answering Peter's direct question. Otherwise, this parable is difficult to understand and will lead Christians into many tangents not intended to be taught. It is an analogy and every detail of analogies do not always fit the teaching of a specific truth.

Jesus begins the story by describing a king who desired to settle accounts with his servants. These were not his slaves in chains but probably provincial governors. They were to pay the king his legal share of their tax revenue in order to support the kingdom. This king discovered that one of his "servants" owed him ten thousand talents. To owe him this much, the governor would have to have kept back the owed tax revenues for many years. It became an impossible sum to pay back. In modern terms, we would owe back taxes, so large that we could not pay them back no matter how long we worked. This man was in a difficult predicament.

The tax revenue of Judea and Samaria together was only two to three hundred talents, so one can imagine the great sum ten thousand would be. The point is simple: it was an impossible sum to ever pay back. When the king discovered the discrepancy, he would have known that the servant had been cheating the king for a very long time. This would have made him extremely angry. Since he obviously couldn't pay, the king ordered him to be sold into slavery with his whole family. Then whatever he owned would be sold, so some payment could be made. This would come nowhere near the amount owed, but the king would take everything.

To take all that the man owned and to sell his family into slavery would never earn the king enough to compensate for all the man had stolen. It would cost the servant everything that he had and beyond. This was a common practice among the nations in the ancient world. Everyone who heard Jesus would understand what was described. So, this official fell to the ground in submission and worship and began to beg for mercy from the king. He cried, "Please, please, be patient and I will repay you!" This would have been impossible, and they both knew it but crying out for the king's patience and mercy was his only hope.

He did not deny his sin or question the king's judgment. He pleaded for mercy! Suddenly, this king felt compassion for the man and released him from the debt. He could have lambasted him for such a ridiculous request, but he did not.

He bestowed complete forgiveness on the man and wiped away his debts. The official walked away a free man and unencumbered from any transgressions. He had pleaded for mercy and received it. Does this not sound like believers who plead for mercy, receive Christ as Savior and Lord, and are released from all the debts of their sin? Yes, it does, and this is the first point Christ is making to Peter.

Then, something utterly hypocritical happened. The man immediately proceeded to behave in a way that was almost exactly opposite of the forgiveness the king had shown him. Obviously, while he was trembling before the patient king, he must have remembered that someone else should actually be trembling before him. Once released, the official decided to search for the man who had owed him some money, and he would not receive the same kind of mercy from him. He did not care that in comparison to the debt that was just forgiven; it was a small amount of only one hundred denarii. When he found him, he grabbed him by the throat since the debtor was on the same level as him (a fellow-servant).

While the first servant's hands were wrapped around his throat choking him, the official demanded payment of what he was owed. So, this fellow servant did exactly what the official had just done to the gracious king. He begged for mercy from him. He fell down to the ground in submission and cried, "Please, please be patient, and I will repay you." Since this amount was so much smaller, this man's payback was actually possible.

Though the official had been shown compassion when he uttered those words, he responded in a completely opposite manner. There was no compassion, no mercy, and absolutely no love. He threw the fellow-servant into prison until this man paid back every denarius he owed. Unfortunately for the official, a group of his own people (fellow-servants to the king) happened to be strolling by. The Lord Jesus described his actions as grieving them terribly, so they all left to report it to the king in detail. They knew that this was unacceptable behavior for someone who had just received so much mercy! When the king discovered what the grievous act his official had committed, the official was summoned.

As this servant stood before him a second time, the king rebuked him and said, "You wicked servant! I forgave all the debt you had because you pleaded with me. Couldn't you have had mercy on your fellow-servant in the same way that I had mercy on you?" Notice this sovereign rebuked the man for not following his example. Then his majesty became angry and commanded that the servant be handed over to the torturers until all of the ten thousand talents had been repaid. Of course, this was impossible, so he would spend his life in prison. At this point the Lord Jesus ends the story and issues a warning, "So will the heavenly Father do to you, if you don't forgive your brother from the heart!" What an indictment! These were stern words from the Master! What could Jesus have meant?

Additional Notes: If asked about the Bible's teaching on showing mercy, here are a few verses:

Matthew 5:7
Blessed are the merciful, for they shall obtain mercy.

James 2:13
For judgment is without mercy to him who has shown no mercy. Mercy triumphs over judgment.

James 3:17
But the wisdom...from above is first pure, then peaceful, gentle, reasonable, full of mercy and good fruits, without partiality, and without hypocrisy.

Colossians 3:12
Put on therefore, as God's chosen ones, holy and beloved, a heart of compassion, kindness, lowliness, humility, and perseverance.

Here Jesus (the master) was talking to Peter and His other disciples! He is not speaking to unbelievers because God is not their heavenly Father! He may be their creator, but He is not their Father. Rather than interpreting every detail of the parable, which is not necessary, let's get to Jesus' second point. The debt of our sin against God is so great that we could not pay it back in an eternity of punishment or a lifetime of good deeds (the torture until paid back). The sins people commit against us, no matter what they consist of, are very small in comparison to our sins against God (ten thousand talents vs. one hundred). As He demonstrated full and complete forgiveness of our sins, we are to do the same to others (the king felt compassion and released him). If not, we will experience the discipline and training of the Lord, and it will not be pleasant (threw him into prison)!

Additional Notes: According to Romans 8:1, as Christians, "there is no condemnation for those who belong to Christ Jesus." Our past, present, and future transgressions are forgiven. Yet, God's discipline in His relationship to us will come upon us. God wants His compassion and mercy shown in forgiveness toward others. This official in the story made distinctions in the person of the fellow servant and the sin. He was unwilling to forgive all sins of all men, but we are different. Like our father, we will make no distinctions and forgive as we are forgiven. You say, "How do I do that?" Once again, you do this by comparing the large weight of your sin against a holy, righteous God with the small weight of another's sins against you. There are times when someone might get upset with his spouse. Then he should stop and say to himself, "You have done much worse to God many times." Then, he should pray and ask the Holy Spirit to help him forgive her. As a believer the spouse should do the same.

A Modern Anecdote

Due to a large immigration movement, the population of the western world now represents many different cultures and values. As people of different cultures meet, fall in love, marry, and raise children in their new country, often there is a clash of cultural values between the children and parents within the family. Though she did not know it at the time, this was the issue that one such young lady was facing when she came in for counseling.

She explained that she had problems in her relationships with men. As soon as she came near to "falling in love," the young lady would inevitably push the men away. She could accomplish this feat by providing numerous "mixed signals." This would utterly confuse the men so they would give up and end the relationship. Though she thought about it often, the young lady could not figure out the real reason for this endless cycle of confusing suitors.

After a short time, we discovered that she had unresolved issues with her father. Though this might not always be the case, it was with her. She felt that her father had treated her mother in a demanding and demeaning way, and she did not like it. When I asked for examples, she told me that her father bossed her mother around and expected her mother to obey every command of his. She described her mother as acting like "like a little puppy dog" following him all around the house. He spoke and she listened. Whatever her father wanted, her mother did. This angered her greatly.

When I probed further, she gave more specific details. He would ask her to get him a drink of water, and she would run to get it. Though he could have gotten up and served himself. Also, he wanted dinner on the table as soon as he got home and refused to ever help her in the kitchen. The daughter was appalled. Sometimes, his tone of voice became harsh and unkind. When she left for college, she was so glad to get out of the house and be rid of him once and for all.

Then she ran out of money and had to move home. Now, she was back in this toxic environment. The father's behavior did appear a bit out of sync with western cultural norms, but it was not abusive. I asked her if he had ever mistreated her, and she said, "Never! In fact, he always treated me better than my mom. It made me suspicious that it was all an act. I don't trust men." Why should she? She thought that the most important man in her life had failed her, why would she trust another man? After discovering that her mother and father were immigrants from different cultures, things began to clear up. We took some time to study how the roles of men and women differed in the cultures of her parents and then the western culture she had embraced.

It dawned on her that her father was simply following the cultural values of the country he came from. Though the mother's values were less restrictive than her husband's, she loved him and enjoyed caring for him. She did not mind acting in accordance with his views. It was the daughter that did not like it. She was viewing the situation from a third western cultural perspective. When she was asked if she had ever shared her feelings with her father, she responded, "No! He is evil and wouldn't understand." I explained to her from the Scriptures that God desired her to gently confront him. He certainly deserved the chance to explain his actions at the very least.

Gentle confrontation is not simply to blast a person for his sin, but to see the situation from both sides. She also needed to consider that she may have been wrong in her view of his behavior over these years which led to her intense bitterness toward him. She might well have been angry because she misunderstood her parents' views of their different cultural roles. She would need to repent of this anger and ask for her father's forgiveness. Whatever she decided to do, God would want her to forgive her father just as He had forgiven her for whatever wrongs she had committed in her life.

When she heard this, she stood up and marched out of my office. I heard her mumbling, "I'll never forgive him!" A month later, she gave me a call to let me know that the Holy Spirit had deeply convicted her for the bitterness. The Holy Spirit always convicts of sin and encourages us to act on it.

So, she decided to go to her father and gently confront the man. After an extremely long conversation, she finally began to understand him better. He explained to her how much he loved her and how sorry he was. She told him how sorry she was for harboring such bitterness for so long. This restored the relationship, and they began the process of building it to a new level. This came about because the young woman was willing to gently confront her father. We must do the same.

Additional Notes: Though all Christians have the same principles to obey, sometimes their cultural expressions are very different. According to Ephesians 5:22-33 and 1 Peter 3:1-7, the divine mandate is for a husband and wife to love, respect, and understand each other. It is up to any couple to work out those expressions within their cultural context as long as no other Scripture is violated. In this case none were. The daughter was viewing the situation through only one cultural lens. The gentle confrontation allowed her to see things from the other two lenses.

AN INSTRUCTOR'S MANUAL

A Personal Response

Dear Heavenly Father,

After studying the principles in this chapter, I realize that I have made distinctions in my forgiveness. I have forgiven others but not (add name) for (add sin). It has been really difficult because of (describe issue). Help me remember how much you have forgiven me on a daily basis. I know I have done much worse to You when I (describe sins). I know the amount my transgressions against you far outweigh (add names)'s sin against me. I am sorry for my hardened heart. Please help me to forgive (add name). I want to honor You in my relationship with (add name) and follow Your Word. I pray this in the name of Jesus. Amen.

Instructor's Notes

AN INSTRUCTOR'S MANUAL

Chapter 1

Forgive as Forgiven

If others sin against us in a relationship, we must forgive them as God forgives us. This applies to any and all sins over the course of the relationship.

In the section, "A Typical Scenario," the author describes a co-worker stealing a Christian's idea and his unwillingness to forgive which will need reconciliation.

What is the scenario about?

A Christian's co-worker stole his idea for the company logo, and he was unwilling to forgive him.

What did the conflict concern?

A co-worker stole the idea of a company logo and a shared it as his own.

What was the relationship between the parties?

They were co-workers.

Have you had a similar experience?

(Various answers should be shared including yours.)

HEALING RELATIONSHIPS THROUGH FORGIVENESS

In the section, "A Scriptural Principle" the author presents an important biblical principle in the forgiveness process which concerns forgiving as we are forgiven.

How would you express this principle in your own words?

The first principle is "we must forgive others as we have been forgiven."

(*Various answers should be shared including yours.*)

How would you rewrite this principle to make it even more personal to your life (using your name and situation)?

(*Various answers should be shared including yours.*)

Why do you think this principle might be important in your life right now?

(*Various answers should be shared including yours.*)

How would you rate yourself on the percentage of times you followed this principle in the past when you did something wrong in a relationship?

(*Various answers should be shared including yours.*)

Directions: Put a horizontal mark and your name where you see yourself on the percentage line.

0%   25%   50%   75%   100%

AN INSTRUCTOR'S MANUAL

In the section, "A Biblical Explanation," the author explains the reasons why we are to forgive as we are forgiven and how to do it.

How do we sometimes make distinctions among people in our forgiveness?

If God forgives the sins of all of us against Him, then we are to forgive the sins against us (this includes both believers and non-believers).

According to Mark 11:25 and Luke 11:4, what key words are used by the Lord Jesus to demonstrate that all people should be forgiven whether they are believers are unbelievers?

In Mark 11:25, on His way to Jerusalem, Jesus told His disciples, "Whenever you stand praying, forgive, if you have anything against anyone." In Luke 11:4, when He was asked how to pray, Jesus Christ delivered the Lord's Prayer for a second time which included the forgiveness of others. He said, "Forgive us our sins, for we ourselves also forgive everyone who is indebted to us." Notice, the Lord makes no distinction between believers and unbelievers in His words. The Lord Jesus uses the inclusive terms "debtors," "anyone," and "everyone." Forgiveness is extended to all.

To aid in our forgiveness process, what kind of comparison should we make concerning our own sins with the sins of those against us?

Now, how does this work in real life? When we become filled with anger and bitterness and unwilling to forgive, we must consider the amount and extent of the transgressions we have committed against God. He has made absolutely no distinctions in forgiveness of us. Then we will discover that the sins against us will look so much smaller in comparison to our large number of sins against God.

If Christians are having a difficult time of forgiving people, what might they not be doing enough of?

They may not be repenting enough. When believers are always throwing themselves before the throne of God and begging Him for forgiveness, they will find greater forgiveness of others. This would include both those who know and love the Lord Jesus Christ and those who do not.

Is the forgiveness of others dependent on their response to us? Why or why not?

Forgiving others is not dependent on their response but only on God's forgiveness of us.

In what ways might these truths impact your relationships?

(Various answers should be shared including yours.)

AN INSTRUCTOR'S MANUAL

In the section, "An Ancient Portrait," the author presents the parable of the servant who was unwilling to forgive.

What was the king's response to his servant's plea?

Since he obviously couldn't pay, the king ordered him to be sold into slavery with his whole family. Then whatever he owned would be sold, so some payment could be made. This would come nowhere near the amount owed, but the king would take everything.

He did not deny his sin or question the king's judgment. He pleaded for mercy! Suddenly, this king felt compassion for the man and released him from the debt. He could have lambasted him for such a ridiculous request, but he did not.

What was the first servant's response to the second servant's plea?

When he found him, he grabbed him by the throat since the debtor was on the same level as him (a fellow-servant).

There was no compassion, no mercy, and absolutely no love. He threw the fellow-servant into prison until this man paid back every denarius he owed. Unfortunately for the official, a group of his own people (fellow-servants to the king) happened to be strolling by.

How were the two responses different from each other and why?

They knew that this was unacceptable behavior for someone who had just received so much mercy! When the king discovered what the grievous act his official had committed, the official was summoned.

What actions did the king take when he found out?

Notice this sovereign rebuked the man for not following his example. Then his majesty became angry and commanded that the servant be handed over to the torturers until all of the ten thousand talents had been repaid. Of course, this was impossible, so he would spend his life in prison.

According to this parable of Jesus why should we forgive as forgiven?

The sins people commit against us, no matter what they consist of, are very small in comparison to our sins against God (ten thousand talents vs. one hundred). As He demonstrated full and complete forgiveness of our sins, we are to do the same to others (the king felt compassion and released him). If not, we will experience the discipline and training of the Lord, and it will not be pleasant (threw him into prison)!

Have you ever been in a situation comparable to the king or either servant's dilemma? How was it different or the same?

(Various answers should be shared including yours.)

AN INSTRUCTOR'S MANUAL

In the section, "A Modern Anecdote," the author discusses a situation in which a young lady struggled with forgiving her father.

Why did the young lady come in for counseling?

As soon as she came near to "falling in love," the young lady would inevitably push the men away. She could accomplish this feat by providing numerous "mixed signals." This would utterly confuse the men so they would give up and end the relationship. Though she thought about it often, the young lady could not figure out the real reason for this endless cycle of confusing suitors.

Why was the young lady bitter toward her father?

After a short time, we discovered that she had unresolved issues with her father. Though this might not always be the case, it was with her. She felt that her father had treated her mother in a demanding and demeaning way, and she did not like it. When I asked for examples, she told me that her father bossed her mother around and expected her mother to obey every command of his.

Rather than confront her father, but what did she do?

Sometimes, his tone of voice became harsh and unkind. When she left for college, she was so glad to get out of the house and be rid of him once and for all.

How did the young lady misinterpret her father's behavior toward her mother?

It dawned on her that her father was simply following the cultural values of the country he came from. Though the mother's values were less restrictive than her husband's, she loved him and enjoyed caring for him.

Why did she not want to forgive her father?

She also needed to consider that she may have been wrong in her view of his behavior over these years which led to her intense bitterness toward him. She might well have been angry because she misunderstood her parents' views of their different cultural roles. She would need to repent of this anger and ask for her father's forgiveness. Whatever she decided to do, God would want her to forgive her father just as He had forgiven her for whatever wrongs she had committed in her life.

Based on the truths learned in this chapter, what would you have done differently if you were the bitter daughter, the unknowing father, or the traditional mother?

(Various answers should be shared including yours.)

In the section, "A Personal Response," the author provides a model you may use for prayer if you find it necessary after discovering the truths in this chapter.

Are you presently in a relationship where you have sinned against another and have not asked God for forgiveness? If not, is there one from the past that still needs this prayer to be prayed?

(Various answers should be shared including yours.)

Based on the truths you have just learned, what will you continue doing in your current relationships and what will you do differently?

(Various answers should be shared including yours.)

What additional thoughts would you like to share with the others?

(Various answers should be shared including yours.)

Instructor's Notes

Chapter 2

Forgive the Forgiven

From practical experience, we know that when Christians have transgressed us, it is not always easy to forgive them. Believers can commit some horrible sins against us that can do great damage to our lives and the lives of those we love. Many people can share stories of believers in a local church who have hurt them.

Additional Notes: Unfortunately, believers must struggle with their flesh upon this earth. Here, Paul referred to the flesh as his "body of death."

Romans 7:24
What a wretched man I am! Who will deliver me out of the body of this death?

Our physical bodies, which contain a sin-principle, can speak horribly damaging words and behave in terribly destructive ways. This is our human condition on earth.

Though we are redeemed in our souls, our bodies groan for their redemption as Paul explains.

Romans 8:23
Not only so, but ourselves also, who have the first fruits of the Spirit, even we ourselves groan within ourselves, waiting for adoption, the redemption of our body.

The church has problems because it is made up of people who have problems. The real question is, "How do we handle these problems when they arise?" We are to forgive.

Sometimes, this is difficult. When this occurs, one way of resolving this dilemma is to consider all the sins that we have committed against God. God has forgiven so much more. We put away any distinctions in who they are or what they have done to us and forgive. In this chapter, we will learn that not only should we forgive believers because we are forgiven, but also because they are already forgiven by the Lord God.

A Typical Scenario

Have you ever had or heard a conversation with a spouse, parent, or friend about another friend that went something like this? You say or hear, "Do you see my magazine? I just loaned it to my friend. His two-year-old son got ahold of it, and now it is destroyed. I was going to pass the magazine to my brother. He loves these things. Every time I have loaned this guy something, it happens again. I am done. I have had enough with him. I am so angry! (Person comments.) What? I don't care if he is a Christian. If he ever comes to me and asks for forgiveness, I'm not forgiving him. And don't quote me any Bible passages. I will never ever forgive him. Do you really understand? Never!"

A Scriptural Principle

We must once again begin thinking differently about the person and the transgression to overcome this problem. This brings us to principle two which is "we must know that believers who transgress us are already forgiven for their sins." This is an obvious truth, but it is not often considered in this type of circumstance. Whether Christians who have transgressed us have asked for our forgiveness or not, our holy God and Father has already forgiven them eternally. Whether those who sin against us have asked Him for forgiveness or not, the Lord will handle that relationally. Whether the saints who have sinned against us have asked for forgiveness or not, God will also handle that issue with them as He handles the issue with us.

That is the direct work of His Spirit. We can confront, but He has to work in their hearts. If we have difficulty forgiving another believer, we must consider that those sins against us were nailed to the cross when they received Jesus as Savior and Lord. We may claim all the forgiveness that God gives to us, but we don't always want to think that the Lord has already forgiven the sins they have committed against us through Christ's death on the cross (Colossians 2:13-14).

A Biblical Explanation

Let us study God's forgiveness, not in the light of our own sins, but in the light of deeds against us by other Christians. In the introduction of this book, I mentioned Exodus 34:6-7. In this passage, Moses asked God if he could see His glory. God could only allow him to see the backside, as it were, so He would not be consumed. As God physically manifested Himself to Moses, you may remember that He also verbally declared his glory with these words, "Yahweh passed by before him, and proclaimed, "Yahweh! Yahweh, a merciful and gracious God, slow to anger, and abundant in loving kindness and truth, keeping loving kindness for thousands."

Now, let's read the last part of God's revelation about His character with the wicked deeds of believers against us in our minds. The Lord is "forgiving iniquity and disobedience and sin" of other saints against us. God's glory is manifested when He forgives the sins of others against us. It is a part of

God's nature to forgive the sin of other believers against us. His forgiveness extends not only to our sins against others but to others' sins against us. One of the primary reasons we are to forgive is that they are already forgiven by our God. They transgressed against Him first. Yet, God had enough grace, mercy, and love to forgive them and so should we.

In Luke 17:3-4, Jesus teaches, "Be careful. If your brother sins against you, rebuke him. If he repents, forgive him." He commands forgiveness of others again. Then Jesus exhorts, "If he sins against you seven times in the day, and seven times returns, saying, 'I repent,' you shall forgive him." Why should we? One reason is that God, our Father, has already forgiven them. In Matthew 26:28, at the last supper, Jesus declared "For this is My blood of the covenant, which is poured out for many for forgiveness of sins." The blood of Christ was not simply poured out for us and the sins we commit against others but also poured out for others and the sins they commit against us. What an amazing change in perspective. So, when I consider the sins of a spouse, parent, child, friend, fellow student, co-worker, or neighbor against me and do not want to forgive, I must remember that if they are a believer God has already forgiven him or her.

In Ephesians 1:7, Paul says, "In Him we have redemption through His blood." That redemption extends to the sins of other Christians against us. Then he adds, "The forgiveness of our trespasses, according to the riches of His grace." The forgiveness according to the riches of God's grace not only extends to our trespasses but those who trespass against us. In Hebrews 9:22, the author describes the impact of Christ's death in these words, "Without shedding of blood there is no forgiveness." The shedding of Jesus Christ's blood on that cursed cross providing forgiveness for all our sins, provided forgiveness for all those saints who have sinned against us.

In 1 John 1:7, the beloved disciple declares, "But if we walk in the light, as he is in the light, we have fellowship with one another, and the blood of Jesus Christ, his Son, cleanses us from all sin." The blood cleanses "us" from all our sins even against each other. Then he continues in 1 John 2:12, "I write to you, little children, because your sins are forgiven you for His Name's sake." The biblical expression "for His Name's sake" carries the idea of "all that He is and has done." The name of a person represented all of whom the person was and did. The sins believers have committed against us have been forgiven in His name and for Him.

Paul was the Lord's classic example in 1 Timothy 1:15-17. The Christians who had loved ones injured or killed because of Paul had to accept him into the church. They had to forgive his atrocities against them and the ones they loved the most. That must have been tough.

Additional Notes: If asked about the details of this story, here is the Bible reference I cite:

1 Timothy 1:15-17
The saying is faithful and worthy of all acceptance, that Christ Jesus came into the world to save sinners; of whom I am chief. However, for this cause I obtained mercy, that in me first, Jesus Christ might display all his patience, for an example of those who were going to believe in him for eternal life. Now to the King eternal, immortal, invisible, to God who alone is wise, be honor and glory forever and ever. Amen.

As we can so clearly see, all of these passages include our forgiveness when we sin against others. We love to rejoice in this truth. Here is another equally important truth: these verses also include the forgiveness of others when they transgress us! In fact, here is a beautiful pattern: we are being forgiven for our sins against the brethren as they are being forgiven for their sins against us. There is forgiveness upon forgiveness. Often, we get stuck and do not want to forgive our brothers and sisters in Christ. Yet, we so desperately want God to forgive our sins against them. We cannot have it both ways. If we are to receive God's forgiveness, so are they! May this truth assist us in forgiving others.

An Ancient Portrait

Let's now take a look at the story of the Prodigal Son. This tale can also be viewed from the perspective of the older brother to gain some insight into why Christians do not forgive their brothers and sisters in the light of the last two principles mentioned. In Luke 15, the older brother was unwilling to forgive his younger brother after he repented. Let's pick up the story when the son returns and the banquet to celebrate began.

Additional Notes: This is much like believers who are unwilling to forgive their spiritual brothers and sisters after they have repented. The first part of the story is not dealt with here but here is a short summary. The younger brother had humiliated his father and whole family by demanding his inheritance early. He took the entire one-third of all that the father had and squandered it on wild living. When the money ran out and a severe famine hit the land, his brother hit rock-bottom. When he found himself longing for the food the pigs were eating, he finally came to his senses. So, in deep repentance and humility, the younger brother returned home. He merely hoped that his father would forgive him enough to allow him to be a day-laborer until he paid back all he had lost. Instead, their father met him outside of town and completely forgave him. Then, he experienced the full love and blessing of his father. As if that were not enough, the father celebrated the son's return to the family by killing a fattened calf. The father served it during a special feast to which the whole town was invited.

The son arrived at the house after a day's work in the field managing the estate. Suddenly, he heard music and dancing which meant people were celebrating something inside his home. There were no servants around. The outside of the estate was empty. All of them were serving the guests. He was standing there completely alone wondering what in the world was going on. He called over one of the boys who were playing outside, since the adults were celebrating, to find out what was happening.

He was the eldest son and should have been presiding over any celebration. Now, he had been reduced to someone asking children what was going on. They explained that his youngest brother had come back, and his father had killed a fattened calf. He may have thought to himself in disbelief, "What? That is impossible? That no good brother of mine is getting the greatest celebration any family can have? I have been faithful to my father all along and I have nothing!"

Then the boys explained further. His father had received his younger brother back safe and sound. The Greek words utilized actually emphasize the father's response to his son's return. The son had been received back in peace and with full restoration. This made the older brother very angry! So, the son absolutely refused to go into his own home! When dad found out, he came running out. What a great, warm, and loving father he was! He would not let the older son stay outside and wallow in his own anger, bitterness, and stubbornness. He pursued the older son in his sin as he did the younger in his. In his love, grace, and mercy, the father pleaded with the older son to come inside and celebrate the return of his dear younger brother. They were all a family again!

HEALING RELATIONSHIPS THROUGH FORGIVENESS

The older son could only think about himself. Instead, He rebuked his merciful father and described how he himself had served his father many years. He had never disobeyed him. The older son had never even been given a young goat, so he could celebrate with his own friends. This response is loaded with meaning. He turned this all around and made it all about him. Why was his father not concerned about his feelings? He had continually served and obeyed him. In his possessions and property, the older son had reduced his relationship with his father to nothing more than servitude and obedience.

He ignored the return of his younger brother and did not even appeal to the father's love for him. Why didn't he say, "Father, we love each other, why haven't you given me a celebration?" Why not even an appeal to love, however weak it would have been? Why? There was no relationship there in the first place. Notice, he tells his father that he has never even had a celebration with his friends, not his family. His buddies were all that mattered to him. He did not seem to care about his father or brother at all.

What a blow to the father! Neither of the two was worth anything to him. Then the older brother lets us in on a little secret. He was keeping tabs on his younger brother all along. He revealed the prostitution his little brother had indulged in and then asked his father why he would give his brother a celebration with a fattened calf. He threw his little brother's squandering of the father's goods into his face and still he was restored. The older son tried to rile his father up and turn his warm heart from compassion to bitterness. There was nothing but accusations.

Not once, did the older son ask how his younger brother was or even if he had repented. The father did not even explain himself. The father simply told him that he had always been with him, and all of his property was his. Then he explained that his little brother had been dead and was now alive; that is, his younger brother was dead to the family and was back. He was lost but now was found. The son was concentrating on the loss of their possessions and property, but his father was focusing on the restoration of their relationships and the rebuilding of their family.

Jesus told this story to point out that the Pharisees (older brother) had hard hearts toward God, our Father. They were concerned only about righteous works and outward religion, pomp, and circumstance. God is concerned about repentance and His gracious forgiveness. They did not truly have an inward, spiritual relationship with God but only an outward temporal relationship. For our purposes, let us focus on the older brother who was unwilling to forgive the younger one.

Additional Notes: The older brother was selfish. The Bible speaks against this sin:

Psalm 119:36
Turn my heart toward your statutes, not toward selfish gain.

Romans 2:8
But to those who are self-seeking, and don't obey the truth, but obey unrighteousness, will be wrath and indignation.

2 Timothy 3:2
For men will be lovers of self, lovers of money, boastful, arrogant, blasphemers, disobedient to parents, unthankful, unholy.

Titus 1:7
For the overseer must be blameless, as God's steward; not self-pleasing, not easily angered, not given to wine, not violent, not greedy for dishonest gain.

HEALING RELATIONSHIPS THROUGH FORGIVENESS

James 3:14
But if you have bitter jealousy and selfish ambition in your heart, don't boast and don't lie against the truth.

First, he was unwilling to forgive because he had never himself asked his father for forgiveness. Why? He thought he had never done anything wrong. He told the father he had never disobeyed him or ever failed to serve him. That is impossible. Since the older son had never gone to his father and begged for mercy, how could he in anyway understand how his father could show mercy to his brother? When we are not continually going before God with our sins begging for his mercy, then it is harder to show mercy to others.

How can we forgive when forgiven, if we think we do not need forgiveness? Those believers who think they are always right and have all of the answers have a tremendous difficulty forgiving the other person in a relationship. If this occurs, God will discipline that person to fully understand what a sinner he or she is.

Second, he would not recognize that his father who was the foremost person transgressed had already forgiven him. The primary person in that family was the father; if he could forgive, then so could all the other family members. The foremost person transgressed in a sin against us is God. If He can forgive them, so can we. When a brother or sister transgresses us, we need to acknowledge that our Father has already forgiven that very transgression on the cross of Jesus Christ. We must view the situation from the perspective of God, not from our perspective. The older brother refused to view the situation from his father's perspective so he would not forgive him.

Third, the older son was looking only at what he had lost. He was focusing on the transgressions against him. As a result, he kept churning the sins over and over again. When his little brother had finally repented, he could not see past the sins. He could not comprehend what would possibly be gained. He could not see that he would gain his little brother back. Yet, this is exactly what the father saw. He looked past the physical and material to the relational. To find the right perspective, we must look beyond the temporal things to the deeper spiritual reality. Since the Lord God had forgiven them already, we must also forgive others.

A Modern Anecdote

One of my counselees grew up with a mother who had a serious alcohol problem. Since his father had passed away when he was about six, his mother did not take it very well. Alcohol was her drug of choice whenever, which was often, she felt overwhelmed by the kids (six of them), her job, the bills, and loneliness. Many times, after a drinking bout, his mother would arrive home and leave their front door wide open. When he awoke to use the restroom, he would see the front door open and think someone was breaking into the house. Other times, she would forget to buy food, and the kids would have to take whatever was in the house and turn it into school lunches. Sometimes, this meant a large piece of cheese or a small cereal box.

Additional Notes: If asked about the Bible's teaching on alcohol, consider these principles:

God allows drinking, but not drunkenness.

Romans 13:13
Let us walk properly...in the day; not in reveling and drunkenness, not in sexual promiscuity and lustful acts, and not in strife and jealousy.

HEALING RELATIONSHIPS THROUGH FORGIVENESS

Ephesians 5:18
Don't be drunken with wine, in which is dissipation, but be filled with the Spirit.

Christians are not to associate with drunken saints or unbelievers.

1 Corinthians 5:11
But as it is, I wrote to you not to associate with anyone who is called a brother who is a sexual sinner, or covetous, or an idolater, or a slanderer, or a drunkard, or an extortionist. Don't...eat with such a person.

Proverbs 23:20
Don't be among ones drinking too much wine, or those who gorge themselves on meat.

Drunkenness is destructive, impairs ones functioning, and causes one to sin.

Genesis 9:21
He [Noah] drank of the wine and got drunk. He was uncovered within his tent.

Lamentations 4:21
Rejoice and be glad, daughter of Edom, that dwell in the land of Uz: the cup shall pass through to you also; you shall be drunken, and shall make yourself naked [drunkenness can make people uninhibited which leads to sin].

Jeremiah 48:26
Make him drunken; for he magnified himself against Yahweh: and Moab shall wallow in his vomit, and he also shall be in derision. (Drunkenness makes you sick].

Proverbs 26:9
Like a thorn bush...goes into the hand of a drunkard, so is a parable

in the mouth of fools [Drunkenness can inhibit your mechanism for feeling pain and can cause injuries to worsen].

There were several incidences where his mother would fall and injure herself, and he would bandage her up. Then, he would fall asleep fearing she would bleed to death during the night. As he got older, the problem just worsened. Often, she would fall asleep on the couch with a lit cigarette in her hand. He would take turns with his other siblings to stay up late and watch her until she had fallen asleep drunk. Then, he would quietly take the cigarette and put it out to prevent the house from burning down. She spent much of the small amount of money they had on liquor and could not pay the bills. When bill collectors came around, they (the children present at the time) would hide behind the couch. This way the person would think no one was home. When he would talk to her about many of these events, she would respond with a long diatribe about the woes of a single parent who was doing the best that she possibly could. At nineteen, the mother finally entered a rehab program and sobered up.

After he had grown up and had his own family, he visited his mother on either Thanksgiving or Christmas every year. Besides this time, he never called her or invited her to any of his children's events and activities. When his last child was close to graduating from college, she casually said to him, "How come you never invited me to any of my grandkid's functions when they were growing up?" This startled him. He could not respond because he did have an answer. For several months, he pondered that question, "Why hadn't he invited her to his children's activities?" He had spent every summer traveling to see his siblings but never his mother.

One day it dawned on him that he had completely walled her off from his heart. He had not invited her because there was no real relationship. He had no feelings for his mother.

In fact, he was angry and bitter and had never forgiven her for what she had done. He had punished her unknowingly by not allowing her into his life or the lives of his children. Then, he decided that she deserved it, and that was that. A year later, the woman came to Christ. In the first year of her salvation, his sister gently confronted His mother concerning all of the problems that she had caused in their growing up years. She told her that she deeply regretted what happened and asked his sister for forgiveness. He decided if she called to reconcile, he would refuse to speak to her or even see her. The pain was too deep and the scares too numerous.

What could he do to break this anger and bitterness that had a death grip upon him before his mother called, so he could forgive her? I explained to him all that we have just studied in this chapter. First, he should compare the sins his mother had committed against him with the sins he had committed against God. God had forgiven Him and desired him to forgive His mother. Secondly, he must recognize that she had sinned against God first as she was sinning against him. God had already forgiven her for what she had done to him on the cross of His Beloved Son. He needed to ask the Holy Spirit to help him grasp these important truths so he could fully forgive her. After much prayer over several days, he was able to open his mind and heart to these truths and forgive her for the sins she had committed against him, as His Lord had already done on the cross.

A Personal Response

Dear Heavenly Father,

I have been harboring a grudge against a fellow brother (sister) in Christ. I have been so angry because (add name) sinned against me by (describe sin). Yet, I know that when your Son died on the cross, He died for that sin also. I realize that you have already forgiven the sin and expect me to do the same. Please give me the wisdom to know whether I should also set up a boundary or provide a consequence for this transgression to help (add name) learn not to continue this sin. I am very sorry for transgressing your righteous law. Help me to honor and glorify you in my relationship with (add name) and follow your Word. I pray this in the name of Jesus. Amen.

Instructor's Notes

AN INSTRUCTOR'S MANUAL

Chapter 2

Forgive the Forgiven

When Christians struggle with forgiving other Christians who have hurt them, they should remember that God has already forgiven those very sins on the cross.

In the section, "A Typical Scenario," the author describes an angry encounter between friends which needed restoration.

What is the scenario about?

A Christian loaned a valuable magazine to a friend and his two-year-old tore it.

What did the conflict concern?

This was not the only time he had loaned his friend something and it was returned damaged.

What was the relationship between the parties?

They were friends.

Have you had a similar experience?

(Various answers should be shared including yours.)

HEALING RELATIONSHIPS THROUGH FORGIVENESS

In the section, "A Scriptural Principle" the author presents an important biblical principle in the forgiveness process which concerns forgiving the forgiven.

How would you express this principle in your own words?

The second principle is "we must know that believers who transgress us are already forgiven for their sins."

(Various answers should be shared including yours.)

How would you rewrite this principle to make it even more personal to your life (using your name and situation)?

(Various answers should be shared including yours.)

Why do you think this principle might be important in your life right now?

(Various answers should be shared including yours.)

How would you rate yourself on the percentage of times you followed this principle in the past when you did something wrong in a relationship?

(Various answers should be shared including yours.)

Directions: Put a horizontal mark and your name where you see yourself on the percentage line.

0%   25%   50%   75%   100%

AN INSTRUCTOR'S MANUAL

In the section, "A Biblical Explanation," the author explains the many reasons why we are to forgive believers who have already been forgiven by God and how to do it.

How does the Lord God's forgiveness of our sins pertain to his forgiveness of other sins against us?

One of the primary reasons we are to forgive is that they are already forgiven by our God. They transgressed against Him first. Yet, God had enough grace, mercy, and love to forgive them and so should we.

According to Luke 17:3-4, is there a limit on the number of times we should forgive?

In Luke 17:3-4, Jesus teaches, "Be careful. If your brother sins against you, rebuke him. If he repents, forgive him."

According to Matthew 26:28, what does the blood of Christ do to the sins that are committed against us by believers?

The blood of Christ was not simply poured out for us and the sins we commit against others but also poured out for others and the sins they commit against us. What an amazing change in perspective.

According to 1 Timothy 1:15-17, how was Paul, the apostle, the Lord's classical example of forgiveness?

Paul had put the church through a terrible persecution but was forgiven.

Why was it so difficult for Paul to be forgiven and accepted by Christians?

The Christians who had loved ones injured or killed because of Paul had to accept him into the church. They had to forgive his atrocities against them and the ones they loved the most. That must have been tough. As we can so clearly see, all of these passages include our forgiveness when we sin against others.

In what ways might these truths impact your relationships?

(Various answers should be shared including yours.)

In the section, "An Ancient Portrait," the author describes the parable of the Prodigal Son from the perspective of the older brother who did not want to forgive.

How did the father show the younger brother his love and forgiveness when he returned?

They explained that his youngest brother had come back, and his father had killed a fattened calf. He may have thought to himself in disbelief, "What? That is impossible? That no good brother of mine is getting the greatest celebration any family can have? I have been faithful to my father all along and I have nothing!"

Then the boys explained further. His father had received his younger brother back safe and sound. The Greek words utilized actually emphasize the father's response to his son's return. The son had been received back in peace and with full restoration. This made the older brother very angry! So, the son absolutely refused to go into his own home! When dad found out, he came running out.

How did the older brother want the father to demonstrate his love to him?

The older son could only think about himself. Instead, He rebuked his merciful father and described how he himself had served his father many years. He had never disobeyed him. The older son had never even been given a young goat, so he could celebrate with his own friends. This response is loaded with meaning. He turned this all around and made it all about him.

Do you think the older brother loved his father and younger brother and how do you know?

He had continually served and obeyed him. In his possessions and property, the older son had reduced his relationship with his father to nothing more than servitude and obedience.

He ignored the return of his younger brother and did not even appeal to the father's love for him.

Notice, he tells his father that he has never even had a celebration with his friends, not his family. His buddies were all that mattered to him. He did not seem to care about his father or brother at all.

What did the older brother want the father to do to the younger brother instead?

He revealed the prostitution his little brother had indulged in and then asked his father why he would give his brother a celebration with a fattened calf. He threw his little brother's squandering of the father's goods into his face and still he was restored. The older son tried to rile his father up and turn his warm heart from compassion to bitterness. There was nothing but accusations.

Not once, did the older son ask how his younger brother was or even if he had repented.

What were the three reasons why the older brother would not forgive the younger brother for what he had done?

First, he was unwilling to forgive because he had never himself asked his father for forgiveness. Why? He thought he had never done anything wrong. He told the father he had never disobeyed him or ever failed to serve him.

Second, he would not recognize that his father who was the foremost person transgressed had already forgiven him. The primary person in that family was the father, if he could ultimately forgive then so could the other family members.

Third, the older son was looking only at what he had lost. He was focusing on the transgressions against him. As a result, he kept churning the sins over and over again.

Have you ever been in a situation comparable to the older brother who had difficulty forgiving or the father who had to handle it? How was it different and how was it the same?

(Various answers should be shared including yours.)

HEALING RELATIONSHIPS THROUGH FORGIVENESS

In the section, "A Modern Anecdote," the author explains a son's struggle to forgive his mother who had come to Christ.

What were the three ways in which the mother traumatized the young man and his siblings growing up?

Many times, after a drinking bout, his mother would arrive home and leave their front door wide open.

Other times, she would forget to buy food, and the kids would have to take whatever was in the house and turn it into school lunches. Sometimes, this meant a large piece of cheese or a small cereal box.

How did the man attempt to help his mother as a child?

There were several incidences where his mother would fall and injure herself, and he would bandage her up.

He would take turns with his other siblings to stay up late and watch her until she had fallen asleep drunk.

When bill collectors came around, they (the children present at the time) would hide behind the couch. This way the person would think no one was home.

How did the man deal with his mother once he had become an adult?

After he had grown up and had his own family, he visited his mother on either Thanksgiving or Christmas every year. Besides this time, he never called her or invited her to any of his children's events and activities. When his last child was close to graduating from college, she casually said to him, "How come you never invited me to any of my grandkid's functions when they were growing up?"

AN INSTRUCTOR'S MANUAL

When the mother came to Christ, why did the man still have difficulty forgiving her?

She told her that she deeply regretted what happened and asked his sister for forgiveness. He decided if she called to reconcile, he would refuse to speak to her or even see her. The pain was too deep and the scares too numerous.

What could he do to break this anger and bitterness that had a death grip upon him before his mother called, so he could forgive her? *I explained to him all that we have just studied in this chapter.*

What was biblical truth that caused the man to change his mind and finally forgive his mother for what she done?

First, he should compare the sins his mother had committed against him with the sins he had committed against God.

God had forgiven Him and desired him to forgive His mother.

Based on the truths learned in this chapter, what would you have done differently if you were the mother who neglected her children or the man who was neglected?

(Various answers should be shared including yours.)

HEALING RELATIONSHIPS THROUGH FORGIVENESS

In the section, "A Personal Response," the author provides a model you may use for prayer if you find it necessary after discovering the truths in this chapter.

Are you presently in a relationship where you have sinned against another and have not asked God for forgiveness? If not, is there one from the past that still needs this prayer to be prayed?

(Various answers should be shared including yours.)

Based on the truths you have just learned, what will you continue doing in your current relationships and what will you do differently?

(Various answers should be shared including yours.)

What additional thoughts would you like to share with the others?

(Various answers should be shared including yours.)

Chapter 3

Forgive the Lost

When people have transgressed us, sometimes it becomes difficult to forgive them. It may take some time. People can do some hurtful and destructive things to us, and we might get stuck in bitterness because we are unwilling to forgive. A way we can get "unstuck" is to consider all the sins we have committed against God. Once we realize that Jesus made no distinctions in forgiving us when we received His Son, it will be easier to make no distinctions ourselves. Why? God did not refuse to forgive us because of who we were or because of the gravity or extent of our sins. So, we are to do the same to others. If those who transgressed us are believers and we are struggling with forgiveness, here is another approach. We must consider this truth: whatever they may have done to us has already been forgiven on the cross. How can we not forgive what God has already forgiven? Regarding those who are unbelievers, we must view them much differently to get unstuck from bitterness. Rather than considering them as just wicked people who deserve punishment, we should see them as lost and desperately in need of salvation. This will be the topic of discussion in this chapter.

A Typical Scenario

Have you ever had or heard of someone looking out the window of his home and having the following conversation with his wife? He says, "Honey, you've got to come and see this! Do you remember that young guy down the street who we shared the gospel with the other day? The neighbor three doors down? The guy that told us he wasn't interested. He has two large garbage bags filled with glass bottles tied to his bike and ran into our car. The bags just broke right in front of our driveway. I can't believe this! Now, there's glass all over the street and a dent in the car. He's trying to pick up the pieces with his bare hands. Those pieces are way too small! Is he crazy? What a fool! Oh, he's going to pay, all right! There will be no forgiveness here! Honey!? What are you doing? Where are you going with that broom?"

This man had been caught in the act of being shamed by his forgiving wife. All he could think about was himself. His wife thought about the neighbor. The man saw his neighbor as a wicked man in need of judgment, and his wife saw him as lost in need of salvation. She ran out to demonstrate the love and compassion of Christ. The husband did not want to forgive him, but his gracious wife already had! This attitude sometimes takes ahold of us. Unbelievers hurt us in some way, and we do not want to forgive them. Then someone like this wife is able to. How does that happen? How could she show such forgiveness and we struggle with it? It simply has to do with perspective. She saw him as lost, not wicked.

A Scriptural Principle

Now we come to the next principle. The third principle is "we must view unbelievers as lost to forgive." This means we should view those who transgress us with the eyes and heart of God. In order to forgive unbelievers for hurting us, we must first see them differently. We must have the divine perspective of our Father in heaven. At this time in salvation history, God sees all unbelievers as lost and seeks to save them in His compassion. On the great Day of Judgment, the Lord God will see them as wicked and seek to punish them in His Holy Wrath. This is an such an important distinction that is well worth discussing.

A Biblical Explanation

We know people should be forgiven for everything they have done against us. The Lord Jesus makes no distinction in their beliefs or relationship to Him. In Matthew 6:12, during the Sermon on the Mount, Jesus declared that our prayers should end with "forgive us our debts, as we also forgive our debtors." In Mark 11:25, He told His disciples, "Whenever you stand praying, forgive, if you have anything against anyone." In Luke 11:4, the Lord stated clearly what the prayers of His people should entail, "Forgive us our sins, for we ourselves also forgive everyone who is indebted to us." There is no distinction between believers and unbelievers. Jesus uses the critical words "debtors," "anyone," "everyone." Forgiveness is extended to all.

This is sometimes easier said than done. Sometimes, we Christians may get stuck in bitterness and be unwilling to forgive. Perhaps, the hurt is so deep inside we cannot seem to get past the hurt. We may become terribly angry and wish harm upon those who hurt us, especially if they do not know the Lord. To overcome this difficulty, Christians must begin to think differently about those who do not know Jesus. When an unbeliever is viewed as a wicked, evil sinner, then it is easy to be bitter and angry. It is simple to curse them into the fire of hell without mercy. This is what happened with James and John, two of the twelve disciples of Jesus.

In Luke 9:51-56, the Lord was on His way to Jerusalem for the final Passover and His ultimate death. He sent some of His disciples into a Samaritan village to obtain lodging. The citizens of the city refused. They hated the Jews and their feasts and Jesus was a Jew on His way to a feast. As far as they were concerned, this Rabbi was not staying the night in their town. When James and John heard of it, they asked the Lord if they could command fire from heaven to consume the town. The disciples were upset and desired judgment on these unrighteous people. Jesus rebuked them explaining that "He had not come to destroy men's lives, but to save them." When Christ came the first time to earth, He came to save the lost. The second time, He will arrive to judge the wicked. The first time, He views them as lost and desires to save them. The second time, He will have given them all the time they needed to repent, and they did not. Then, He will focus on them as wicked and desire to judge them.

In Luke 19:10, the Lord declared His desire, "For the Son of Man came to seek and to save that which was lost." Jesus spoke of unbelievers, especially Israel, as lost sheep, a lost coin, and a lost son. He viewed unbelievers as lost. We are to view them similarly. We might be in various relationships with unbelievers. At times, they may sin against us. When this happens, to help us in the forgiveness process, we must see them as lost. What does it mean to say the unsaved are lost? When someone is lost, they do not know where they are or where they are going. They cannot find their way. In many places in the New Testament, people are described by the inspired writers in their unbelieving state. For example, in Ephesians 2:1-4, Paul describes the unsaved as being dead in sin and sons of disobedience. He portrays them as living in the lusts of their flesh and walking according to the course of this world. He characterizes them as ruled by the prince of the power of the air and servants of Satan.

In Ephesians 4:17-19, he continues by describing these lost souls as being completely futile in their mind, darkened in their understanding, excluded from the life of God, ignorant, hard of heart, callous, and given over to sensuality and the practice of every kind of impurity with greediness. In 1 John 2:11, John paints a picture of the unsaved lost as walking in the darkness, not knowing where they are going because the darkness has blinded their eyes. They are stumbling around in the darkness of their own sin and wickedness and the lies and falsehoods of the Devil. When we are in relationships with unbelievers, we must understand that they are totally lost. They have no life in God (Romans 6:13), no Holy Spirit inside of them (1 Corinthians 6:19), and no Lord Jesus Christ to follow (Mark 9:41). These poor people have no spiritual power to change (Philippians 2:12-13), no desire to be holy or righteous (1 Peter 4:3), and have centered their lives on themselves (2 Timothy 3:2). The lost live by the impulses of their flesh. They don't get it, but we do! They are lost.

Additional Notes: If asked about the spiritual state or condition of unbelievers, here are the Bible references I cite:

Ephesians 2:1-4
You were made alive when you were dead in transgressions and sins, in which you once walked according to the course of this world, according to the prince of the power of the air, the spirit who now works in the children of disobedience; among whom we also all once lived in the lust of our flesh, doing the desires of the flesh and of the mind, and were by nature children of wrath, even as the rest. But God, being rich in mercy, for his great love with which he loved us.

Ephesians 4:17-19
This I say therefore, and testify in the Lord, that you no longer walk as the rest of the Gentiles also walk, in the futility of their mind, being darkened in their understanding, alienated from the life of God, because of the ignorance that is in them, because of the hardening of their hearts...having become callous gave themselves up to lust, to work all uncleanness with greediness.

1 John 2:11
But he who hates his brother is in the darkness, and walks in the darkness...doesn't know where he is going, because the darkness has blinded his eyes.

HEALING RELATIONSHIPS THROUGH FORGIVENESS

Romans 6:13
Also, do not present your [bodily] members to sin as instruments of unrighteousness, but present yourselves to God, as alive from the dead, and your members as instruments of righteousness to God.

1 Corinthians 6:19
Or don't you know that your body is a temple of the Holy Spirit which is in you, which you have from God? You are not your own.

Mark 9:41
For whoever will give you...water to drink in my name, because you are Christ's, most certainly I tell you, he will in no way lose his reward.

Philippians 2:12-13
So then, my beloved, even as you have always obeyed, not only in my presence, but now much more in my absence, work out your own salvation with fear and trembling. For it is God who works in you both to will and to work, for his good pleasure.

1 Peter 4:3
For we have spent enough of our past time doing the desire of the Gentiles, and having walked in lewdness, lusts, drunken binges, orgies, carousings, and abominable idolatries.

2 Timothy 3:2
For men will be lovers of self, lovers of money, boastful, arrogant, blasphemers, disobedient to parents, unthankful, unholy.

So, if we have a relationship with an unbeliever, why do we expect them to constantly behave like us? Why don't we anticipate them to act lost? Often times, our expectations are too high which makes us even more bitter and angry. You may say, "Aren't they also responsible for their actions?" Of course they are. If they do not come to Christ, they will be judged for every single unkind word or action they commit toward us. They desperately need Christ. Don't they? We could constantly condemn these people as truly wicked and wallow in our anger and bitterness. Or we can share Christ with them and continue in prayer for them. This does not excuse any of their actions toward us, nor the consequences for them. It does not mean they may treat us poorly. This simply has to do with our heart's forgiveness of them.

In Luke 23:34, the Lord Jesus was hanging on the cross, dripping with blood from the crown of thorns and the nails in his hands and feet. In His pain and humiliation, as He was slowly dying, He cried to His Father. For what? He asked Him to forgive His persecutors because they did not know what they were doing. He saw all of these people in the light of their lostness. They were dead, hard, calloused, and blind, but, most of all, ignorant. The Romans, who were doing the dirty work the Jews could not do, did not realize that they were crucifying the King of Kings. This crowd of Jews who were standing around the cross throwing insults and curses at Him did not understand this was their own Messiah. The frightened disciples, who had hidden from the mob, did not fully comprehend that as His death was at hand, so was His forgiveness of all on the cross. From His death would come the resurrection to a new life in Him. Even many of these rulers, who were caught up in their religious self-righteous pride, did not perceive that a new covenant in His blood had come. They did not see that a new and final priest was now making a final sacrifice for the sins of all men.

In the midst of this horrible chaos, Christ knowing all of this, looked down at their lostness and cried out for the Father's forgiveness. This obviously implies the Lord's own forgiveness in His humanity. Christians know through their understanding of the Scriptures that this prayer could only be fulfilled if all of these lost people received the soon to be risen Son of God as Savior and Lord. Yet, implied in the merciful cry to His Holy Father, is a God who became truly man, and as a man forgave His persecutors, tormentors, and scoffers. How could He do that? How could He keep from becoming bitter and angry, refusing to forgive? He saw them as lost!

In Acts 7:54-60, When Stephen preached before the Jewish council, he indicted them for their sin. They responded by rushing him, dragging him out of the city, and stoning him to death. He kneeled down, and cried loudly, "Lord, don't hold this sin against them!" Then he passed away. In his final words, Stephen took up Christ's compassionate mantle and begged his God for their forgiveness. Why? They were so utterly lost and blind. Once again, forgiveness from God must be obtained through and only through His Son. Once again, implicit in his words is his own forgiveness of these killers. Stephen was willing to forgive them because he saw them as lost. This sense of lostness brings deep compassion. The Lord God has a heart for the unsaved and Christians are to possess the same heart and compassion for all those they know who are not believers.

In 2 Peter 3:9, the apostle wrote in light of those who were scoffing that Christ had not yet come, "The Lord is not slow concerning his promise, as some count slowness; but is patient with us, not wishing that any should perish, but that all should come to repentance." The apostle asserts that God is holding off His judgment day for the wicked in order to allow more lost people into His kingdom. Why does God do this? He has great mercy and compassion. This is God's time to pour forth His love, grace, and mercy. This is our time to pour forth our love, grace, and mercy. There will be a time for judgment upon the wicked (Hebrews 9:27), and in some way we will have a place as judges (1 Corinthians 6:1-4), but it is not now. This is the day of salvation, a time to forgive.

In Matthew 5:43-48, Jesus corrects the mistaken notion that one should love his neighbor but hate his enemy. The Jewish leaders taught that one should love his neighbor until he transgresses him, then he could hate him. Instead, our Lord commands us to love our enemies because we are sons of a Father who loves His enemies. We are to love, bless, pray, do good to, and meet the needs of those who hurt us. Why? God loves them and does the same. He causes the sun to rise and the rain to fall on the righteous and unrighteous. God looked down upon the world, saw so many lost people, felt compassion for them, and then sent His only Son to die for them (1 Peter 1:3). Remember, we were lost when Christ died for us! We needed someone to view us as lost, so we could hear the gospel message and receive Christ as Savior and Lord. Only then, could we find real forgiveness through Him. Can we even imagine if the person designated by the Lord to bring the gospel to us, looked at us, was appalled at our wickedness and sin, and then turned away?

An Ancient Portrait

This is what happened when Jonah viewed the people of Nineveh. In the book of Jonah, God had told him to go and preach to them; instead, he was repulsed and fled. He did not want them to be forgiven. They deserved judgment and he was going to make sure they got it. Why?

Additional Notes: The last thing he wanted was to see them receive the compassion of God and be saved. Why? The city of Nineveh was the capital of Assyria and infamous for its cruelty. Moses explains that the city of Nineveh was built by Nimrod who also founded Babel.

HEALING RELATIONSHIPS THROUGH FORGIVENESS

Genesis 10:6-12
The sons of Ham were: Cush, Mizraim, Put, and Canaan. The sons of Cush were: Seba, Havilah, Sabtah, Raamah, and Sabteca. The sons of Raamah were: Sheba and Dedan. Cush became the father of Nimrod. He began to be a mighty one in the earth. He was a mighty hunter before Yahweh. Therefore it is said, "like Nimrod, a mighty hunter before Yahweh". The beginning of his kingdom was Babel, Erech, Accad, and Calneh, in the land of Shinar. Out of that land he went into Assyria, and built Nineveh, Rehoboth Ir, Calah, and Resen between Nineveh and the great city Calah.

It was perhaps the largest city in the ancient world. Here are some references which indicate this:

Jonah 1:2
Arise, go to Nineveh, that great city, and preach against it, for their wickedness has come up before me.

Jonah 3:
Arise, go to Nineveh, that great city, and preach to it the message that I give you.

Jonah 3:3
So Jonah arose, and went to Nineveh, according to Yahweh's word. Now Nineveh was an exceedingly great city, three days' journey across.

Jonah 3:4
Jonah began to enter into the city a day's journey, and he cried out, and said, "In forty days, Nineveh will be overthrown!"

Jonah 3:5
The people of Nineveh believed God; and they proclaimed a fast, and put on sackcloth, from their greatest even to their least.

Jonah 3:6
The news reached the king of Nineveh, and he arose from his throne, and took off his royal robe, covered himself with sackcloth, and sat in ashes.

Jonah 3:7
He made a proclamation and published through Nineveh by the decree of the king and his nobles, saying, "Let neither man nor animal, herd nor flock, taste anything; let them not feed, nor drink water.

Jonah 4:11
Shouldn't I be concerned for Nineveh, that great city, in which are more than one hundred twenty thousand...who can't discern between their right hand...their left hand; and also much livestock?

Nimrod was most likely the leader of the revolt at Babel where the multitude refused to scatter over the earth and instead wanted to stay together and make a name (national name), a city (capitol city, and a tower (false religion) for themselves. This caused God to scatter them according to Moses.

Genesis 11:4
They said, "Come, let's build ourselves a city, and a tower whose top reaches to the sky, and let's make a name for ourselves, lest we be scattered abroad on the surface of the whole earth."

These people were terribly wicked.

Additional Notes: Read what Nahum said about these terrifying and barbarous people.

Nahum 3:1-3
Woe to the bloody city! It is all full of lies and robbery. The prey doesn't depart. This city was so vile that they saw their prey [the innocent] as almost limitless....Nahum described the sounds of their sins as never ceasing, "The noise of the whip, the noise of the

rattling of wheels, prancing horses, and bounding chariots, the horseman mounting." Then he spoke of the lights of their terror, *"And the flashing sword...glittering spear."* Lastly, he concluded with a portrayal of death everywhere, *"And a multitude of slain, and a great heap of corpses, and there is no end of the bodies. They stumble on their bodies.*

Yet, the Lord saw them as lost and desired to give them grace.

Additional Notes: These people were butchers and slaughterers of innocent people. Yet, God saw them as lost and desired to give them grace. Jonah knew God was merciful and did not want them to be forgiven. He wanted them punished for their atrocities. Then God commanded Jonah to travel to the city of Nineveh and preach against the city.

Then God commanded Jonah to travel to the city of Nineveh and preach against the city.

Additional Notes: This prophet was to tell them that the true God of Israel had seen their sin and wickedness and was displeased. The people were to immediately repent and believe in the only true God of Israel. If they did not, He would judge them by destroying their city and everything in it. Though this might not sound like much of a message of mercy and compassion for the lost, it absolutely is. Forgiveness cannot come without someone's recognition of his sin with repentance and belief following. Jonah's response was quick and straight-forward; he ran from the Lord and this command.

So, Jonah boarded a ship at [the city of] Joppa that was headed for Tarshish. This city was about as far away from Nineveh as one could get at the time. I am sure that Jonah had hoped God would give up on him since he was too far away.

While on his sea voyage, the Lord sent a great storm. This put the ship on the verge of breaking apart. The ship's crew started throwing the cargo overboard to lighten the ship's load. Then they cried out to their gods for help. While all this commotion was happening, where was the prophet? Jonah was asleep below in the cargo area. How could Jonah be fast asleep? Why wasn't he afraid? Most likely, the prophet knew God may punish him, and frankly he did not care. He would rather die than go to that evil city! Though he was calm in his resolve, the captain of the ship was not. The captain came down and screamed at him. He told him to wake up and call on his God to save them. He refused to do it. Then they cast lots to see which crew member or passenger had caused this storm? The lot fell on Jonah. They demanded him to explain who he was and what he had done. Can you imagine the tension in the crew as they stood there with this stranger that was causing all this havoc?

Jonah declared that he was a Hebrew who feared the God of heaven and earth. He immediately explained that he was a believer in the true God. Then he told them he was on the run from God because he didn't want to obey His command. They must have known right then that this man was special. He wasn't any ordinary Jew, and he wasn't disobeying any ordinary command. Something was seriously wrong. Then, they begged him to explain what the crew could do to calm the storm. I am sure they expected him to repent and offer something to "his god." This was a storm that was about to destroy them all. Even they knew this should be done. Jonah probably startled them by his calm and almost ridiculous response. He told them to throw him overboard. It was his fault and he needed to go. Why didn't Jonah simply repent? God would have calmed the sea, and he could have shared the gospel with this amazing backdrop of God's power and grace.

The prophet could only think about those dirty, wicked, evil Ninevites. Nothing else mattered. The Ninevites were not going to be forgiven if he could help it, even if it cost him his life. Though unbelievers, the crew did not have the heart to follow his advice and throw him overboard. Instead, they tried furiously to row the boat to shore. This was a vain and useless attempt, but they could not kill him. The storm only got worse! So, they begged the Lord God not to hold what they were about to do against them and threw Jonah into the sea. Immediately the storm ceased.

Additional Notes: We cannot be sure that they now believed in the true God, but they certainly did some things that made it appear that way. The author described the men as fearing God, offering sacrifices to God, and making vows of obedience to God. Notice, they did this after the storm, not during it. The sea was calm and there was no need for some desperate attempt to appease a god they did not believe in.

This rebellious prophet Jonah could have been used to bring many on that ship to the true God even though he was disobeying Him at the time. God will use us in spite of ourselves. He is sovereign and will even use our mistakes to bring others to Him. He cannot be stopped!

Now Jonah was flailing and thrashing about in his own stubbornness in the ocean all alone. The Lord could have left him there to die, but that has never been God's way.

He showed Jonah the forgiveness Jonah did not want the Ninevites to receive. God sent a great fish to swallow him. He was in the stomach of that fish for three days and three nights. While trapped there, Jonah began to reflect on what just happened. He remembered that he been in the depths of the ocean, the currents had engulfed him, and the waves of the ocean were passing over his body. At the same time, the weeds had wrapped around his head, and he had come to the edge of life and death. In that moment, he had felt far from the presence of the Lord. He knew he was exactly where he had desired to be. He was away from the Lord. Unfortunately, it was not what he had expected. It never is. As he was about to lose all consciousness, he turned back to his God and cried out in anguish with a desperate prayer for mercy.

He was literally lost in his own sin and stubbornness. Haven't we all been there before? He desperately needed some compassion from God, and Jonah was begging for His forgiveness. Though these Ninevites were lost also in their stubbornness and sin, Jonah hadn't thought that they might deserve either. Perhaps, the time had come to rethink this obvious contradiction. After having been swallowed up in the depths of the sea by a huge creature, he remained in its belly for three days and nights. It was here that Jonah began to ponder these amazing things. Then, he repented and thanked God for his gracious rescue.

When Jonah had finally submitted to the Lord God and decided to obey Him, God commanded the fish to vomit Jonah onto the shore. It was time to go to Nineveh. Again, the Lord issued His command to Jonah: preach to the city of Nineveh. These Ninevites were lost, and God wanted them found. So, Jonah arose and went to the city. Then, he walked from one end of it to the other proclaiming God's merciful message. He declared that they were to repent of their evil deeds or be destroyed in forty days.

This city was the capitol of Assyria which was the most powerful nation on earth. Who could overthrow them with such power? Humanly speaking, no individual or nation could, but Jonah was speaking for the Lord. His God can do anything that He desires. His God meant business. When the

King of Nineveh heard Jonah's message, he arose from his royal throne, threw off his royal robe, covered himself in sackcloth and ashes, and issued a proclamation in the land.

The king commanded that all people and animals put on sackcloth and ashes and fast out of sorrow and repentance for their wicked and violent ways. They should then pray that Jonah's God would have mercy on them and withdraw His burning anger and wrath of judgment upon them. The one hundred and twenty thousand people of the city obeyed from the greatest to the least with sincerity. So, God stopped the calamity that was about to come upon the Ninevites and showed them mercy.

Additional Notes: Yet, Jonah was displeased and angry. He knew this would happen! He knew the Lord was a God of mercy and compassion. He knew the Lord God would relent if the Ninevites repented and believed. The prophet Jonah's response was quick and straightforward. He begged the Lord to take his life. Had Jonah forgotten all he had learned in the belly of the fish? Yes, they were wicked, and he still desired them to be punished. These unrighteous souls must be crushed for their sin. God's mercy was too much to bear! Then he cried for the Lord to bring his death quickly!

The Lord gently asked him whether he had a legitimate reason to be angry. Then Jonah left the city and sat east of it to observe what would happen next. Perhaps, he was hoping that God would change His mind and finally obliterate these wicked people. As he sat in his own stubbornness, it became hotter and hotter there. Patiently, the Lord God caused a plant miraculously to grow up over him and provide shade from the sun. Here Jonah was stewing over God's gracious act concerning the Ninevites. Yet, he was experiencing God's act of grace in providing shade for him. Why didn't God just smite him? God is merciful and patient in his instruction. The prophet was stubborn and needed a different approach. While Jonah was sitting in the sun shaded from the heat, he felt happy about this plant. Suddenly, a worm slithered up the plant and attacked it. As a result, the plant withered and died. This made Jonah angry. He loved that simple plant. He felt so much compassion for that plant and did not want it to die.

Again, the sun beat down on his head and God sent a scorching wind to torment him. This was enough! Jonah was so angry about the plant and the horrible wind that all he wanted to do was die. Then the Lord God spoke to Him. He chastised him for having such compassion upon a plant that he had put no effort in growing and was only in existence for one day. It was just a lowly plant! He felt mercy for it and didn't want it to be destroyed. Yet, his God was not allowed to have mercy on one hundred and twenty thousand people who were so spiritually ignorant that they didn't know their right hand from their left. They were lost in their ignorance! They were not steeped in hard heartedness but were lost and needed to be found.

Sometimes, like Jonah we view the unsaved as only evil and wicked. When they commit a transgression against us, we do not want to forgive them, nor do we desire them to come to Christ. Let them die in their sins! Our Father is not like this. He has tremendous compassion for them as He had for us. Must we forgive the evil, especially when it hurts us? How about when it hurt God's only righteous, beloved, holy Son? This is a total game changer in perspective toward all who are unbelievers. It changed Jonah's perspective, and now it must also change our perspective. God desires for us to see them as He sees them. The unsaved are lost and walk in darkness. All unbelievers do not spiritually know their right hand from their left. They should be forgiven.

A Modern Anecdote

Problems with fathers date back a long time. Every family has had one or more male family members who choose not to fulfill their responsibilities as fathers. They discovered it was quite easy to have children but extremely difficult to care for them. For the children, this often leads to issues in later life. One such child, now a man, came in for counseling. As he entered my counseling office, I was introduced to an upbeat, happy, and seemingly fulfilled man who didn't seem to have a care in the world. He was successful and happily married. His children were all grown up, educated, happily married, and successful also. He had become a believer in his twenties and desired to love the Lord with all his heart and obey him. His wife and children were believers, and his first grandson had just received the Lord Jesus Christ.

After our first session, I discovered that all was not what it seemed. He had glaring issues in his life which were under the surface, unseen by others, including his own family. He felt inadequate as a husband, uncomfortable as a father, and inferior as a man. He was so tired of these feelings but could not rid himself of them. No amount of prayer or bible study could solve this problem, and he did not know why. When feelings come up without present circumstances warranting them, then it's time to look into the past. During several sessions, we discovered that he had issues with his father.

His father was a heavy drinker and could be violent with anyone who disagreed with him when he was in this state. When the son was seven years old, his parents divorced over it. Then, his father moved out. As alcohol took over his father's life, he almost never visited his son. As a result, his son never learned the mechanical skills that he possessed, received any advice on the childhood or adolescent issues he faced, only saw his father shouting at his mother when they had to interact, and eventually forgot any relationship they had had before the divorce. In his son's mind, he was always a dark shadow which was lurking in the background never showing himself.

Sometime after the son had graduated from college, the father finally sobered up. The son thought perhaps now he would come around, but he did not. Suddenly he passed away. The son refused to go to his funeral and mourn him. In fact, deep down the son was glad that he was gone. As we spoke about his father, the son became angrier and angrier, until he burst into tears. He suddenly realized he was full of bitterness for this man who was supposed to be his father, and he was now dead. The anger and bitterness began to pour out of him like dark, murky water. He quickly became aware that he blamed his father for his feelings. His father had not been the example necessary for him to learn how to be a husband and always felt inadequate.

His father had not demonstrated how to be a parent to his children. As a result, he always felt like he could be a better father when he was actually a great "dad." His father had not taught him the mechanical skills that he so desperately needed to even fix the simplest of problems with his house or car. This made him feel like less of a man. He had not realized that every time one of these feelings occurred, he blamed his father. He felt like his father had robbed him of his needed preparation for manhood which led to his inability to experience the full joy of being with his family. This could not be recompensed. He could never have these precious years back.

I told him that he was completely justified in his feelings. It was the father's responsibility to fulfill his role in his son's preparation for his adult life, and his father had completely failed him.

Additional Notes: The father had responsibilities he did not fulfill. Here are some Bible references:

Ephesians 6:4
You fathers, don't provoke your children to wrath, but nurture them in the discipline and instruction of the Lord.

Proverbs 3:12
For whom Yahweh loves, he reproves; even as a father reproves the son in whom he delights.

Hebrews 12:7-9
It is for discipline that you endure. God deals with you as with children, for what son is there whom his father doesn't discipline? But if you are without discipline, of which all have been made partakers, then are you illegitimate...not children. Furthermore, we had the fathers of our flesh to chasten us, and we paid them respect. Shall we...be in subjection to the Father of spirits, and live?

Now, he [the father] was gone and could never reconcile the relationship, but he still needed to forgive his father. Once this was done by faith, then the feelings would slowly fade away. When I discovered that his father was an unbeliever, I shared the principles in this chapter with him and we read the story of Jonah aloud. As we read that story, I could hear him quietly mumbling and muttering to himself. The Holy Spirit began opening his eyes to see that he was facing the same issues as Jonah. At the end, he announced, "I know what I have to do, please go with me." Several days later, we drove to his father's gravesite, and the man confronted his dead father and then forgave him. He had understood how lost his father truly was and how desperately he needed to be found.

AN INSTRUCTOR'S MANUAL

Additional Notes: The Lord wants parents honored regardless of what their parenting skills are. Here are some Bible references:

Proverbs 1:8
My son, listen to your father's instruction, and don't forsake your mother's teaching.

Proverbs 4:1
Listen, sons, to a father's instruction. Pay attention and know understanding.

Proverbs 4:3
For I was a son to my father, tender and an only child in the sight of my mother.

Proverbs 6:20
My son, keep your father's commandment, and don't forsake your mother's teaching.

Proverbs 10:1
A wise son makes a glad father; but a foolish son brings grief to his mother.

Proverbs 13:1
A wise son listens to his father's instruction, but a scoffer doesn't listen to rebuke.

Proverbs 20:20
Whoever curses his father or his mother, his lamp shall be put out in blackness of darkness.

Proverbs 23:22
Listen to your father who gave you life, and don't despise your mother when she is old.

A Personal Response

Dear Heavenly Father,

    I have not fully understood how lost (add name) is. I now know that I am to forgive those who do not know you as much as those who do. Please help me to see (add name) as someone who is lost and desperately needs to be found, rather than as wicked who deserves eternal punishment. I ask You to soften my heart so I may forgive (add name) as You forgave me. Give me the wisdom to know whether I should provide a consequence or set up a boundary for this transgression to help (add name) learn not to continue this sin. I am very sorry for transgressing your righteous law. Help me to honor and glorify you in my relationship with (add name) and follow your Word. I pray this in the name of Jesus. Amen.

AN INSTRUCTOR'S MANUAL

Chapter 3

Forgive the Lost

If Christians have difficulty with forgiving those who do not know Christ, they should see them as lost in desperate need of salvation rather than as wicked in need of judgment.

In the section, "A Typical Scenario," the author contrasts the reaction of a husband with his wife's toward the mistakes of a neighbor.

What is the scenario about?

A neighbor spilled a bag of recyclable bottles in front of his house and a Christian's wife went to help.

What did the conflict concern?

A Christian was angry that his neighbor rejected the gospel and then spilled a bag of recyclable bottles in front of his house.

What was the relationship between the parties?

They were spouses and a neighbor.

Have you had a similar experience?

(Various answers should be shared including yours.)

HEALING RELATIONSHIPS THROUGH FORGIVENESS

In the section, "A Scriptural Principle" the author presents an important biblical principle in the forgiveness process which concerns viewing unbelievers as lost rather than wicked.

How would you express this principle in your own words?

The third principle is "we must view unbelievers as lost to forgive."

(*Various answers should be shared including yours.*)

How would you rewrite this principle to make it even more personal to your life (using your name and situation)?

(*Various answers should be shared including yours.*)

Why do you think this principle might be important in your life right now?

(*Various answers should be shared including yours.*)

How would you rate yourself on the percentage of times you followed this principle in the past when you did something wrong in a relationship?

(*Various answers should be shared including yours.*)

Directions: Put a horizontal mark and your name where you see yourself on the percentage line.

0%   25%   50%   75%   100%

In the section, "A Biblical Explanation," the author explains the reasons why we are to view unbelievers as lost in order to forgive them and how to do it.

In Luke 9:51–56, what did James and John want to do to the Samaritan village for rejecting Jesus and what was the Lord's response?

He sent some of His disciples into a Samaritan village to obtain lodging. The citizens of the city refused. They hated the Jews and their feasts and Jesus was a Jew on His way to a feast. As far as they were concerned, this Rabbi was not staying the night in their town. When James and John heard of it, they asked the Lord if they could command fire from heaven to consume the town. The disciples were upset and desired judgment on these unrighteous people.

How is the concept of man being lost and blind related?

In Luke 19:10, the Lord declared His desire, "For the Son of Man came to seek and to save that which was lost."

When someone is lost, they do not know where they are or where they are going.

In 1 John 2:11, John paints a picture of the unsaved lost as walking in the darkness, not knowing where they are going because the darkness has blinded their eyes. They are stumbling around in the darkness of their own sin and wickedness and the lies and falsehoods of the Devil.

If those who sin against us receive Christ, what will happen to those sins?

Christ will forgive all of their sins of against us.

What are two groups who participated in Christ's crucifixion and how did He view them in order to forgive them?

The Romans, who were doing the dirty work the Jews could not do, did not realize that they were crucifying the King of Kings.

This crowd of Jews who were standing around the cross throwing insults and curses at Him did not understand this was their own Messiah.

The frightened disciples, who had hidden from the mob, did not fully comprehend that as His death was at hand, so was His forgiveness of all on the cross. From His death would come the resurrection to a new life in Him.

Even many of these rulers, who were caught up in their religious self-righteous pride, did not perceive that a new covenant in His blood had come. They did not see that a new and final priest was now making a final sacrifice for the sins of all men.

Though Christ asked God, the Father, to forgive them, could they be forgiven without receiving Christ? Why or why not?

Christians know through their understanding of the Scriptures that this prayer could only be fulfilled if all of these lost people received the soon to be risen Son of God as Savior and Lord.

In what ways might these truths impact your relationships?

(Various answers should be shared including yours.)

AN INSTRUCTOR'S MANUAL

In the section, "An Ancient Portrait," the author portrays the struggle of the prophet Jonah to obey God's command.

Why did Jonah run when commanded to preach the gospel to the Ninevites and what was God's response?

In the book of Jonah, God had told him to go and preach to them; instead, he was repulsed and fled. He did not want them to be forgiven. They deserved judgment and he was going to make sure they got it. Why? These people were terribly wicked.

While on his sea voyage, the Lord sent a great storm. This put the ship on the verge of breaking apart.

After the storm came, what did the ship's crew finally decide to do with Jonah when they discovered it was his fault?

Though unbelievers, the crew did not have the heart to follow his advice and throw him overboard. Instead, they tried furiously to row the boat to shore.

This was a vain and useless attempt, but they could not kill him. The storm only got worse! So, they begged the Lord God not to hold what they were about to do against them and threw Jonah into the sea. Immediately the storm ceased. Now Jonah was flailing and thrashing about in his own stubbornness in the ocean all alone. The Lord could have left him there to die, but that has never been God's way.

After some time in the belly of the great fish, why did Jonah finally repent?

He showed Jonah the forgiveness Jonah did not want the Ninevites to receive....He was literally lost in his own sin and stubbornness.

He desperately needed some compassion from God, and Jonah was begging for His forgiveness.

Though these Ninevites were lost also in their stubbornness and sin, Jonah hadn't thought that they might deserve either. Perhaps, the time had come to rethink this obvious contradiction.

After having been swallowed up in the depths of the sea by a huge creature, he remained in its belly for three days and nights.

It was here that Jonah began to ponder these amazing things. Then, he repented and thanked God for his gracious rescue.

What contradiction in the Prophet Jonah's thinking led him to be hypocrite when it came to God's mercy?

He needed some compassion from God, and Jonah was begging for His forgiveness. Though these Ninevites were lost also in their stubbornness and sin, Jonah hadn't thought that they deserved either. Perhaps, the time had come to rethink this obvious contradiction.

What was the response of the Ninevites to Jonah's message and what does this tell us about God?

The one hundred and twenty thousand people of the city obeyed from the greatest to the least with sincerity. So, God stopped the calamity that was about to come upon the Ninevites and showed them mercy.

Have you ever been in any situation comparable to Jonah's wicked perspective or the Ninevite's desperation? How was it different and how was it the same?

(Various answers should be shared including yours.)

AN INSTRUCTOR'S MANUAL

In the section, "A Modern Anecdote," the author describes a man angry and bitter against his father and how he learned to forgive him.

Why was the son so angry and bitter against his father?

His father was a heavy drinker and could be violent with anyone who disagreed with him when he was in this state. When the son was seven years old, his parents divorced over it. Then, his father moved out. As alcohol took over his father's life, he almost never visited his son. As a result, his son never learned the mechanical skills that he possessed, received any advice on the childhood or adolescent issues he faced, only saw his father shouting at his mother when they had to interact, and eventually forgot any relationship they had had before the divorce.

How did the son demonstrate his bitterness?

The son refused to go to his funeral and mourn him. In fact, deep down the son was glad that he was gone. As we spoke about his father, the son became angrier and angrier, until he burst into tears. He suddenly realized he was full of bitterness for this man who was supposed to be his father, and he was now dead.

Was the father a Christian, why or why not?

Now, he was gone and could never reconcile the relationship, but he still needed to forgive his father. Once this was done by faith, then the feelings would slowly fade away. When I discovered that his father was an unbeliever, I shared the principles in this chapter with him and we read the story of Jonah aloud.

HEALING RELATIONSHIPS THROUGH FORGIVENESS

How did the believing son need to view his father in order to fully forgive him?

He had to see them as lost not wicked.

Since the father had passed away, how should the son finally decide to outwardly demonstrate his forgiveness?

At the end, he announced, "I know what I have to do, please go with me." Several days later, we drove to his father's gravesite, and the man confronted his dead father and then forgave him. He had understood how lost his father truly was and how desperately he needed to be found.

Based on the truths learned in this chapter, what would you have done differently if you were the son who was neglected or the father who did the neglecting?

(Various answers should be shared including yours.)

AN INSTRUCTOR'S MANUAL

In the section, "A Personal Response," the author provides a model you may use for prayer if you find it necessary after discovering the truths in this chapter.

Are you presently in a relationship where you have sinned against another and have not asked God for forgiveness? If not, is there one from the past that still needs this prayer to be prayed?

(Various answers should be shared including yours.)

Based on the truths you have just learned, what will you continue doing in your current relationships and what will you do differently?

(Various answers should be shared including yours.)

What additional thoughts would you like to share with the others?

(Various answers should be shared including yours.)

Instructor's Notes

Chapter 4

Keep No Records

If we have a broken relationship with our spouse, partner, boyfriend, girlfriend, child, parent, friend, neighbor, fellow student, or co-worker, or even an acquaintance, we learned the Lord God desires that we go to him or her and reconcile the relationship through forgiveness. This includes what we do with past sins. The next step concerns any mental records we may want to keep.

A Typical Scenario

Have you ever had or heard a conversation with a spouse that went something like this? You say, "Wow! I have been waiting for this coffee all morning. (Sip coffee). Yuck! No cream. Honey! Did you remember to purchase the cream? (Person responds in the negative.) No! Why not? I gave you one thing to do and once again you forgot. This is the third time in a month you forgot the cream for my coffee. Last week, you forgot my shirts at the cleaners. The week before that, you also forgot to pick up the kids at school. I cannot depend on you for anything. (Talk to yourself.) The next time she needs me to do something, I'm going to forget! Let's see how she likes that! That'll teach her!" Notice, the spouse mentions the past mistakes over and over. Why do we keep bringing up the past? Why do we keep tabs on people who have hurt us? Why must we continue to punish our spouses, children, parents, friends, co-workers, or even neighbors who may have offended us again and again? It discourages them and makes us angry and bitter. This leads to the break-up of relationships, not the building up of them.

A Scriptural Principle

Once forgiveness comes, we must take the next important step. The fourth principle is "we must not keep records of the sins against us." Simply, we should forgive and forget. Obviously, we cannot actually forget, but we are to treat past offenses as if the transgressions are over, finished, and done with. When Paul describes Christian love in 1 Corinthians 13:5, he uses these very words to characterize it. He declares that love "takes no account of evil." This English phrase is two words in the Greek which mean "makes no record of it" or "no longer takes it into account." It was a banking term in the ancient world speaking of keeping a record of deposits and withdrawals in an account. It means keeping a record of someone's wrong.

Paul is indicating that love does not keep records. People do not demonstrate true love by keeping a record in their minds and memories of others' transgressions against them for the purpose of punishing them. Through forgiveness, the transgressions are forgotten and permanently removed from the ledger of our minds. This is a supernatural, divine act. Our memories of hurtful words or actions of a loved one may be triggered by a movie, book, song, or event, yet we make that memory of no account. It comes back up into the ledger of our minds, and through a conscious effort, we erase it once again. Every time it surfaces, we erase it. This is what God does for us.

A Biblical Explanation

This constant record keeping begins in the mind, not from the mouth. Our minds indulge in the continual rehearsing of what others have done to us, and this produces much anger and bitterness. These negative feelings bring forth strife and conflict as they transform themselves into harsh words and actions. Centuries ago, Solomon described this very process in Proverbs 30:33 when he penned, "For as the churning of milk produces butter, and the wringing of the nose produces blood; so, the forcing [churning] of wrath produces strife." A barrage of our transgressions is thrown at us or vice versa which destroys and demolishes our relationships. Why? This cannon fire leads to fighting, arguing, and quarreling which never builds and renews relationships, only crushes them.

In Proverbs 10:12, the king asserts, "Hatred stirs up strife, but love covers all wrongs." Real love does not write wrongs down upon the heart in order to use it against someone later; it covers over all of them. The recording of transgressions in our minds and repeating them in our words causes hatred of the offenders leading to disputes, clashes, and altercations. In Proverbs 17:9, he continues, "He who covers an offense promotes love; but he who repeats a matter separates best friends." Here Solomon is speaking of (covering over) not revealing the offense of one friend against another. This will promote love between them. When the offense is revealed, the one offended separates from the offender.

This can easily describe what happens in a relationship when people keep bringing up (revealing) the past offenses again and again, never "covering it over" in love. Suddenly, they will find themselves alone. In 1 Peter 4:8, the apostle reiterates this same important principle when he entreats his readers, "And above all things be earnest in your love among yourselves, for love covers a multitude of sins." Notice, Peter describes an effort that is earnest in our love for one another. This covering over in love requires an earnest effort to really love someone. It is so easy to keep bringing things up instead of holding our tongues. It is difficult and requires much effort to keep silent in love and forgiveness. This lack of record-keeping does not involve the consequences and necessary restitution one may require for the transgression. This does not in any way mean that the transgressor has a free ticket to do whatever they want and then say, "Sorry, you have to forgive and forget." This does not at all mean that we should never alter our behavior or set up boundaries in our relationships when sin continues to occur over and over.

Instead, this lack of record-keeping involves the response of forgiveness itself.

Additional Notes: If asked about boundaries, here are two Bible references:

Acts 4:19-20
But Peter and John answered them, "Whether it is right in the sight of God to listen to you rather than to God, judge for yourselves, for we can't help telling the things which we saw and heard."

Acts 5:40-42
They agreed with him. Summoning the apostles, they beat them and commanded them not to speak in the name of Jesus and let them go. They therefore departed from the presence of the council, rejoicing that they were counted worthy to suffer dishonor for Jesus' name. Every day, in the temple and at home, they never stopped teaching and preaching Jesus, the Christ.

Once our sins [all of them] are forgiven, we should not have the transgressions brought up over and over again, so we have to relive them or experience the consequences again and again. When this occurs, it usually produces anger or grief that will lead to a real despair in the relationship. It will make us feel as if we will be held accountable for what we did the remainder of time we partake in the relationship. How can someone live in a relationship with another who says, "I may never get over this!" The reverse will also be true. We cannot put others through this torment and torture.

When Paul visited Corinth, someone had opposed him vehemently to his face. He had questioned Paul's motives and actions in ministry. After the church had disciplined this instigator, the man repented. Then Paul was very concerned about the man's restoration back into the fellowship. In 2 Corinthians 2:7, he admonished the church to "forgive him and comfort him, lest by any means such a one should be swallowed up with his excessive sorrow." The apostle was worried that after this one who opposed him had repented, the church would not fully accept him back. He did not want the church to shun him or avoid him. The saints were not to bring up his past actions against Paul because this would only lead to the man's excessive sorrow. If we keep bringing up an offense over and over, we are indicating to the other person that we have not fully forgiven him. This may lead to the transgressor being swallowed up in sorrow or despair.

This principle of forgiving and forgetting comes right out of the character of our merciful and compassionate God. Once people have received Jesus as their Lord and Savior, their sins are not only forgiven but forgotten. In Isaiah 43:25, God describes this process in the following words, "I, even I, am he who blots out your transgressions for my own sake; and I will not remember your sins." In Jeremiah 31:34, the Lord again proclaims, "And they shall teach no more every man his neighbor, and every man his brother, saying,' Know Yahweh; for they shall all know me, from their least to their greatest, says Yahweh: for I will forgive their iniquity, and their sin will I remember no more." In Hebrews 8:12, God announces, "For I will be merciful to their unrighteousness. I will remember their sins and lawless deeds no more." Now, it is not that the Lord does not actually remember; instead,

He renders it of no account. It is over and done. It will never be brought up again.

In Isaiah 44:22, the Almighty God of Israel proclaims this, "I have blotted out, as a thick cloud, your transgressions, and, as a cloud, your sins. Return to me, for I have redeemed you." This passage describes the Lord's forgiveness utilizing a powerful analogy. He says that He puts a thick cloud over our sins so He cannot see them. All Christians must do the same when it comes to the sins of others against them. Is God going to bring up our past sins in heaven? When we die, will he bring up all our past sins and transgressions against Him over and over again into eternity? No!

Our sins have been nailed to the cross and remembered no more. Christ's judgment will be only for our reward. In 1 Corinthians 4:5, Paul describes it as a day of judgment which brings praise. The past sins were erased from God's ledger.

Additional Notes: If asked this judgment of praise, here is the Bible reference I cite:

1 Corinthians 4:5
Therefore judge nothing before the time, until the Lord comes, who will both bring to light the hidden things of darkness, and reveal the counsels of the hearts. Then each man will get his praise from God.

Our evil deeds are gone. The wasteful deeds will fall away, and our righteous, holy deeds will be rewarded. So, when someone hurts us, we need to act like God does toward us. We need to forgive them and forget the offense by rendering those offenses as of no account in our minds. They won't be brought up again.

AN INSTRUCTOR'S MANUAL

An Ancient Portrait

The best example of someone who did not keep records is Jesus Christ Himself. When the Lord encountered Martha and Mary a second time on the way to raising their brother from the dead, He didn't bring up the past mistakes Martha had made. You may remember the first story of Martha and Mary in Luke 10:38-41. Mary was seated at the feet of Jesus listening to Him teach, while her sister Martha was in the kitchen making preparations. She became so overwhelmed that she stormed into the presence of Jesus and demanded that He command Mary to help her. Patiently, Jesus refused and explained to Martha that Mary had chosen the better part which was teaching over service. Mary was seen later at the house of Simon the leper anointing Jesus with oil in worship and adoration.

Their next recorded encounter together is found in John chapter eleven. It begins after the public ministry of Jesus had ended. Lazarus, Martha and Mary's brother, was very ill and deteriorating rapidly. The Lord received a message from Martha and Mary saying, "Lord, the one whom you love is sick." Jesus loved all three of them and they knew each other well. They believed He was the Savior. They knew He had healed so many people in Palestine, many of whom He did not even know. Now, their brother, someone He knew and loved, was extremely sick.

Additional Notes: Notice they addressed Him as Lord indicating they were true saints. They also knew He was the master of all things and had the power over life and death. This word that the sisters used to describe the love Jesus had for their brother spoke of a brotherly love. It was a deep affection between two friends.

They did not need to identify their brother Jesus would know immediately who the person was. Since they were informing the

HEALING RELATIONSHIPS THROUGH FORGIVENESS

Lord directly, their brother must have been at death's door. They did not even ask the Lord to come and heal him. Jesus would know what needed to be done. He knew all things. I'm sure these sisters thought, "He'll find out, come right away, and heal him as He has done so many times for multitudes. This time it would be better than all the others, because Lazarus was a real friend. Jesus won't let us down."

After receiving the message, Jesus casually remarked to His disciples that the sickness of His dear friend wasn't for the purpose of bringing on his death but for the purpose of demonstrating the glory of God. This was information only Jesus as God could know. He knew the world was about to see something so dramatic that people would speak of it for many years. To present His great glory to the world, Lazarus unfortunately would have to die for a short time, so Jesus stayed two more days. Though the Lord loved Martha and Mary, they would now have to endure one of man's most difficult experiences, the death of a family member.

Additional Notes: Several questions arise. Would they still trust Him? Would they still believe in Him? Would they be angry and bitter that He had not come earlier? He knew that He would raise Lazarus from the dead so in the end all would be joyful. We must realize that sometimes God makes us go through difficulties for a higher purpose which is His purpose. Martha and Mary would have to watch their own brother slowly, painfully pass from this life knowing that just a short distance away, the solution to all their problems dwelt. Two very difficult days went by for them, then Jesus declared that it was time to go to Judea. He doesn't say it was time to go to Lazarus.

All is downplayed to demonstrate the divine confidence of Jesus in what He was about to do. The disciples warned Him that the last time He went into Judea the people tried to stone Him. He explained to them that His light must shine in that region again.

Also, Lazarus was asleep (dead), and He was going to wake (raise) Him. They most likely were quite puzzled by His reply.

By the time Jesus arrived, Lazarus had been in the tomb four days. A crowd of people had gathered around Martha and Mary attempting to console them. When Martha heard that Jesus had finally arrived, she came running, and she wasn't planning on their reunion being pleasant. Martha stood before the Lord and questioned Him as to why He did not arrive earlier and save her brother! She then implied that he could still raise Him from the dead if He so desired, since God always answered His prayers.

Before I mention what Jesus said to her, I want to take a moment to mention what He did not say. Jesus did not say, "Well, here we go again, Martha. The last time we saw each other you complained about Mary and her unwillingness to help you in the kitchen. This time, you are complaining that I did not come quick enough to save your brother. We are done. I have had enough! Let Lazarus rot in the grave for all I care."

Jesus did not respond in this way because the Lord was not keeping a record of all her wrongs. Instead, the Lord had forgiven her other transgression and was not going to bring it up again. This is critical to building strong relationships and is a good example of the principle we are studying. He did not allow what happened in the past to get in the way of the present. Instead, Jesus explained to Martha that Lazarus will rise again. Martha responded that she knew he would be resurrected on the last day and affirmed her faith in Him. He did not say he was going to raise her brother. After their time together, he asked for Mary.

Additional Notes: Jesus reaffirmed who He was by stating that He was the resurrection and the life and anyone who believed in Him would never die. He implied that this included their dear brother Lazarus. Jesus asked Martha if she believed this. She once again reaffirmed her belief in His deity by declaring that He was the Christ, God's only begotten Son who had come into the world. Yet, this theological truth did not provide enough comfort because her brother was still in the grave. Instead of disclosing the fact that He was about to demonstrate that He truly was the resurrection and the life by raising her brother from death, He decided to keep her wondering. She was too tied to the present, temporal life, when it was their spiritual, eternal life that really mattered. They knew that their brother Lazarus possessed eternal life and they would see Him again for eternity, but he was gone now.

I am sure that she left disappointed. She then went and sent Mary to Jesus secretly because Jesus wanted to see her. Perhaps, she thought Mary could talk some sense into Him, so He would raise their brother from the dead. They wanted him back! That is all they could think about.

Additional Notes: At this point, they did not want a theological discussion on the deity of Christ, but Jesus did. When the Jews who were comforting her saw her leave, they followed her thinking she was going to the tomb to weep.

When Mary saw Jesus, she fell at His feet and questioned Him in the exact manner that Martha had done. Once again, if Jesus had come when they called, Lazarus would still be alive today. They had seen His power, they knew He could heal him, but He didn't. Notice, Jesus does not rebuke her for her temporal blindness (not seeing his death in the light of heaven).

Additional Notes: Notice, Jesus did not explain why He didn't come. God doesn't feel the necessity to explain everything He does. When Jesus therefore saw her weeping, and the Jews who came with her doing the same, he was deeply moved in His spirit and was troubled. The Greek word which is translated "troubled" is reflexive indicating that He troubled Himself. In His humanity, Jesus allowed Himself to be troubled. The meaning of the word indicates a stirring of deep emotion and agitation in His inward person. They couldn't put on those spiritual eyes to see the beauty of his death as a doorway to his new life. The physical had such a powerful grip on them. Then the Lord wept. The sadness of it all overwhelmed Him in His humanity. Yet, when the Jews saw His tears, they questioned Him in their own minds as to why he didn't heal Lazarus, if He had such affection for Him. How could He make blind men see and not heal a beloved friend? Knowing what was in their hearts only added to His troubled spirit. When would they see that there is so much more to life than the physical?

Then, Jesus traveled with the sisters and the crowds of people to the cave where the brother had been buried. When he arrived, Jesus commanded them to move away the stone that was covering the entrance to the brother's tomb. Martha once again interjected. She commented that there would be a great stench because he had been in the tomb four days. This implied that the Lord Jesus simply wanted to see the body and perhaps say goodbye. Again, Jesus doesn't bring the record up and blast her for this third infraction. Instead, He simply reminded her that He said if she believed in Him, she would see His glory. Of course, she thought it would be on the last day not a few moments later. Since Lazarus had been in the grave for so long, all would know that what they saw was not a magician's trick. Jesus could raise even the dead!

When they removed the stone, Jesus thanked the Father and then commanded loudly, "Lazarus, come out!" Can you imagine the hush among the people? What? Did He just say what they thought He said? Just as suddenly, the dead man came hobbling out still being bound hand and foot by the wrappings that encompassed him. Jesus told them to free him, and let the man go. Nothing was said about Martha or

Mary's indiscretion before the Lord. The Lord had forgiven them, and He did not keep records. Many believed in Him. So, when people sin against us, we are to forgive and not keep mental records of the offenses. This frees us from the torment of churning it over and over and keeps them from excessive sorrow or despair in the relationship. We are to forgive and forget.

Additional Notes: If asked about the original encounter Jesus had with Martha and Mary, here is Bible reference:

Luke 10:38-41
As they went on their way, he entered into a certain village, and a certain woman named Martha received him into her house. She had a sister called Mary, who also sat at Jesus' feet, and heard his word. But Martha was distracted with much serving, and she came up to him, and said, "Lord, don't you care that my sister left me to serve alone? Ask her therefore to help me." Jesus answered her, "Martha, Martha, you are anxious...troubled about many things, but one thing is needed. Mary has chosen the good part, which will not be taken away from her."

A Modern Anecdote

A teenage daughter stomped angrily into my office with her mother in tow and demanded, "I want to go first." She explained that as far back as she could remember her mother took detailed mental notes on every "bad thing" (her words) she had done. If the daughter repeated even one of these, out of her mother's mouth would come a long list of infractions she had committed. It overwhelmed her and made her feel really stupid. She admitted that she was a bit clumsy and didn't always pay attention to what she was doing. I asked if she could give me several concrete examples. At seven, she was playing the game of Hide and Seek in the living room and knocked over a lamp which put a small chip at the base. She was reprimanded and spent the evening in her room. She told her mother how sorry she was. Then the daughter promised her mother that the next time she would be much more careful.

Two years later, the daughter was removing a box of her princess dolls out of the top of the closet, lost her balance, and the box came tumbling to the ground spilling out all the dolls. One of the dolls took flight and hit a figurine that her mother had purchased for her on a trip and broke its finger off. When her mother heard all the commotion, she stormed into the room, saw the broken figurine, and then screamed, "Okay, that's twice now. What is wrong with you?" After a detailed description of what she had done to the lamp, the mother marched her down the stairs and pointed to the chip. The young lady had felt so upset that she ran to her room, shut the door, and sobbed. The mother shouted through the door, "You are grounded for three days young lady! Once that figurine is repaired, it will be put away. That way you cannot destroy it."

At twelve, she made herself a snack and went to watch television in the family room. Her mom had told her many times to be careful with any food she brought in. The carpet was new. She decided to watch a scary movie and eat some nachos. In the movie, a monster jumped out from behind a corner and startled her to such an extent that she threw the plate up into the air. As the nachos, cheese, and salsa landed on the carpet, she gasped. She quickly ran to the linen closet, grabbed a towel, wet it, and began to wipe it up. The more she wiped, the worse the stains became. In desperation, she covered the stain with a small carpet she had in her room. She knew this was a dumb idea but could not come up with anything else.

HEALING RELATIONSHIPS THROUGH FORGIVENESS

When her mother arrived home, as always, she marched around the house checking to see if everything was in its place. The mother noticed the dishes in the sink, the towel with the nacho cheese, salsa, and bits of chip sticking out of the hamper in the hall, the small carpet on the family room floor, and her daughter nervously lying on the couch. She calmly walked over to the small carpet, lifted it, and gasped. The mother looked at her daughter sternly and whispered, "I told you to be careful. This house is full of your clumsiness." Then she rattled off a long list of the daughter's mistakes and sent her to her room. In response, the daughter sprang up and screamed, "This is all your fault. Everybody has to be perfect around here. I'm sick of it! I'm sorry, sorry, sorry! There! Does that make you happy?" As she left the room, her mother yelled, "I have standards!" From that time forward, it became one battle after another. When she was finished, she slumped in the chair sobbing, "I can't ever please you. I'm such a screw up."

This ended the session. In the next one, mom defended herself. After some time discussing the importance of not keeping records, the mother stared blankly at her daughter. Then with tears in her eyes, she responded, "That must have been horrible growing up and feeling like you can never please me. I love you! I am so proud of you and who you have become. I am really sorry for bringing up all those past mistakes." After this very moment, we began the restoration process. The mother had seen the importance of not keeping records.

Additional Notes: If asked about the training of children patiently and without exasperating them, here are some Bible references:

Ephesians 6:4
You fathers, don't provoke your children to wrath, but nurture them in the discipline and instruction of the Lord.

Proverbs 22:6
Train up a child in the way he should go, and when he is old he will not depart from it.

Proverbs 31:28
Her children rise up and call her blessed. Her husband also praises he.

A Personal Response

Dear Heavenly Father,

I am very sorry I have been keeping records on the many transgressions of (add name) against me. I am so thankful that you are not keeping any records on me but instead are forgiving and forgetting my sins against you. Please aid me in this same process with (add name). Help me to let go of (list the sins) he (she) has committed against me and truly forgive (add name). I want to honor and glorify You in my relationship with (add name) and follow your Word. I pray this in the name of Jesus. Amen.

Instructor's Notes

AN INSTRUCTOR'S MANUAL

Chapter 4

Keep No Records

To fully forgive others means not only forgiving, but also forgetting. We should not keep records of past offenses in order to punish others over and over.

In the section, "A Typical Scenario," the author describes a man's harshly reminding his wife of her past mistakes which will require a reconciliation.

What is the scenario about?

A husband gets angry that his wife forgot the cream for his coffee and brings up past incidents where she has forgotten things.

What did the conflict concern?

The husband was constantly bringing up past mistakes that his wife made.

What was the relationship between the parties?

They are spouses.

Have you had a similar experience?

(Various answers should be shared including yours.)

HEALING RELATIONSHIPS THROUGH FORGIVENESS

In the section, "A Scriptural Principle" the author presents an important biblical principle in the forgiveness process which concerns forgiving and then forgetting the offenses.

How would you express this principle in your own words?

The fourth principle is "we must not keep records of the sins against us."

(Various answers should be shared including yours.)

How would you rewrite this principle to make it even more personal to your life (using your name and situation)?

(Various answers should be shared including yours.)

Why do you think this principle might be important in your life right now?

(Various answers should be shared including yours.)

How would you rate yourself on the percentage of times you followed this principle in the past when you did something wrong in a relationship?

(Various answers should be shared including yours.)

Directions: Put a horizontal mark and your name where you see yourself on the percentage line.

0%   25%   50%   75%   100%

In the section, "A Biblical Explanation," the author explains the reasons why we should never keep records of the sins others have committed against us and how to do it.

What does the "churning" over and over others' sins against us result in?

Our minds indulge in the continual rehearsing of what others have done to us, and this produces much anger and bitterness. These negative feelings bring forth strife and conflict as they transform themselves into harsh words and actions.

The recording of transgressions in our minds and repeating them in our words causes hatred of the offenders leading to disputes, clashes, and altercations.

This could easily describe what happens in a relationship when people keep bringing up (revealing) the past offenses again and again, never "covering it over" in love.

When the Bible says "keep no records," what two things does it involve? What does it not involve?

Paul is indicating that love does not keep records. People do not demonstrate true love by keeping a record in their minds and memories of others' transgressions against them for the purpose of punishing them.

This lack of record-keeping does not involve the consequences and necessary restitution one may require for the transgression. This does not in any way mean that the transgressor has a free ticket to do whatever they want and then say, "Sorry, you have to forgive and forget." This does not at all mean that we should never alter our behavior or set up boundaries in our relationships when sin continues to occur over and over.

HEALING RELATIONSHIPS THROUGH FORGIVENESS

What can happen to our relationships if we constantly bring up the sins of the past?

When this occurs, it usually produces anger or grief that will lead to a real despair in the relationship. It will make us feel as if we will be held accountable for what we did the remainder of time we partake in the relationship. How can someone live in a relationship with another who says, "I may never get over this?" The reverse will also be true. We cannot put others through this torment and torture.

In 2 Corinthians 2:7, what was Paul's response when church members kept bringing up the repentant man's offense?

He did not want the church to shun him or avoid him. The saints were not to bring up his past actions against Paul because this would only lead to the man's excessive sorrow. If we keep bringing up an offense over and over, we are indicating to the other person that we have not fully forgiven him.

Does our Father, God, bring up our transgressions against Him over and over? Why or why not?

Is God going to bring up our past sins in heaven? When we die, will he bring up all our past sins and transgressions against Him over and over again into eternity? No!

Our sins have been nailed to the cross and remembered no more. Christ's judgment will be only for our reward.

In what ways might these truths impact your relationships?

(Various answers should be shared including yours.)

AN INSTRUCTOR'S MANUAL

In the section, "An Ancient Portrait," the author describes the how Jesus did not hold Martha's previous sin against her when she confronted Him about allowing Lazarus to die.

What happened the first time Martha confronted the Lord?

Mary was seated at the feet of Jesus listening to Him teach, while her sister Martha was in the kitchen making preparations. She became so overwhelmed that she stormed into the presence of Jesus and demanded that He command Mary to help her. Patiently, Jesus refused and explained to Martha that Mary had chosen the better part which was teaching over service.

He knew the world was about to see something so dramatic that people would speak of it for many years. To present His great glory to the world, Lazarus unfortunately would have to die for a short time, so Jesus stayed two more days.

After receiving a message from Martha, why did Jesus wait two more days before he began the journey to Lazarus?

He allowed Lazarus to die in order to raise him from the dead.

When Martha chastised the Lord for not arriving in time, how did Jesus respond? How could He have?

Instead, Jesus explained to Martha that Lazarus will rise again. Martha responded that she knew he would be resurrected on the last day and affirmed her faith in Him. He did not say he was going to raise her brother.

The last time we saw each other you complained about Mary and her unwillingness to help you in the kitchen. This time, you are complaining that I did not come quick enough to save your brother.

HEALING RELATIONSHIPS THROUGH FORGIVENESS

We are done. I have had enough! Let Lazarus rot in the grave for all I care."

When Mary took the same approach to Jesus as her sister, how did Jesus respond? How could He have responded?

Once again, if Jesus had come when they called, Lazarus would still be alive today. They had seen His power, they knew He could heal him, but He didn't. Notice, Jesus does not rebuke her for her temporal blindness (not seeing his death in the light of heaven).

Why didn't Jesus hold the previous confrontation against the sisters and refuse to resurrect Lazarus from the dead?

Many believed in Him. So, when people sin against us, we are to forgive and not keep mental records of the offenses. This frees us from the torment of churning it over and over and keeps them from excessive sorrow or despair in the relationship. We are to forgive and forget.

Have you ever been in a situation comparable to the Lord's second chastisement or Martha's constant confrontation? How was it different and how was it the same?

(Various answers should be shared including yours.)

AN INSTRUCTOR'S MANUAL

In the section, "A Modern Anecdote," the author shares the deep struggle of a daughter with her mother's reminders of her past mistakes.

What three transgressions of the daughter were on the list of her mother's mental records of sins against her?

I asked if she could give me several concrete examples. At seven, she was playing the game of Hide and Seek in the living room and knocked over a lamp which put a small chip at the base.

Two years later, the daughter was removing a box of her princess dolls out of the top of the closet, lost her balance, and the box came tumbling to the ground spilling out all the dolls.

At twelve, she made herself a snack and went to watch television in the family room. Her mom had told her many times to be careful with any food she brought in. The carpet was new. She decided to watch a scary movie and eat some nachos.

How did the harsh reminders impact the daughter?

From that time forward, it became one battle after another. When she was finished, she slumped in the chair sobbing, "I can't ever please you. I'm such a screw up."

When the mother was gently confronted about what she had done, what was her initial reaction?

This ended the session. In the next one, mom defended herself. After some time discussing the importance of not keeping records, the mother stared blankly at her daughter.

HEALING RELATIONSHIPS THROUGH FORGIVENESS

What was the mother's final response?

Then with tears in her eyes, she responded, "That must have been horrible growing up and feeling like you can never please me. I love you! I am so proud of you and who you have become. I am really sorry for bringing up all those past mistakes."

What was the next step the mother had to take after this final response?

After this very moment, we began the restoration process. The mother had seen the importance of not keeping records.

Based on the truths learned in this chapter, what would you have done differently if you were the record-keeping mother or the discouraged daughter?

(Various answers should be shared including yours.)

AN INSTRUCTOR'S MANUAL

In the section, "A Personal Response," the author provides a model you may use for prayer if you find it necessary after discovering the truths in this chapter.

Are you presently in a relationship where you have sinned against another and have not asked God for forgiveness? If not, is there one from the past that still needs this prayer to be prayed?

(Various answers should be shared including yours.)

Based on the truths you have just learned, what will you continue doing in your current relationships and what will you do differently?

(Various answers should be shared including yours.)

What additional thoughts would you like to share with the others?

(Various answers should be shared including yours.)

Instructor's Notes

Chapter 5

Restore Through Action

Once the transgressions are forgiven by both parties, it becomes time to begin the real restoration process to rebuild the relationship. Sometimes, it can be brought to the same level as it was before the incident. At other times, it returns to a lower level. Sometimes, it can actually be brought to a higher level of functioning with real effort on both sides. It depends on the effort of all involved as the Holy Spirit pours forth power into their lives.

A Typical Scenario

Have you ever had or heard a conversation with a spouse, sibling, or friend that went something like this? You say, "Hi! Well, today I finally worked things out with my mom. After all these years of struggle, I finally confronted her about all the things that she did in my childhood which were so hard on me. I was as gentle as possible without holding anything back. She apologized. Now I feel this huge burden lifted off of me, but I don't feel closer to her. I thought for sure things would feel different between us, but I still feel very little love for her when she is around."

If this were a scene from a movie, or a verse from a song, or chapter in a romance novel, then all the feelings would come flooding back. Then we would go off into the sunset and live happily ever after. This is pure fantasy and does not work that way in real human relationships. Neither is the opposite true. Once you have offended someone in a certain way, the feelings do not necessarily have to remain forever.

The person can get over what happened and the relationship can be restored. The past can be overcome. Getting "stuck in the past" may create a great dramatic moment in a movie, song, or story but never has to come true. Instead, any kind of relationship can be rebuilt if both parties desire it and will make the effort.

A Scriptural Principle

We now a critical and often left out step in this important process of forgiveness and reconciliation. The fifth principle is "we must restore the relationship through words and actions and allow the feelings to follow." In Galatians 6:1, Paul explains this important concept when he exhorts the saints in Galatia, "Brothers, even if a man is caught in some fault, you who are spiritual must restore such a one in a spirit of gentleness." These "brothers" Paul refers to could be sinning against us.

Additional Notes: He finishes his thought with an important warning, "Looking to yourself so that you also aren't tempted."

The Greek word translated "transgression" is used by our Lord Jesus in the context of forgiveness. In Matthew 6:14-15 and Mark 11:25-26, Christ uses the word to speak of the sins "we are to forgive as we are forgiven." Isn't this what we are talking about? Sins against ourselves or sins we have done to others that need to be forgiven.

What do we do with these brothers who sin? "Restore" them. Here Paul is saying that as Christians, when we see someone caught in any sin, those who are spiritual should "restore" the person. The word translated "restore" not only encompasses restoration with God but all others who have been transgressed. In the apostle's context, the restorer is a

Christian who sees a believer in sin. Yet, there are actually two other people who also might restore. These are the two people involved in a relationship that has gone awry: the one transgressed or the transgressor. This might occur after they have reconciled with the Lord God and now desire to reconcile with the other. In any of these three cases, there has been a transgression, and a restoration is warranted. This restoration must always begin with the Lord first. After this, the ones we have transgressed should then be addressed. This is God's divine way.

A Biblical Explanation

The next step in this forgiveness process is to restore. Sin destroys relationships and the Lord God desires for them to be restored. The Greek word translated "restore" means "to render fit, sound, or complete; to mend or repair what has been broken; to equip or prepare someone for something; to complete." In this context, it means to mend or repair what was broken. The word is used of a physically broken fishing net. In Mark 1:19 and Matthew 4:21, when Jesus called James and John into ministry with Him, they were in the process of "mending" their fishing nets. They were removing the holes in their net that would allow the fish to fall through. In 1 Corinthians 1:10 the Greek word is used of Christians being "complete" in the same mind and judgment. They are not to have any holes in their unity. The disagreement had to be mended, so all agreed.

In his first letter to the Thessalonians, Paul described his desire to return to them and complete what was lacking in their faith. He needed "to mend" their faith, until it was like a whole "net." In this way, their faith would be complete and mature (1 Thessalonians 3:10).

HEALING RELATIONSHIPS THROUGH FORGIVENESS

Additional Notes: If asked about these Bible references to mending, here they are:

Mark 1:19
Going on a little further from there, he saw James the son of Zebedee, and John, his brother, who were also in the boat mending the nets.

Matthew 4:21
Going on from there, he saw two other brothers, James the son of Zebedee, and John his brother, in the boat with Zebedee their father, mending their nets. He called them.

1 Corinthians 1:10
Now I beg you, brothers, through the name of our Lord, Jesus Christ, that you all speak the same thing and that there be no divisions among you, but that you be perfected together in the same mind and in the same judgment.

1 Thessalonians 3:10
Night and day praying exceedingly that we may see your face, and may perfect that which is lacking in your faith?

When a relationship has been broken, it has to be mended. All the holes *[between the two parties]* must be patched and repaired so the relationship is whole again. How does this happen? What do we actually do to mend or restore the relationship? Well, forgiveness is the first step which begins the mending process. Jesus gives us another key to the mending process in Revelation, when He demands that the Ephesians mend their broken relationship with Him. As the risen Lord explains to them how to accomplish this, we learn how we can do this very same thing in our relationships.

In the book of Revelation, Jesus directs the apostle John to send seven letters to seven different churches. In His letter to

Ephesus, He begins with a description of their strengths as a church. In Revelation 2:1-3, Jesus comments, "I know your works, and your toil and perseverance, and that you can't tolerate evil men, and have tested those who call themselves apostles, and they are not, and found them false. You have perseverance and have endured for my name's sake and have not grown weary." Notice, the Lord Jesus began with a complement. He listed the things that He most appreciated about them and their relationship to Him.

To restore our relationships with others, we must begin with complements that describe the wonderful qualities that the person has and how much these contribute to our lives and relationships with them. This restoration process begins with the recognition that the ones we have transgressed or have transgressed us have made many contributions to our lives. I like to take some time to contemplate their qualities and contributions, before I start spouting off things that are of no consequence, insincere, or simply not true. This is not just "to butter them up" as one might say. These are true and sincere complements and reminders of their importance to us. This is step one.

Then the Lord Jesus mentions their exact transgressions. In Revelation 2:4, He admonishes, "But I have this against you, that you left your first love."

Additional Notes: The Greek word translated "left" means "to send away, to neglect, to desert, and to abandon." The Greek word translated "first" means "first in time or place, and chief or principal one." The Greek word translated "love" is a noun which means a valued or prized person, place, thing, or idea. They were in the midst of some amazing actions for their Lord, but they had left or neglected what they valued the most or first in their lives. Obviously, the "what" is not a "what at all. It is a "who."

The Lord obviously means Himself. Though they [*the church*] had endured persecution and stood against false teachers, they had stopped loving Him. They had gotten so caught up in the battle that they had forgotten who they were battling for.

We know the words we must use; now what actions does the Lord require of them to rebuild their relationship with Him? In the first part of Revelation 2:5, He describes their action, "Remember therefore from where you have fallen." The first action is inward. The Lord asked them to think back and to remember the time before they had fallen into their broken relationship. Why? They need to remind themselves of how good it was and how far they were from it. This is step two. We must remember from where we have fallen. I would think back to how great things were before the break down of the relationship.

Additional Notes: Since several sinful incidents may have actually occurred, I may have to go further back than simply the last one. Relationships often break down after a series of problems, not just one. I would ask myself, "How good was it? How wonderful was it?"

Once this was accomplished, we would then compare the past with the present. It is not as good nor is it as fulfilling, because we have gotten so far away from each other. This is what is implied in the word, "fallen." When we have become upset, our flesh will plant thoughts in our minds like, "I never loved him," or "I never really had a relationship with her that was healthy," or "my parents and I really never got along." This body of death (the flesh) will drum up these sweeping statements and rewrite our history with the person to match our present feelings. This is not God's way. These thoughts only cause despair in the relationship and its quick destruction. This remembrance of the past relationship will provide hope for the future. It will also encourage us to put out the effort required to restore the relationship, so we can return to those wonderful former days. Once we had it "so good," we can have it again that way.

Our initial step, we have already discussed is found at the end of verse five, Jesus continues, "And repent and do the first works." Then the Lord Jesus asks them to repent. This we have already discussed. Suffice it to say, restitution and accepting the consequences should be inserted here as deeds of restoration. Then Christ commanded them to go and "do the first works or deeds" they had done from the beginning with Him. They must return to the beginning actions. It is these deeds that should take place again. The focus is not on the actions of love one does in the middle of a relationship, but the ones done at the beginning. This is a huge difference. This restoration requires the new, fresh, more intense deeds one does as a relationship is beginning to blossom. These are the actions that quickly build relationships. Therefore, step three is to do the beginning deeds. Notice, the Ephesians had to mend their relationship with their actions. He does not appeal to their feelings. Our mind decides what is right; then our actions follow. Once the actions have commenced, the feelings will follow them.

Additional Notes: He does not say, "Repent and try to feel love for me again. I want you to get excited about me. I'm Jesus, the King of Kings and the Lord of Lords." No. He commands them to act, not feel. Often times, people let their feelings dictate many of their attitudes and actions. I feel miserable, so I will be grumpy and mean. I feel happy, so I will be smiling and encouraging. I feel sad, so I will withdraw from people and be silent. Of course, our emotions are important but are never considered when developing attitudes or actions concerning obedience to the Lord. Our mind decides what is right; then our actions follow. Once the actions have commenced, the feelings will follow them.

HEALING RELATIONSHIPS THROUGH FORGIVENESS

If we study the many letters of the apostle Paul, he always begins with how Christians are to think about something from God's perspective, and then he asks them to obey God. He never adds the caveat, if they feel like it, nor does he deal with the feelings at all. Why? Feelings will come once actions begin. Even if they don't, then Christians are guided not by feelings but by submission and obedience to the Lord. In John 14:15, Jesus described how He desired to be loved, "If you love me, keep my commandments." He did not say, "If you love me, feel love for me! Be excited about me!" As you can see, Jesus didn't appeal to feelings either.

My clients always ask me this question, "If I do something that I don't feel like doing or don't want to do, isn't that hypocritical?" The answer is no. If we don't feel like obeying the Lord in something but do it anyway, this is one of the greatest forms of sacrifice and obedience one could give. In this passage (Revelation 2:1-3), the Lord Jesus did not ask the Ephesians to feel something different; he told them to do something different.

Here is the Bible reference:

Revelation 2:1-3
To the angel of the assembly in Ephesus write: "He who holds the seven stars in his right hand, he who walks among the seven golden lamp stands says these things: 'I know your works, and your toil and perseverance, and that you can't tolerate evil men, and have tested those who call themselves apostles, and they are not, and found them false. You have perseverance...have endured for my name's sake, and have not grown weary.'"

If I don't particularly feel emotional love toward the Lord but continue to obey him then I am showing Him love. It is the same in our human relationships. This is distinct from begrudgingly doing something while we are grumbling and murmuring under our breadth. This is hypocritical; instead, we show love to the person whether the feelings are there or not by restoring the relationship. We do this by returning to the initial deeds of love.

Now, what were these initial actions that the church did? They are the same actions and deeds every church did when it was established. In Acts 2:42, Luke describes them in these words, "They continued steadfastly in the apostles' teaching and fellowship, in the breaking of bread [communion], and prayer." They were praying (talking to God) and reading His Word (letting Him talk to them). The saints were receiving communion (remembering Jesus Christ's great sacrifice with thanksgiving) and fellowshipping with others (serving and supporting the saints in words and deeds). Apply this to our human relationships now. Our first deeds would be for us to talk with the people who need restoration and really listen to them. This is the word and prayer. We should look at their good qualities and the great relationship we had with them in the past and be grateful for them. This is like communion. Then, we should serve them and support them with words and deeds of kindness. Finally, we should be around people who would encourage our relationships. This is referred to as fellowship in the Body of Christ.

Additional Notes: These deeds were verbal and physical. Initially, how many times did we tell the Lord Jesus how much we loved Him and how thankful we were for His grace and mercy in salvation? How many times did we tell Him how important He was to us? All of these deeds, I call the building of bridges in a relationship.

Whenever we take the time to have a conversation with, listen to, complement, show appreciation and gratitude, or serve those we have offended or have offended us, we mend a small hole in the relationship net. We must keep doing this until all the holes are mended, and the relationship is whole again. We should realize that this will take time to mend too.

These nets were large and were spread out on the rocks and mended carefully. Why? They could not afford for the net to break again.

To restore a relationship properly means that we have to spread the net out and understand where the holes are. We must take our time to carefully mend them. The worse the transgression, the bigger the hole is. The bigger the hole is, the more time it may take to mend it. It does not matter what their response is when we begin the mending process, nor does it matter what our feelings are. We should keep doing the many beginning deeds of love and expect the previous feelings to return. Normally, this will be to their previous level. If we continue to do these deeds, then we may actually increase the feelings and bring them to a higher level.

The Christian life is a mutual exchange of work and effort in our growth to maturity in Christ. In Philippians 2:12-13, Paul explained this principle, "Work out your own salvation with fear and trembling. For it is God who works in you both to will and to work, for his good pleasure." Here Paul is not speaking of doing good works to become saved. Paul is speaking about putting out real human effort while God is working His power in us. This assists us in growing toward Christian maturity, but it also assists us in all areas of our Christian lives. This would include our relationships. In our context, as we are rebuilding, power will be released from the Holy Spirit. We can only do our part and must allow God to work in the life of the other person. As we obey His principles, our feelings will follow.

It is important to note that someone has to begin building the cycle upward in the relationship, rather than letting it continue downward. It takes two to argue and fight; one cannot. The other party must spar alone.

If the feelings do not return and the deeds are being done, then it is time to pray for divine intervention on both our parts. The effort on both sides makes the difference. If we have an open heart and the willingness to put out the needed effort, the Spirit can do the rest. If we do this, we will have gained back our spouse, sibling, parent, neighbor, or co-worker. If they don't respond, we will have honored the Lord. In Matthew 18:15, Jesus declared, "If your brother sins against you, go, show him his fault between you and him alone. If he listens to you, you have gained back your brother." When we restore relationships, it allows us to gain back everything the other parties have contributed. This coincides with step two.

Additional Notes: The Greek word translated "gain" is used several times in the New Testament for financial gain. In Matthew 25:16-17, the word is used in the parable of the talents, when Jesus spoke of the servants who gained more talents.

Matthew 25:16-17
Immediately he who received the five talents went and traded with them, and made another five talents. In the same way, he also who got the two gained another two.

It is used of material profit or gain in Matthew 16:26. In that passage, the gospel writer spoke of gaining all that the world had to offer but losing one's immortal soul (Mark 8:36; Luke 9:25).

Here are the references:

Mark 8:36
For what does it profit a man, to gain the whole world, and forfeit his life?

HEALING RELATIONSHIPS THROUGH FORGIVENESS

Luke 9:25
For what does it profit a man if he gains the whole world, and loses or forfeits his own self?

The word is used spiritually in 1 Corinthians 9:19-20 of gaining or winning people to Christ. The term is also used in Philippians 3:8 for gaining Christ as more important than gaining prestige and achievement in the world.

Here are the Bible references:

1 Corinthians 9:19-20
For though I was free from all, I brought myself under bondage to all, that I might gain the more. To the Jews I became as a Jew, that I might gain Jews; to those...under the law, as under the law, that I might gain those who are under the law.

Philippians 3:8
Yes most certainly, and I count all things...loss for the excellency of the knowledge of Christ Jesus, my Lord, for whom I suffered the loss of all things, and count them nothing, but refuse, that I may gain Christ.

Another aspect of this restoration is found in Scripture's discussion of the "reconciliation" process. This word is found in Matthew 5:23-24, Jesus says, "If therefore you are offering your gift at the altar, and there remember that your brother has anything against you." We are on our way to church and suddenly we remember that another believer has something against us (whether we offended them, or they offended us), we must stop and then go and reconcile with them. Jesus continues at the end of the passage, "Leave your gift there before the altar, and go your way. First be reconciled to your brother, and then come and offer your gift." It indicates that we are to stop everything and "reconcile." The Greek word translated "reconciled" means "to make changes." This comes from a root word that is a banking term meaning to "render accounts the same." If there was any discrepancy between two ledgers, they would have to find the mistakes and fix them. Both ledgers had to be the same. We express this as "being on the same page." Just because someone will ask for forgiveness, doesn't mean that the cause of the argument or disagreement can be dropped. It must be fully reconciled. This is critical. Otherwise, the issue that caused the strife will never be fully resolved, and the strife is stirred up over and over.

The question then arises, who will start this restoration process? The answer is found in Galatians 6:1. Paul states, "Brothers, even if a man is caught in some fault, you who are spiritual must restore such a one in a spirit of gentleness; looking to yourself so that you also aren't tempted." When we transgress, we have to mend the relationship and bring it back to completeness. We must make the relationship full and strong again. Who begins the process? The first one who is spiritual! Paul says, "You who are spiritual." I always say, "First one filled with the Spirit has to take the first action to restore." The first one in the relationship who is filled with the fruits of the Spirit begins the restoration (Galatians 5:22-23).

Additional Notes: Since this is truly a divine act that requires supernatural strength, one needs to be filled with the Spirit to restore. To be filled with the Spirit may require time in His Word and prayer.

The Lord also expects the more mature Christian to take the lead if needed. If we have a broken relationship and we have been a believer longer, then we need to go.

This principle should also involve the many relationships we have with those who are unsaved. If we have a broken relationship with a non-believer, we are the spiritual ones and we need to take the first step.

Additional Notes: In fact, in Ephesians 4:18, Paul says that they are "darkened in their understanding, excluded from the life of God." In 1 Corinthians 2:14, the apostle Paul indicates that the natural man (non-Christians) cannot even understand these spiritual things. So, it becomes the Christian's responsibility to take the first step. So, then who is to go? The Spirit-filled, the spiritually mature, or the Christian is to reconcile.

Here are the Bible references:

Ephesians 4:18
Being darkened in their understanding, alienated from the life of God because of the ignorance...in them, because of the hardening of their hearts.

1 Corinthians 2:14
Now the natural man doesn't receive the things of God's Spirit, for they are foolishness to him, and he can't know them, because they are spiritually discerned.

It does not matter who started it, or whose fault it is, once we are spiritual, we must seek to restore the relationship with all the parties involved.

Additional Notes: Why must we do it when we are spiritual? The "spiritual ones" thinking is clear, pure, and Spirit-filled. In our context, we have confessed our sins to the Lord Jesus and accepted His forgiveness. Also, we have gone to the other person or persons and humbly asked for their forgiveness if we have transgressed them. We have forgiven the others if they have transgressed us. Now, we are fully filled with God's Holy Spirit, so we need to restore the relationship. If we are the more spiritually mature in Christ, then we bear more of the responsibility than the immature or new in Christ to take the first step in restoration. Why? We are the grown-up in the relationship spiritually. We know better.

Notice, it is to be done "in a spirit of gentleness." We should restore relationships in gentleness. We must not lord it over them because we are suddenly filled with the Spirit, more mature, or even are believers. Instead, we are to be gentle. Why? Paul asserts that we are simply a fellow, humble sinner before the Lord. Paul continues by saying, "looking to yourself, so you also aren't tempted." This means we could also be tempted to be bitter or not desire to make the first move. We could have just as easily been on the other side. Also, as we restore, we could fall back in the conflict again. The restoration could tempt us to be angry and bitter or get into argument again. So, we need to be careful.

An Ancient Portrait

In Genesis, Moses described a sibling relationship which had been broken for over twenty years. It had been between twin brothers who would not speak to each other because of one's deceit and the other's spite. Yet, twenty years later God would set up a series of circumstances that would force a reconciliation between these two brothers.

Additional Notes: If asked about the details of this story containing Jacob's two acts of deceit, here are the Bible references:

Incident One:
Genesis 25:27-34
The boys grew. Esau was a skillful hunter, a man of the field. Jacob was a quiet man, living in tents. Now Isaac loved Esau, because he ate his venison. Rebekah loved Jacob. Jacob boiled stew. Esau came in from the field, and he was famished. Esau said to Jacob, "Please feed me with that same red stew, for I am famished." Therefore his

HEALING RELATIONSHIPS THROUGH FORGIVENESS

name was called Edom. Jacob said, "First, sell me your birthright." Esau said, "Behold, I am about to die. What good is the birthright to me?" Jacob said, "Swear to me first." He swore to him. He sold his birthright to Jacob. Jacob gave Esau bread and stew of lentils. He ate and drank, rose up, and went his way. So, Esau despised his birthright.

Incident Two:
Genesis 27:1-10
When Isaac was old, and his eyes were dim, so that he could not see, he called Esau his elder son, and said to him, "My son?" He said to him, "Here I am." He said, "See now, I am old. I don't know the day of my death. Now therefore, please take your weapons, your quiver and your bow, and go out to the field, and take me venison. Make me savory food, such as I love, and bring it to me, that I may eat, and that my soul may bless you before I die." Rebekah heard when Isaac spoke to Esau his son. Esau went to the field to hunt for venison, and to bring it. Rebekah spoke to Jacob her son, saying, "Behold, I heard your father speak to Esau your brother, saying, 'Bring me venison, and make me savory food, that I may eat, and bless you before Yahweh before my death.' Now therefore, my son, obey my voice according to that which I command you. Go now to the flock, and get me from there two good young goats. I will make them savory food for your father, such as he loves. You shall bring it to your father, that he may eat, so that he may bless you before his death."

The Response:

Genesis 27:42-43
The words of Esau [swore to kill Jacob after his father's death], her elder son, were told to Rebekah. She sent and called Jacob, her younger son, and said to him, "Behold, your brother Esau comforts himself about you by planning to kill you. Now therefore, my son, obey my voice. Arise, flee to Laban, my brother, in Haran.

These two were Jacob and Esau and the reconciliation occurs in Genesis 32-34. Though Jacob and Esau were twins, since Esau was born first, he stood to inherit two-thirds of all that His father Isaac owned. Yet, Esau cared little about it. One day Esau was famished, so his twin brother Jacob offered him a bowl of lentil soup in exchange for his inheritance. Foolishly, Esau agreed.

Later, Jacob impersonated his brother before an almost blind father by putting animal skins on his arms to also steal his blessing. This he did and left nothing but a curse for his older brother. Esau had had enough of it. He swore that he would kill Jacob as soon as his father had died. Once his mother, Rebekah, found out, she sent Jacob to her brother Laban's family for protection. Then his twin brother Esau then left the household in disgust.

During the course of those twenty years, the both of them prospered financially and materially. They grew very large families and had households full of servants. Finally, it was time for Jacob to depart from his uncle's land and move back to his father's territory. To do this, he had to travel through Esau's land which was extensive. There was no way around it. He wanted to avoid a confrontation, but God's way has always been reconciliation and restoration, if at all possible. So, in God's providence, Jacob had to cross the land. Don't we do that? A holiday arrives, and we do everything we can in order to avoid a face-to-face meeting. We might even be in the same room but never speak to one another. The Lord God never acts this way towards us and does not expect us to act this way towards any others. Instead, He expects us to restore relationships through action.

So, Jacob took action. He set up camp near his property and devised plans for their reconciliation. Jacob selected gifts of his herds and flocks of animals for Esau: goats, sheep, camels, colts, cows, bulls, and donkeys. He divided them up into three groups according to their herds and flocks and sent a messenger ahead of them in each group. On three different occasions, Esau would be greeted with gifts of reconciliation. Each time, his brother Esau was addressed as "Lord Esau" and was told that Jacob was behind them hoping that these gifts would calm and satisfy him, so he would accept Jacob when they met face to face. After the third set of gifts, the time had arrived for the face-to-face meeting.

Jacob spent the last night before his encounter wrestling with an angel. Here God reiterated His covenant with Jacob and changed his name to Israel which would become the name of the nation in his loins. God assured Jacob that he did not have to worry about Esau because the Lord would protect him. The next day, Esau arrived. Jacob bowed to the ground seven times as he was approaching his twin brother. Here he was honoring him and demonstrating submission and sorrow over what he had done. This clearly indicated that Jacob desired reconciliation. Suddenly, Esau began to run toward Jacob. Would he kill him or embrace him? He grabbed him, hugged him, fell on his neck, and kissed him on the cheek. He saw the women and children who were with him and immediately inquired as to who they were. Then both his wives and their families bowed down. Esau asked why they had all come. Jacob replied that he wanted to find favor in Esau's sight and travel through his land on his way home. The implication was crystal clear he wanted to restore their relationship.

Esau then did something that could only have occurred through the providence of God. He declared that he did not need his gifts because God had provided for him. Then Jacob insisted that he keep them because he saw in Esau the face of God. God was at work because Esau had welcomed him favorably. Finally, his brother Esau had accepted the gifts. Then, Esau suggested that they journey through his land together, and Esau would travel ahead of him. Jacob had to refuse because the herds and flocks had to travel at their own pace. Esau then suggested that he leave some of his men with him to assist in the journey. Again, Jacob refused. He did not feel the need, and so Esau departed. Then, Jacob followed at his own pace through Edom. The two brothers worked things out.

I do not think we see all of God's steps of reconciliation in this story because Jacob and Esau were never very close as brothers. Mom and dad had seen to that through their acts of favoritism. Also, they were extremely different people. The story does accent some of the most important points. Jacob did restore the relationship through his actions. There was gift giving and signs of respect. They stumbled over each other in their recognition of God's blessing upon each of them. Esau offered support for Jacob's journey through his land. They parted as reconciled brothers. This is all they desired. They both did what was right. They restored what they had through actions and allowed their feelings to follow. This is all God requires.

A Modern Anecdote

One day, a set of adult triplets (two men and a woman) walked into my office and described how distraught they were over the deteriorating relationships among themselves and their families. This occurred after their mother became completely incapacitated from a stroke. Since their father had passed away, they decided to allow their mother to stay in the family home with a live-in nurse. During this critical time, they each visited her separately or the two brothers would see her together but never the three of them. Then she passed away. When they met and began discussing funeral arrangements, it turned into an argument. This argument led to accusations concerning the future of their family home, furnishings, and savings. Once they reached an impasse, the sister went to complain to her pastor who referred them to me.

As the discussion began, it was not long before the two brothers were accusing the sister of trying to control and dominate them; in return, she was accusing them of ganging up against her. It was almost as if they were about twelve years old arguing over who would get the last piece of pie. It became very obvious that they had grown up in constant conflict. I asked them to describe their mother's interactions with them. They all agreed that their mother was a strong and domineering woman whose solution to every problem was simply shouting, "Stop fighting and go to your rooms." She never once took the time to discover what they may have been arguing about. This action led to a great amount of conflict occurring behind their mother's back. They began to learn very quickly to deal with things themselves which often led to many instances of physical confrontation. Since the sister always had her own room and she was a girl, the battle lines were easily drawn. The two boys constantly challenged the sister or vice versa. It would get so chaotic at times that things around the house would be broken. When their mother would demand an explanation, all three would stick together and claim that they had no idea what she was talking about.

This fighting and arguing continued until the sister got married and then moved out of the house. Then the mother would have monthly family dinners at her house, and she would accept no excuse for not attending. Either the three of them alone, with their spouses, or with their children would sit there as if everything were fine. When they left, the two brothers would not speak to their sister again until a holiday or these cold, bitter family dinners occurred. When their mother passed away, the pretense was over, the anger and bitterness poured forth, and the fighting once again began.

I explained to them that I could and would help facilitate the decisions that had to be made concerning the mother's funeral, but I would like to meet with them afterward. They had some serious relationship problems and needed to work these out for the sake of their children and their children's children. Often a dominant mother with children who have difficulty getting along will usually separate after her death. Thereafter, the aunts and uncles, nieces and nephews, and cousins will no longer interact with one another. Multiply that by several generations, and this family no longer exists. Though they were hesitant to act, everyone agreed when the children were mentioned. Once the funeral was over, they made an appointment to see me. It required some time to go through the reconciliation process, but it was well worth it. Once they had forgiven each other, we developed a strategy for them to restore their relationships through action. Then plans were created to strengthen all the various relationships among their families. Once these actions began, new feelings of love toward one another also began.

Additional Notes: If asked about the mother's responsibility, one Bible passage we have not discussed can be cited:

Proverbs 31:1-2
The words of king Lemuel; the revelation which his mother taught him. "Oh, my son! Oh, son of my womb! Oh, son of my vows!

Proverbs 31: 10-13
Who can find a worthy woman? For her price is far above rubies. The heart of her husband trusts in her. He shall have no lack of gain. She does him good, and not harm, all the days of her life. She seeks wool and flax, and works eagerly with her hands.

Proverbs 31:26-30
She opens her mouth with wisdom. Faithful instruction is on her tongue. She looks well to the ways of her household, and doesn't eat the bread of idleness. Her children rise up and call her blessed. Her husband also praises her: "Many women do noble things, but you excel them all." Charm is deceitful, and beauty is vain; but a woman but a woman who fears Yahweh, she shall be praised.

A Personal Response

Dear Heavenly Father,

    I do desire to reconcile my relationship with (add name). Give me the wisdom to know what words and actions I can use to restore the relationship. Please provide me with the courage and strength to rebuild the relationship with those words and actions. Soften (add name)'s heart to receive my bold attempts to mend the net we have together. Help me to honor and glorify you in my relationship with (add name). I pray this in the name of Jesus. Amen.

AN INSTRUCTOR'S MANUAL

Chapter 5

Restore Through Action

Once our sins have been dealt with through forgiveness, we begin the restoration process. This will involve a change in our words and actions allowing the feelings to follow.

In the section, "A Typical Scenario," the author describes a broken relationship between a man and his mother which needed reconciliation.

What is the scenario about?

A Christian gently confronts his mother for past mistakes.

What did the conflict concern?

He thought that gently confronting his mother and having her ask for forgiveness would change his feelings toward her, but it didn't.

What was the relationship between the parties?

They were son and mother.

Have you had a similar experience?

(Various answers should be shared including yours.)

HEALING RELATIONSHIPS THROUGH FORGIVENESS

In the section, "A Scriptural Principle" the author presents an important biblical principle in the forgiveness process which concerns the restoring of relationships through action.

How would you express this principle in your own words?

The fifth principle is "we must restore the relationship through words and actions and allow the feelings to follow."

(Various answers should be shared including yours.)

How would you rewrite this principle to make it even more personal to your life (using your name and situation)?

(Various answers should be shared including yours.)

Why do you think this principle might be important in your life right now?

(Various answers should be shared including yours.)

How would you rate yourself on the percentage of times you followed this principle in the past when you did something wrong in a relationship?

(Various answers should be shared including yours.)

Directions: Put a horizontal mark and your name where you see yourself on the percentage line.

0%   25%   50%   75%   100%

AN INSTRUCTOR'S MANUAL

In the section, "A Biblical Explanation," the author explains the reasons why we must restore the relationship through actions and how to do it.

What is the first step in mending a broken relationship?

To restore our relationships with others, we must begin with complements that describe the wonderful qualities that the person has and how much these contribute to our lives and relationships with them.

In the second step of the mending process, what should we remind ourselves of?

Why? They need to remind themselves of how good it was and how far they were from it. This is step two. We must remember from where we have fallen. I would think back to how great things were before the break down of the relationship.

In the third step of this process, what kind of actions should be taken?

Therefore, step three is to do the beginning deeds.

This restoration requires the new, fresh, more intense deeds one does as a relationship is beginning to blossom. These are the actions that quickly build relationship.

As we mend the holes in our relationships, should we focus on our feelings? Why or why not?

Notice, the Ephesians had to mend their relationship with their actions. He does not appeal to their feelings. Our mind decides what is right; then our actions follow. Once the actions have commenced, the feelings will follow them.

If the feelings do not return and the deeds are being done, then it is time to pray for divine intervention on both our parts.

According to Galatians 6:1, who should start the restoration process?

Who begins the process? The first one who is spiritual! Paul says, "You who are spiritual."

The first one in the relationship who is filled with the fruits of the Spirit begins the restoration (Galatians 5:22-23).

In what ways might these truths impact your relationships?

(Various answers should be shared including yours.)

AN INSTRUCTOR'S MANUAL

In the section, "An Ancient Portrait," the author describes Jacob's reconciliation with Esau.

What was the initial problem between Jacob and Esau which caused the rift in their relationship?

Yet, Esau cared little about it. One day Esau was famished, so his twin brother Jacob offered him a bowl of lentil soup in exchange for his inheritance. Foolishly, Esau agreed.

Later, Jacob impersonated his brother before an almost blind father by putting animal skins on his arms to also steal his blessing.

Why did Jacob have to finally face Esau? Do you think God was behind this and why?

There was no way around it. He wanted to avoid a confrontation, but God's way has always been reconciliation and restoration, if at all possible. So, in God's providence, Jacob had to cross the land. Don't we do that?

What steps did Jacob take to reconcile with his brother?

He set up camp near his property and devised plans for their reconciliation. Jacob selected gifts of his herds and flocks of animals for Esau: goats, sheep, camels, colts, cows, bulls, and donkeys. He divided them up into three groups according to their herds and flocks and sent a messenger ahead of them in each group. On three different occasions, Esau would be greeted with gifts of reconciliation.

He grabbed him, hugged him, fell on his neck, and kissed him on the cheek. He saw the women and children who were with him and immediately inquired as to who they were. Then both his wives and their families bowed down. Esau asked why they had all come.

HEALING RELATIONSHIPS THROUGH FORGIVENESS

There was gift giving and signs of respect.

They stumbled over each other in their recognition of God's blessing upon each of them.

How did Esau respond?

Suddenly, Esau began to run toward Jacob. Would he kill him or embrace him?

Did the brothers become close after this restoration? Why or why not?

Esau then suggested that he leave some of his men with him to assist in the journey. Again, Jacob refused. He did not feel the need, and so Esau departed. Then, Jacob followed at his own pace through Edom.

I do not think we see all of God's steps of reconciliation in this story because Jacob and Esau were never very close as brothers. Mom and dad had seen to that through their acts of favoritism.

Have you ever been in any situation comparable to Jacob's deceit or Esau's contempt and yet have to face the other person? How was it different and how was it the same?

(Various answers should be shared including yours.)

AN INSTRUCTOR'S MANUAL

In the section, "A Modern Anecdote," the author explains the difficulties a set of triplets were experiencing with each other and how they were able to reconcile.

How did these siblings handle their conflicts while growing up?

This action led to a great amount of conflict occurring behind their mother's back.

They began to learn very quickly to deal with things themselves which often led to many instances of physical confrontation. Since the sister always had her own room and she was a girl, the battle lines were easily drawn.

How did the mother respond?

They all agreed that their mother was a strong and domineering woman whose solution to every problem was simply shouting, "Stop fighting and go to your rooms." She never once took the time to discover what they may have been arguing about.

When the triplets became adults, how did they handle the family interactions?

This fighting and arguing continued until the sister got married and then moved out of the house. Then the mother would have monthly family dinners at her house, and she would accept no excuse for not attending. Either the three of them alone, with their spouses, or with their children would sit there as if everything were fine.

Why was it important for the children of the triplets to have their parents reconcile?

When they left, the two brothers would not speak to their sister again until a holiday or these cold, bitter family dinners occurred. When their mother passed away, the pretense was over, the anger and bitterness poured forth, and the fighting once again began.

They had some serious relationship problems and needed to work these out for the sake of their children and their children's children.

When did some feelings of love for one another finally begin to appear?

Once they had forgiven each other, we developed a strategy for them to restore their relationships through action. Then plans were created to strengthen all the various relationships among their families. Once these actions began, new feelings of love toward one another also began.

Based on the truths learned in this chapter, what would you have done differently if you were one of the triplets or the mother?

(Various answers should be shared including yours.)

AN INSTRUCTOR'S MANUAL

In the section, "A Personal Response," the author provides a model you may use for prayer if you find it necessary after discovering the truths in this chapter.

Are you presently in a relationship where you have sinned against another and have not asked God for forgiveness? If not, is there one from the past that still needs this prayer to be prayed?

(Various answers should be shared including yours.)

Based on the truths you have just learned, what will you continue doing in your current relationships and what will you do differently?

(Various answers should be shared including yours.)

What additional thoughts would you like to share with the others?

(Various answers should be shared including yours.)

HEALING RELATIONSHIPS THROUGH FORGIVENESS

Instructor's Notes

AN INSTRUCTOR'S MANUAL

Conclusion to Group Study and Workbook Part 3

As we conclude this book, I would like to leave us with some final thoughts about our God of forgiveness and what His Son did on the cross for us. First, if we understand the full extent of what was wrought for us on that cursed tree in order to forgive us, it will become so much easier to do the same thing for others. Second, if you read this entire book and realized that you do not understand salvation or have never received Christ as Lord and Savior, then I would like to provide that opportunity. Please do not skip this section; it may be the most important in your life.

From all outward appearances, humans seem "good" and attempt to live decent lives. This is man's concept of himself. This is not God's concept. The Almighty's view is that people all over the world and throughout the ages sin, sin, and sin again (Romans 3:23). This is a terrible and utterly destructive condition. Yet, they have ramifications that are far worse. These sins condemn us to everlasting divine retribution.

Though described briefly in the Old Testament, the Lord Jesus Christ clearly announced and proclaimed the future punishment to come. Contrary to popular belief, Jesus did not only speak of love, grace, and mercy, He also spoke of the coming judgment for sin. He declared that the judgment of sin would be everlasting punishment in a place He called "Hell." The Lord portrayed this place as an eternal inferno (Matthew 18:8) where there would be the weeping (from the sorrow) and gnashing of teeth (from the agony and anguish of suffering) continually into eternity (Matthew 8:12; 13:42, 50; 22:13; 24:51; 25:30; Luke 13:28).

HEALING RELATIONSHIPS THROUGH FORGIVENESS

Why must people face this horrific punishment? Though God is a God of love, grace, and mercy, He is also a God of great holiness, righteousness, and justice (Psalm 89:14,18). These attributes are just as much a part of His divine nature as His love, grace, and mercy. You have broken God's law as we all have, and the penalty must be paid. This began with the first man Adam (Genesis 3:1-7). When this occurred, His love, grace, and mercy surfaced, and a provision was made. Someone else would have to take man's place and pay the penalty. Someone who had never transgressed Him, who would never deserve punishment, and would fulfill all of God's Laws, would be substituted in man's place. This was the Son of God, Jesus Christ.

As the God-Man, He would pay the penalty for our sins in His death on the cross. Once done, the Lord God made only one provision for people to appropriate what His Son had done on the cross for them. This provision is receiving Jesus Christ as Savior and Lord. Though I cannot possibly share with you this good news in the confines of this book, I would love for you to consider purchasing my book entitled, *Finding The Light: The Kingdom of Heaven and How To Enter It*. It can be found for sale on Amazon.com. It is inexpensive and contains the full gospel message for your consideration. This message is so important and extensive that it cannot adequately be contained in a few pages at the end of a book.

If you are a believer, you must go out into the world and forgive as you are forgiven. These principles are to be lived and shared with others. You now have the tools to make your relationships last a lifetime. Go live them out and share them with others!

AN INSTRUCTOR'S MANUAL

Conclusion to this Manual

In the book of Second Kings a story is recorded describing the reign of a king of Judah named Josiah. Due to Solomon's idolatry and his son Rehoboam's reckless decision-making in God's sovereign judgment, Israel split into two kingdoms. There was the kingdom of Judah which contained the two tribes of Judah and Benjamin and the kingdom of Israel which contained the ten other tribes. First and Second Kings tells the tale of this horrible split and the kings that reigned before Israel was destroyed by the Assyrians and Judah by the Babylonians. Most of the kings were wicked with only a few who were righteous.

One of the righteous ones reigned in Judah whose name was Josiah. He ascended the throne at the tender age of eight. Due to the constant idolatry of God's people over the years, the temple had fallen into disarray, was filled with idols, and was in desperate need of repair. At twenty-six, King Josiah ordered Hilkiah the high priest and Shaphan the scribe to oversee this repair by taking the money which had been deposited by the people in the house of the Lord and use it to clean up and repair the temple.

During this process, Hilkiah made an amazing discovery. In 2 Kings 22:8, the inspired author describes it in these words, "Then Hilkiah the high priest said to Shaphan the scribe, 'I have found the book of the law in the house of the LORD.' And Hilkiah gave the book to Shaphan who read it. Shaphan the scribe came to the king and brought back word to the king and said, 'Your servants have emptied out the money that was found in the house, and have delivered it into the hand of the workmen who have the oversight of the house of the LORD.' Moreover, Shaphan the scribe told the king saying, 'Hilkiah the priest has given me a book.' And

Shaphan read it in the presence of the king. When the king heard the words of the book of the law, he tore his clothes. Then the king commanded Hilkiah the priest, Ahikam the son of Shaphan, Achbor the son of Micaiah, Shaphan the scribe, and Asaiah the king's servant saying, 'Go, inquire of the LORD for me and the people and all Judah concerning the words of this book that has been found, for great is the wrath of the LORD that burns against us, because our fathers have not listened to the words of this book, to do according to all that is written concerning us.'"

Isn't that amazing? God's people had lost the Scriptures. The reading and study of the scriptures had become so unimportant to the lives of the Jewish people that had misplaced their "Bible" and found it in of all places the temple. And notice the result - he discovered that they were not following the ways of God, but man's. Some may have even thought they had been following the Lord, but they were not because they were not reading and studying the Word.

Our greatest tool in the living of our Christian lives and serving the Lord as He desires is His Scriptures. The most powerful solutions to solving our problems, dealing with our temptations, and handling our distress are in the Bible. Yet often times in bible studies, life groups, circle groups, or whenever Christians meet to study the Scriptures, very little of the Scriptures are taught and instead is replaced by the discussion of ideas and opinions that are often filled with human wisdom and even concepts contrary to God's truth. The Bible is often sprinkled in the group study books and questions and taken out of context and portraying even wrong assertions about God's truth. The purpose of my books is to bring the Bible back into the group study of His church. May this instructor's manual help you in this great endeavor.

AN INSTRUCTOR'S MANUAL

ABOUT THE AUTHOR

Dr. Donald Jones is currently a Christian Pastoral Counselor with thirty-eight years of experience in the fields of pastoral ministry, public education, and Christian counseling. He carries degrees and certificates from four major universities and from a variety of educational institutions. He has been a professor of Languages and Bible, a television commentator, and a featured speaker at a variety of events and seminars at churches, schools, and other organizations across the United States. He is a member in good standing of several secular and Christian professional organizations. Dr. Jones has been a published author since 1976. For further information view his website at www.donjonesphd.com.

www.ingramcontent.com/pod-product-compliance
Lightning Source LLC
Chambersburg PA
CBHW020632230426
43665CB00008B/141